EVERYTHING I EVER
NEEDED TO KNOW ABOUT
*
_____
I LEARNED FROM

Also by Brian Cogan

*Deconstructing South Park: Critical Examinations of
Animated Transgression (editor)*
The Punk Encyclopedia

Also by Jeff Massey

*Heads Will Roll: Decapitation in the Medieval and
Early Modern Imagination (co-editor)*

EVERYTHING I EVER NEEDED TO KNOW ABOUT

*

I LEARNED FROM

MONTY PYTHON

*HISTORY, ART, POETRY, COMMUNISM, PHILOSOPHY, THE MEDIA, BIRTH, DEATH, RELIGION, LITERATURE, LATIN, TRANSVESTITES, BOTANY, THE FRENCH, CLASS SYSTEMS, MYTHOLOGY, FISH SLAPPING, AND MANY MORE!

Brian Cogan, Ph.D.
and Jeff Massey, Ph.D.

THOMAS DUNNE BOOKS St. Martin's Press New York

THOMAS DUNNE BOOKS.
An imprint of St. Martin's Press.

EVERYTHING I EVER NEEDED TO KNOW ABOUT _____* I LEARNED FROM MONTY PYTHON.
Copyright © 2014 by Brian Cogan, Ph.D., and Jeff Massey, Ph.D. All rights reserved. Printed in the United States of America. For information, address St. Martin's Press, 175 Fifth Avenue, New York, N.Y. 10010.

www.thomasdunnebooks.com
www.stmartins.com

Designed by Steven Seighman

Library of Congress Cataloging-in-Publication Data

Cogan, Brian, 1967–
    Everything I ever needed to know about _____* I learned from Monty Python :
*including history, art, poetry, communism, philosophy, the media, birth, death,
religion, literature, latin, transvestites, botany, the French, class systems,
mythology, fish slapping, and many more! / Brian Cogan, Ph.D., and Jeff Massey,
Ph.D. — 1st. ed.
        p. cm.
    ISBN 978-1-250-00470-3 (hardcover)
    ISBN 978-1-4668-4216-8 (e-book)
 1. Monty Python (Comedy troupe)   I. Massey, Jeff.   II. Title.
    PN2599.5.T54C64 2013
    791.45'028'0922—dc23

                                                                2013033511

St. Martin's books may be purchased for educational, business, or promotional use. For information on bulk purchases, please contact Macmillan Corporate and Premium Sales Department at 1-800-221-7945, extension 5442, or write specialmarkets@macmillan.com.

First Edition: March 2014

10 9 8 7 6 5 4 3 2 1

Jeff hereby dedicates every even-numbered word in this book to his good lady wife, Kristin, whose love, patience, and support helped bring to fruition (a) his half of the manuscript and (b) his children, Ian and Mallory ("Sir and Lady Not-Appearing-in-this-Book"), whose first years of life were peppered with outrageous accents and silly walks.

Brian, in turn, forthwith dedicates every odd-numbered word in this book to his own personal "Carol Cleveland": his beautiful wife, Lisa, whose love and support—plus the initial suggestion that "this is the next project!"—helped get this puppy off the ground.

CONTENTS

ACKNOWLEDGMENTS

As with all such projects, there are many to thank for their support and inspiration.

Obviously, a debt of gratitude goes out to the Pythons themselves, for corrupting two New York *youts* and inspiring us to such nonsense as this. In particular, Cogan would like to thank all of the pompous professor-types that the Python portrayed, who—for some reason—actually made him want to join academia: "Thanks? I think." Meanwhile, Massey would like to thank Terry Jones, who almost-kinda-sorta makes it cool to be a medievalist. Well, at least to other medievalists.

On a more practical level, we are grateful for the compilers of *The Complete Monty Python's Flying Circus: All the Words vols. I and II* (all *Flying Circus* sketches cited hereafter are drawn from these two volumes) and Python expert Darl Larsen, whose encyclopedic *Monty Python's Flying Circus: An Utterly Complete, Thoroughly Unillustrated, Absolutely Unauthorized Guide to Possibly All the References From Arthur "Two Sheds" Jackson to Zambesi* (the first massive edition, not the silly abridged version) was ever a valuable and enlightening resource . . . even if he does tend to spell "Tolkien" phonemically.

Personally, Massey would like to thank his cronies back home who have shared his love for Python, who quoted (and mis-quoted) their sketches together back when vinyl was king, and who still sometimes laugh at his over-edumacated absurdities. Partial blame for the latter goes to Stuart Wood and Kathleen Clemenz, two teachers who permitted—nay, encouraged—Pythonic thinking in a public high school, and to Marilyn Mumford, who demonstrated that watery tarts and killer rabbits belong in the college classroom as well. So endeth the lesson!

The Pythons also corrupted Cogan early. For some reason his parents encouraged this and by the age of twelve or so, he was one of "those people" who relentlessly recited favorite episodes over and over and over and . . . well, you get the drift. So thanks Mom and Dad for raising him right. Thanks as well to all his Python loving friends, particularly John Pillarella, Mike Salzano, Martin Perrin, Jim Murray, Sal Cannestra, and his brothers Sean and Joe Cogan, all of whom starred in his Python inspired public access cable show and who kept the lumberjack song more or less in tune every time. Also special thanks to Canadian DJ extraordinaire Jason Lamb, who somehow translated Python into Canadian.

A professional tip of the hat goes to the Faculty Scholarship and Academic Advancement Committee of Molloy College, who helped defray the cost of our "research": never was money so well spent. Special thanks as well to Erica Krilov and Pat Shand—glamour stoogents extraordinaire!— without whom we'd be relatively factoid-less, and to Trisha O'Neill of the Royal English Department, who made sure we delivered the goods on time.

And finally, special acknowledgments go out to our agent, Jim Fitzgerald, for finding us a home, and to our kindly editors, Nicole Sohl and Brendan Deneen, for making that home user-friendly.

Ni!

P.S.: Brian would also like to thank Jeff for the absolute pleasure of working together on a book for two years without any rancor whatsoever, except for that brief skirmish over the ceremonial Balinese dagger; but aside from that, it was absolute bliss to write with you, my boon companion!

P.P.S.: You dare bring up the dagger incident again, you secondhand electric donkey bottom biter? Have at thee!

UPDATE! UPDATE!

THIS JUST IN . . .

Just when we thought that there was nothing left for Python to teach us, they surprised us yet again. After a few days of Twitter hints, on 21 November 2013, the surviving members of Monty Python (Cleese, Gilliam, Idle, Jones, and Palin . . . and possibly the urn containing the ashes of Graham Chapman) announced what had been unthinkable even a year earlier: they were getting back together for a reunion! It's the Spanish Inquisition all over again!

According to an early press release, the troupe's first reunion performance at London's O2 Arena—to be called "Monty Python Live (almost)"—sold out in 43.5 seconds. Owing to what John Cleese has called the "very, very silly" fan response, extra shows were almost immediately added; as of this writing the troupe will be performing for ten nights in London, and rumors continue to fly about further performances being added in London and America, should aged hips and modern humours prove amenable.

The shows, which will be directed by Idle, promise "a little comedy, a lot of pathos, a lot of music, and a tiny bit of ancient sex and maybe some cross dressing"; they will certainly be carefully scrutinized by ardent fans, most of whom have never seen Python perform live. While many fans were ecstatic at the news, some cynics suggested that the reunion was prompted by Cleese's latest expensive divorce and a 2012 court case in which former *Monty Python and the Holy Grail* producer, Mark Forstater, successfully sued the surviving Pythons for a share of *Spamalot*'s recent profits. Terry Jones in fact admitted that this was partly the case, but also noted that *South Park* mega-fans Trey Parker and Matt Stone had suggested doing a project with the surviving Pythons, which led the troupe to consider working together again.

Whatever the reason for Python getting back together, the fact remains that they would be performing live again on stage for the first time (in England) in forty years. At the time of this publication, no one knows what material the Pythons will perform, but old favorites and new material have been promised. It would be easy to take the cynical outlook and think of this as a cheap monetary grab, destined to fill up the old comics' coffers and put some more filthy lucre in the trust funds of the grandkids (although Chapman certainly doesn't need the money . . .) but we prefer to look at the reunion more optimistically.

To the authors of this weighty tome, the Python reunion is not (just) a money grab and not (just) a final victory lap for the vanguards of surrealistic comedy. We see this reunion as a final lesson from Python to all of us. This is Python defying age to show us that we are never too old, too rich, or too set in our ways, to become unabashedly and gleefully silly. In touring one last time, Python teaches us that, while we will age, we don't ever have to really grow up, that being an adult does not mean leaving the sheer wonder and glory of silliness behind. Prepare the comfy chair!

INTRODUCTION

INTRODUCTION (Trade)

Have you paid your bleeding twenty-five dollars for this book yet? Are you looking through the book in a bookstore (homeless, eh?) or—God forbid—a library (shudder) instead of buying the damn thing and reading it in the privacy of your dorm room (squat/lean-to/cardboard box on the side of the road) kipping under the ratty poster of 'N Sync that no one thinks you still have up?

Seriously, put this book down, you git, and *go!* Buy a copy *right now* before the dirt and acid on your grubby little fingers get these pristine pages dirty, rendering them completely unreadable to the many gentlemen and ladies of superior breeding who will no doubt give this book a proper home next to their leather-bound copies of the works of Thomas Hardy displayed on the rich mahogany bookshelves that they no doubt imported at great expense into their tastefully decorated town houses. You appall us: leave now and do something useful with your life, like joining the growing army of those "working" in television. Stupid git!

INTRODUCTION (*Executive Edition*)

Good evening. We apologize for the indelicacy of the previous introduction. It was clearly not intended for *you,* the suave and sophisticated

The cast of *Monty Python's Flying Circus* (left to right): John Cleese, Terry Gilliam, Terry Jones, Graham Chapman, Michael Palin, Eric Idle.
The Pythons in "character"—upper-class twit, naked man, Pepperpot, the Colonel, Gumby, sleazy emcee.

purchaser of the *Executive Edition* of *Everything I Ever Needed to Know About* _____* *I Learned from Monty Python* book. Clearly, you are not some common street urchin wearing a spotty trench coat and evidencing a nervous tic, sneaking furtive glances at cheap paperbacks in bookstores instead of adding this fine, weighty tome to your personal library. No, you are a reader who appreciates not just books about Monty Python, but a volume that echoes the sophistication and fine breeding that goes into collecting books for one's own private library. Note the crispness of the paper, the stylishness of the font, and the cut of the jib in the book that you now legally possess. Note, too, how every page in front of you has been numbered in appropriate sequence! Ah, luxury!

Or, if you have chosen to download the extra-special *Executive Electronic Edition* of this book (a welcome literary respite from the near-constant stream of epicurean, terpsichorean, and Sapphic fantasies populating your gold-clad operating terminal), notice that instead of pedestrian binary computer code (10100110011 indeed!) your *Executive Electronic Edition* includes—as a testament to your extraordinary sophistication—several extra "2s" a few "3s" and one especially cultivated "4." After all, you deserve them!

For those discerning few willing to pay more for luxury, the *Executive Edition* has been dutifully crafted with the sophisticated literary palate in mind, developed by designers of the best possible breeding, writers educated in the most exclusive boarding schools, and manservants possessing only the finest digital dexterity. We have made this fine literary work available for people like yourself, those select few who know real luxury when they see it, bold individuals possessing the warmth and grace of true savants. We welcome you to this fine and weighty tome, a truly excellent addition to your household. We know that you will spend many an evening sipping the finest brandy (delivered reverently by your own manservant), chuckling at the bon mots contained within this book, no doubt nodding in recognition at the cogent analysis of the Hundred Years' War, or the way in which the British class system (lower classes only, of course!) is satirized by Python. So sit back, relax; have a sip of that brandy. What's that you say? One hundred years old? Ah, we certainly expected that from *you*, sir and/or madam, a true connoisseur of all of life's great joys. Well, we shan't keep you any longer in the introduction! Please now move on to what we in the industry call the "body" of the book. (You can of course, call it whatever you like! After all, you purchased the *Executive Edition*! Indeed, for a modest additional charge, you may even send it back and we shall rechristen it "Horatio" or "Ralph" should you wish.) You have made a wise choice, and, as always, we salute you for your patronage. As you turn the page, please note the slight but tasteful scent of lilacs that clings to your fingers for a moment. Just a little extra touch, one that you, a person of taste, class, and breeding will assuredly appreciate. And no, *you're* welcome.*

---

* For those who purchased the *Executive Electronic Edition*, a special code has been enclosed containing a link to an exclusive Web site accessible only to people of taste and breeding (and certain skilled hackers of substantial lineage). On this special site, you will be able to download an "app" that will enable your phone or e-reader to transmit the smell of genetically modified lilacs directly to your orbitofrontal cortex. *Science!*

INTRODUCTION (The "Real-as-it-Gets" Version)

Since its BBC premiere on October 5, 1969, *Monty Python's Flying Circus* has consistently been regarded as one of the most innovative, surrealistic, and groundbreaking programs in television history. During their four seasons on British television (and well into the troupe's movie sequels and assorted solo projects), Monty Python became a worldwide icon of surrealistic comedy, not only for taking serious subjects and making them seem silly but also for treating silly subjects with the same consideration that the Oxford- and Cambridge-educated members once took their Latin and Greek lessons.* Monty Python did not simply epitomize intellectual surrealism; they also provided a treasure trove of erudite "in" jokes for those viewers who watched closely, offering sly allusions to subjects as diverse as T. S. Eliot's *Murder in the Cathedral* (as part of a commercial for a weight loss product), William Shakespeare's lesser-known foray into specialty porn (*Gay Boys in Bondage*), and even how to conjugate Latin properly (as helpfully explained by a staid Roman centurion to a rebellious Jewish graffiti artist). It was this combination of uniquely high-brow (but never pedantic) humor and simultaneously silly deconstructive comedy that inspired a legion of sometimes-inspired followers.† As Matt Stone—who, alongside Trey Parker, is responsible for the biting social commentary of *South Park*—has observed, "They'll do that joke that they know that only 20% of the audience is going to get so you know 80% is not going with you but you know that 20% is going to follow you to the grave" (*Monty Python Conquers America*). Significantly, no matter how seemingly esoteric Python's subject matter may have initially appeared to viewers, *MPFC* always mixed an underlying erudition with surrealistic but ultimately accessible comedy, thus appealing

---

* Extensive research suggests that the Pythons—unlike Shakespeare—were not, in fact, born with a thorough knowledge of Latin and ancient Greek.
† The American *Saturday Night Live*, for example, was certainly influenced by *Monty Python's Flying Circus*, even featuring members of the Pythons early on, and the Canadian *Kids in the Hall* troupe enacted anarchic and sometimes-interconnected skits while in Pythonesque Pepperpot guise.

to a legion of fans who—to this day—strive to "get" Python's myriad references.

Yet despite their acknowledged cultural influence, while Python has been looked at separately from various individual critical perspectives, no major work (other than Darl Larsen's laudable compendium *Monty Python's Flying Circus: An Utterly Complete, Thoroughly Unillustrated, Absolutely Unauthorized Guide to Possibly All the References from Arthur "Two Sheds" Jackson to Zambesi*) has yet analyzed the complex and nuanced way in which Monty Python deconstructed hundreds of years of theory, culture, history, art, and so forth ... until now. This book thus serves as a needed corrective, providing not only critical analyses of Monty Python's many rich allusions but also theoretical guides to understanding the context of many references, both obscure and obvious, in a rigorous but accessible fashion.

Everything we ever needed to know we learned from Python? Perhaps not *everything*, but certainly watching Python at different stages of our lives has taught us much about the world, and certainly much of our imagination and desire to learn even more about esoteric topics came from early television experiences with Python; experiencing the program for the first time, we laughed, but without understanding the implications or backstory of many sketches. The Pythons laced a dizzying barrage of "learned" factoids into their comedy, but they never stopped— or stooped—to explain themselves to their audience. As the actor David Hyde Pierce (who played Sir Robin in the opening run of *Spamalot*) has noted, "It's a gesture of great respect to an audience because it says we trust that you're smart enough that you're going to going to get this— either now or eventually—and that you'll laugh" (*Monty Python Conquers America*). That's not to say that you *need* to know firsthand the intricacies of the British class system or have seen the ultraviolent works of American film director Sam Peckinpah to know that a British upper-class twit, staggering about with a set of piano keys bisecting him, blood spurting everywhere and ruining the picnic, is incredibly funny ... but it helps.

So what makes Monty Python so damnably, and eternally funny? What remains so different about Python? Well, for a start, almost everything. While many critics have described Python as the most influential comedy show ever made (and its legions of fans are as diverse as the Beatles, the Who, David Hyde Pierce, Robin Williams, the casts of *Saturday Night Live* and *The Whitest Kids You Know,* as well as *South Park* creators Trey Parker and Matt Stone),* Python has no direct descendants. There are a few programs over the years that have attempted the level of sophistication and silliness inherent in Monty Python (the Canadian absurdist sketch comedies *The Kids in the Hall* and *Second City Television* may be its likeliest descendants), but most programs—even those made by Python members after the demise of *MPFC*—would not (and could not) follow the Python formula. The trick with Python is that no one could ever really copy Python; it stood boldly on its own, waiting for a fresh contingent of intelligent, bizarre, and groundbreaking comedians to rush up the hill after it ... but sadly, no one followed. According to John Cleese:

> Python certainly changed comedy, but in a rather negative way because instead of people taking our stuff to the next stage, they avoided it. So it had a rather disappointing effect, which was to close off an avenue for a particular type of humor and I'm surprised that's the way it happened. (Pythons 2003, 350)

Whether out of sheer awe or because Python had painted themselves (and comedy) into a dead end, there was almost no way to take the Python formula to its (il)logical conclusion. As some have suggested, perhaps the show was too ahead of its time, too English, or simply too counter-formulaic to be duplicated or imitated overseas. Ultimately, Python had many fans, but few who dared to replicate the original. As Cleese has sadly mentioned,

> ... the strangest thing I think about Python is how few people tried to copy it. When you think of most of show business, if anything is successful, people immediately begin to copy it, but there was something about Python that had the immediate reverse ef-

---

* Yeah, a lot of white ones, we know.

fect. It was very successful and nobody tried to copy it. (Pythons 2003, 170)

Such reticence seems atypical—if not anathema to—the Hollywood entertainment model; a seemingly endless string of successful British programs have been "Americanized" over the years (*Steptoe and Son, Man About the House, The Office, Coupling, Pop Idol, Being Human,* and *Top Gear,* * to name but a few), but *Monty Python's Flying Circus* has remained oddly sacrosanct, influencing many but standing on its own as a show almost impossible to copy or even reimagine.

One reason Python cannot really be replicated or even adapted terribly well is that *MPFC* occurred at the end of a unique era in history and was part of the primal DNA or "selfish gene" of television comedy then evolving and replicating. Python came out in an age when astounding social changes were happening in both England and America; it would be difficult to name another television program that clearly stands out as the vanguard of something so startlingly *new* but that also so clearly identifies itself as of its particular time and place. *MPFC* marks the end of a historical era: it relentlessly mocks both perceived authority figures *and* the conventions of television so completely that—for anyone who has ever watched the show—it is simply impossible to take those figures and conventions seriously again. Python is not only the forefather of modern television but the forefather of modern culture . . . in ways that are both very good and also very bad. Python is the progenitor of the "modern" genre-splicing *mash-up.* It is relentlessly intertextual, in the way that it takes history, literary studies, or philosophy and does not simply use them as topical references but as new ways of looking at the potential of comedy for newer, more sophisticated audiences. In retrospect, it seems as though as an audience with their own absurdist tendencies was growing up along with *Monty Python's Flying Circus* and the Pythons were ready to amuse—and confuse—that audience, much to their mutual delight. To paraphrase an ancient joke: "How many times do people laugh

---

* *Sanford and Son, Three's Company, The Office, Coupling, American Idol* ("Oh, there's a giveaway!"), *Being Human,* and *Top Gear,* respectively.

at a Monty Python sketch? Three times: once when they see it, a second time when a friend explains it to them, and a third time when they finally get it." This doesn't mean that mere mortals are too dense to get the many layers of meaning in the Python oeuvre, but that to get certain jokes a deeper knowledge of various non-comedic subjects is often required. It's not that watching various contestants utterly fail to summarize Proust isn't in and of itself hilarious; it's just that knowing how incredibly long-winded Proust was in his books gets you a little closer to the full humor of the situation. Michael Palin has talked about how episodes of *Monty Python's Flying Circus* are "rich" with meaning:

> It's like a thick, well-filled comic book. People are always finding new things in Python, it was layer after layer, because one person would write the basics, someone else would have an idea, someone else would say, "While you're doing that let's have something on the wall that looks good." (Johnson 1999, 184)

Of course, such comic layering encouraged obsession among a receptive fan base. Palin continues: ". . . if one sees it forty-five times like some people in America have, they get around to noticing the things on the wall. So there's always something new" (Johnson 1999, 184). Historical figures dislocated from their original contexts (Attila the Hun and his family starring in a canned-laughter American sitcom, communist leaders vying for prizes on a game show, philosophers playing soccer, and so forth) are not simply referents for a punch line, but by being taken out of context, reimagined, and mashed up, history itself is made fresh and new. As we will discuss in the chapter on history, Python did not simply illustrate how our linear version of history, as memorialized by great figures starring in epochal events, was a lot more random than we thought; they used the medium of television as the basis for history (or philosophy, or sports, and so forth) essentially making everything viewed through that lens—no matter how "traditionally" serious—seem silly. As we will discuss, McLuhan had a point when he said the medium is the message.

Python often overtly made the importance of medium and genre a part of their humor—they led the charge—but why wasn't television different after them? Or even comedy on television? It's not as though the awful laugh track–based sitcom has vanished. Python should have started a new golden age of comedy, but the fact is—despite how many ardent fans profess their undying love (evidenced by their often uncanny ability to recite entire sketches line by line)—there was never anything quite like Python afterwards. Even shows that deliberately take deconstruction and mash-ups as their starting points—such as *Tim and Eric's Excellent Show*, the self-aware dead-on silliness of early *Simpsons* episodes, and later the intertextual and self-referential gags of *Family Guy**—no one really traced Python's absurdly successful footsteps. They couldn't really, after Python; the only real response to the utter deconstruction of *MPFC* was a return to form, as shown in the plethora of unimaginative sitcoms in both England and America that persist to this very day. Yet Python does not just deconstruct comedy; it enables attentive viewers to see a world unbound by earlier notions of linearity and coherence. In many ways Python anticipates nothing so much as mash-up culture, *Girl Talk*, the remix, and even the field of media studies, where they served as not just a cultural barometer (like an Anglicized version of Marshall McLuhan's intuitive reappraisal of the field of media studies), but also in pointing out that the *form* of television was equally (or sometimes more) important as the content they anticipated works such as Neil Postman's seminal *Amusing Ourselves to Death* (1985). In *Amusing*, Postman's critique of the way in which television inherently reduces the serious to the trivial reiterates Python's point. Python saw a world amuck under a system of authority, class, and hierarchy, normalized by a form of mass media that contained equally ridiculous assumptions and biases towards decontextualizing serious thought. Echoing Postman's point years later, Cleese observed, "Someone once told me that they couldn't watch the news after Python, it all just seemed so ridiculous" (Pythons 2003, 350). By challenging the way in which we accept the world as real instead of as a social construction, Python asks us to consider what writers, philosophers, artists, and musicians have been asking for

---

*Which, as *South Park* has suggested (via manatees!), is sometimes all *Family Guy* has to offer in terms of humor.

thousands of years: why do we witness things that are patently absurd and silly and, instead of laughing, go on about our daily business as if all is normal?

Much of Python's ability to intuitively grasp the inherent ridiculousness of modern life came from specific historical circumstances (where they were from, where they went to school, what topics they chose to pursue before and after graduation) but also the style of comedy and expression that they were already accustomed to before they created *MPFC*. Terry Gilliam, the lone American in the troupe and the man singularly responsible not just for the brilliant animation that helped define *MPFC* but also for the overall look and design of Python's many later projects (from television to film to stage), grew up devouring the anarchic humor of *MAD* magazine and various underground comics. Gilliam has said:

> What I loved is in late '65, when I was back in L.A. after being around Europe: The American underground comics had taken off—Shelton, Crumb, everybody out there—but the French were the ones that really amazed me. People like Moebius . . . and *Metal Hurlant* and *Fluide Glacial* and *L'Echo des Savanes*. This was extraordinary stuff! Beautiful looking, funny, sharp, sci-fi on a level that you really want to work at. (Marsh 2012)*

Gilliam, the son of a carpenter who at one point wanted to become a Presbyterian missionary, evolved and became more radicalized in the sixties, so much so that by the time he graduated from college (with a degree in political science) he was already extremely anti-authoritarian, a trait that continued throughout his tumultuous Hollywood career. The other Pythons already had absorbed not just the staid parts of British culture but also some of the subversive humor that had miraculously made its way into British radio in the 1950s. A *lot* of Python comes from their uniquely British class system–based upbringing; but much was in-

---

*For more on Gilliam's particular contributions to Monty Python, see the interstitials, conveniently stuck between each major part of this book.

spired by the comedic anarchy featured on the irreverent and surrealistic radio program *The Goon Show,* wherein the Pythons realized "that you could have a literate form of comedy, an informed comedy, that was influential in making something you felt was worth doing" (Pythons 2003, 85).

(A Brief Note on) THE GOONS

The Pythons did not come out of nowhere; along with their education, social position, and individual interests, a key factor that guided the comedic development (of the British members at least) was their devotion to a BBC radio program that first blazed a trail for them: *The Goon Show.* *The Goon Show* ran on BBC radio from 1951 to 1960 and featured the contributions of comedic giants Peter Sellers, Spike Milligan, and Harry

The cast of *The Goon Show*: (left to right): Peter Sellers, Harry Secombe, and Spike Milligan.
The Goons' anarchic radio program (1951–1960) was a major early influence on the Pythons.

Secombe (and early on Michael Bentine). For Palin, the Goons "saw behind this thin veneer of civilization and pushed these characters to limits, which I just thought was exciting and revealing, not just funny but also imaginative and brilliant" (Pythons 2003, 35). Palin had found a program completely unlike anything he was used to from the often-stodgy BBC radio: it was, in short, "a glimpse of madness ..."

As Palin has mentioned:

What's special about them was they broke rules. And most of the other shows, however funny they were, behaved in a certain way, conformed to certain prejudices, reflected the social order and conventions of my parents' generation. Sketch shows were sketch shows, they just reflected the way the world was. (Pythons 2003, 35)

The Goons not only awakened the Pythons' comedic sensibilities but also taught them a valuable lesson about authority. As Palin put it, "Generally speaking, authority has to win respect now, when in those days, it was automatically granted." This was something new; as Palin recalls, "I felt that they were saying, look behind everything, and don't take anything at face value" (Pythons 2003, 35). Terry Jones also shared a fascination with the Goons; what he loved was "the way they broke up the conventions of radio and played with the very nature of the medium" (Pythons 2003, 46). Cleese was also a huge fan: "I was obsessed with the Goons in the same way that people were later obsessed by Python—so I understood their behaviour!" (Pythons 2003, 41). Later on when the Pythons were established and Milligan had befriended them, Palin recalled talking to Spike Milligan about the Goons: "His answers to questions about the Goons are almost identical to the answers I always give when asked about the Pythons—we did it to make ourselves laugh, to laugh at authority, we always had a love/hate relationship with the BBC, etc." (Palin 2006, 263). Partially due to both their position at the BBC and their debt to *The Goon Show,* Python references a tendency in British comedy of the sixties, where "the dissolution of respect found a focal point in comedy" and a new style that "embraced change, that made fun of authority figures" (Topping 1999, 9).

The Goons were not the only ones making subtle (and not so subtle) jabs at conformity before *MPFC*. For example, a Harvard (and then later MIT and eventually UC Santa Cruz) mathematics professor with a knack for the piano, Tom Lehrer, was satirizing the conventions of American culture during the Pythons' formative years. Palin had heard Lehrer and, to him, Lehrer's songs were satire of a sort he had never heard from an American comedian. "There was an edge to them, which was quite different to a lot of the comedy I'd grown up with" (Pythons 2003, 36).* Over in America, Gilliam was also experiencing disgust with contemporary culture. Gilliam learned a lot about the tedium of mechanization while working on the Chevrolet assembly line: "I worked nights and I said, 'Fuck this, I'm never going to work for money ever again in my life'" (Pythons 2003, 92). To understand Gilliam's sensibility is to understand his delight in both creating works of art and also simultaneously destroying them. A great deal of Gilliam's artwork was collage based, resembling nothing so much as the work the Situationists were engaging in (un)creating in France in the 1960s. Even the famous first-season opening montage of *MPFC* was simultaneously a work of fine art and something that demonstrated Gilliam's attitude towards art itself; when in doubt, destroy something: "You create something beautiful and then you crush it" (Pythons 2003, 145).

Python members, already growing up on absurdist and deconstructive comedy (and rock and roll, as will be mentioned later) came of age as all around them traditional ways of life were gradually changing and one of the (supposedly) most vital parts of British culture—respect for authority and tradition—was being questioned. A key to fully appreciating the humor of Monty Python is not just to know *what* they are mocking but also to know *why* they are mocking. Python did not strive to simply point out how perceived authority was silly; they strove to make authority (in its many guises) look so patently absurd that one could not

---

*Echoes of Lehrer may be heard—however indirectly—in the Pythons' later musical bits, such as Jones' send-up of "Isn't it Awfully Nice to Have a Penis," and in their many "list" skits, which recall Lehrer's "Element Song."

help but look at the world in a radically different way after watching *MPFC*.

But perhaps some *very* general information for the young'uns may be in order, eh?

Monty Python's Flying Circus is the broader term for the original television show of a comedic collective known as Monty Python. The troupe of five British actors—Graham Chapman, John Cleese, Eric Idle, Terry Jones, and Michael Palin—and one American, Terry Gilliam, was first launched in the British television program that ran for four seasons from 1969 to 1974; the troupe also launched four movies, at least ten albums of original material, and several live shows that were recorded for release as records or live concert films. Despite their flurry of creative production in the late sixties and seventies, the group did not create any substantial new material after the release of the film *The Meaning of Life* in 1983 and the group's activities more or less came to a close with the death of Graham Chapman in 1989. Today the other members are very active in various pursuits, including film, television, promotional videos, commercials, travel specials, books, plays, and musicals (including the wildly successful *Spamalot*). Despite their widely flung personal projects, members of Python still sometimes work together in smaller groups or appear in one another's films. Most recently, the surviving members lent their voices to Jones' live-action/animated sci-fi film, *Absolutely Anything*, and most are recording sequences for an animated version of Graham Chapman's aptly named memoir, *A Liar's Autobiography*.

Monty Python came together when either Barry Took (of the BBC) or John Cleese had the idea to split the more creative members from the writing and performing staffs of two BBC programs, *Do Not Adjust Your Set* and *At Last the 1948 Show*, and combine them. Chapman and Cleese (who had attended Cambridge and started a writing team there) were working on *At Last the 1948 Show*; meanwhile, the writing team of Palin and Jones (both from Oxford), along with Chapman and Cleese's Cambridge classmate Eric Idle, had worked together on *Do Not Adjust Your Set*. Gilliam had contributed animation to *Do Not Adjust Your Set* and Cleese had previously worked with him in New York City on a *fumetti* (a type of photocomic), and recommended him to the rest of the group. At first, a veritable plethora of names were suggested for the television show, including *Owl Stretching Time, Toad Elevating Moment,* and *Gwen Dibley's Flying Circus,* before the name coalesced into *Monty Python's Flying Circus*... largely because it sounded like the kind of show a sleazy television promoter would concoct. The first episode premiered on Sunday, October 5, 1969—with prescient irony—"in a slot usually reserved for religious programmes" (Topping 1999, 13).

MPFC was unlike anything else on television at the time and was initially baffling not only to the BBC but to early audiences as well. As Michael Palin said, "It didn't all work, but the general feeling was that you could imagine almost anything, and it could be done if it worked. There were absolutely no rules or limits" (Pythons 2003, 143). According to Terry Jones, "The BBC took pride in not only *not* looking at the scripts—they didn't look at the shows before they went out" (Pythons 2003, 164). And as Gilliam has mentioned about the first Python audience at the live tapings: "There was just the sound of hundreds of jaws dropping, it seemed to me" (Pythons 2003, 166).

As noted, *MPFC* took its inspiration from the free-form association of *The Goon Show,* a radio show that completely transcended the limits of radio in the fifties. But Python was also a reaction to the sixties, and because the BBC essentially put them on in a slot when there were traditionally few viewers, at first they were free to do whatever they pleased and to create new ways of imagining comedy outside the staid boundaries of then-popular British sitcoms. Yet while they were largely left to their own devices at first, eventually the BBC began to exert its "authority," leading the Pythons to engage in a feud with the BBC in 1970, when the BBC began trying to exert more control over the show while simultaneously ignoring their new hit program. This included, at one point, putting *MPFC* in an "opt out" slot so no viewers in Scotland, Ireland, the midland, or the south could see the show. This infuriated the normally unflappable Michael Palin so much that he wrote in his diary that "there is to be a break after three episodes where Python will be replaced by 'horse of year show'" (Palin 2006, 35). The BBC was right to be worried: Python was the most revolutionary show on the air at the time, and revolution rarely arises from complacency or shows self-restraint. Partially due to their fringe position at the BBC and their debt to *The Goon Show*, Python reflected a nascent tendency of British comedy in the sixties: anti-authortarianism.

Terry Jones cites the "college divide" as the initial source of Python's uniquely combative comic dynamic. To Jones, "the first series was very much a fight between the Oxford contingent ... trying to push this stream of consciousness into the thing, and the Cambridge group" (Morgan 2005, 31). The Cambridge Pythons were, in many ways, very "structured and pragmatic, Oxford very 'wooly' and romantic" (Topping 1999, 10). Ultimately, "no matter how silly the Pythons were, they still had their roots in the scholarly pursuits of Oxbridge" (Topping 1999, 40).

But whatever their alma maters,* all the Pythons shared one thing in common: a complete and utter lack of respect for the conventions of television. Cleese was tired of formats (Morgan 2005, 30) and Gilliam noted that the idea of Python was to "get rid of punch lines" (Morgan 2005, 37). More generously, Eric Idle has said, "... we didn't have a clue what we were trying to do, except please ourselves" (Morgan 2005, 37). As a result, to this day the cult of Python is made up of laughing people who "get" their humor and others who simply stare aghast. To Palin, "Python seemed to fit into this niche of daring, irreverent, therefore only accessible to those of a certain sort of intellectual status" (Morgan 2005, 70). According to Terry Gilliam, "people are *passionate* about Python" and, like comic-book fans, "all feel like outsiders, they're never given respect" (Morgan 2005, 73). After the program was over, many of the Pythons did not have breakout careers as solo stars because they were used to the writing conditions facilitated by Python. Michael Palin commented on how hard it was to write for others, because "Monty Python spoilt us in so far as mad flights of fancy, ludicrous changes of direction, absurd premises and the illogicality of writing were the rule rather than the exception" (Palin 2006, 14).

To Cleese, the Pythons "seem like a rugby team which kept changing the ground rules and moving the goal posts and still played a smashing

---

* Or *Almae Matres*, for the Roman centurion reading along.

game—one could barely keep up with them" (Morgan 2005, 2). The program repeatedly violated the conventions of television, breaking the fourth wall, showcasing characters who seemed to be aware that they were characters working on a television show, and exhibiting surrealistic self-referentiality. By show six of the first season, "characters just walk on and move the show forward by simply halting the sketch and starting another one" (Topping 1999, 20). Also violating the usual rules were episodes where "characters ask if they can have any more lines to read, while others check the script to see if they can leave" (Topping 1999, 29). Towards the end of *MPFC*, it was almost as though the show had run out of things to deconstruct, and many, especially Cleese—who did not return for the fourth season—thought that by the end of the third season there was nothing left to deconstruct but the deconstructions (Topping 1999, 42). While many fans still look fondly back at the last season of *MPFC*, it even seemed to some of the Pythons as though "the world had caught up with them" (Topping 1999, 45).

In the end, what makes Python different from any comedy program before or since is the unique combination of individuals working together in a context and time period where challenging authority was possible and supervision was minimal. As Eric Idle has said:

> The Python six had a gut feeling about what was funny and you didn't have to explain that really. We knew we had to keep it tight. It was a laugh that dare not speak its name, we couldn't really say quite why it worked, but it did, and we knew that once we spread it out it would lose something, I mean, it was extraordinary enough to get six people who had that kind of harmony, and that was what I think we wanted to preserve and why we said, "Let's do everything." Plus we also liked dressing up as women! (Pythons 2003, 143)

Although Python is frequently mentioned as a touchstone for many comedians, including Hollywood mainstays Robin Williams, Steve Martin, and Jim Carrey, it is surprising how few comedians have tried to re-create the Pythons' style in any substantial way. Barry Took thought Python would be influential, but "I was utterly wrong because it wasn't influential at all—nobody else apart from undergraduates copied it" (Morgan 2005, 315). Of course, undergraduates eventually become graduates, and some even become professors, who—if they dare not copy the comedy "that dare not speak its name"—will damn well obsess over it.

ANTI-AUTHORITARIANISM
"What have the Romans ever done for us?"

Again, one key element to understanding Python is recognizing that they were not just well-educated folk pointing out the obvious silliness in life, but that they were intentionally revolutionary and that they were often very, very angry. Python, while not overtly political as a group (with singular exceptions), created an incredibly politicized show, one that was anarchistic in the broadest sense: they were anti-authority on *all* levels. The members of Python did not just dislike authority; they hated it and devoted much of their material to trying to convince the audience that the trappings of power and authority that people encountered on a daily basis were absurd and needed to not just be laughed at but also directly questioned.

Yet it is also inadequate to simply state that Monty Python was a combination of well-educated comedians with an absurdist and revolutionary stance regarding their own culture. Python was not just mocking; Python was actively dedicated to undermining and demolishing the institutions that controlled so much of society. The five English Pythons were all not just the products of formalized (indeed, exceptional) education; they were also products of their time period, reared in the particular cultural malaise that had beset postwar England. After years of rationing (which didn't end in England until 1954), the final dissolution of the British Empire, and the cultural and political movements of the 1960s, it seemed as 1970 approached that genuine change might have been in the air. And, in a country that made it almost a badge of honor to be reserved and hide your real feelings, Python was not afraid to point out not just how silly authority is but how blatantly useless much of it was as well.

Another reason Python was able to succeed so well at parodying and satirizing the upper classes was because they resembled (and in some cases came from) those classes. According to Michael Palin, one of the Python's secret weapons was John Cleese. As Palin astutely observed, Cleese was (and still is) tall, well built, and repressed; this epitome of the British class system was great at visually representing the upper classes and was especially adept at showing "this wonderful process of an establishment character undermining the Establishment" (Morgan 2005, 77). Because of his height and command and reassuringly normal presence, Cleese "epitomized the ruling establishment of Britain; he looked like the bishop or the bank manager, a man of authority. He looks just right to undermine it as successfully as he did" (Morgan 2005, 78). Whenever a sketch called for someone to get up and portray the absurdity of someone in charge going about his business—whether or not his "business" made any sense—Cleese was cast, as he was the "archetypical English, respectable, responsible person attacking from within" (Morgan 2005, 78). Whether it was his role as the Minister of Silly Walks or as an interviewer tormenting a cringing Graham Chapman by counting down and ringing a bell in a job interview, Cleese was a perfect representation of the bureaucrat doing his job not simply because he was following orders or reluctantly taking part in the system but because he in some ways *knew* that he was engaged in pointless repetitive behavior and, instead of resenting it and quitting, took the reins and used his position to suck all of the joy and life from the surrounding atmosphere: "He was a headmaster who had gone mad" (Morgan 2005, 78).

A good example of the Cleeseian "knowing bureaucrat" appears in the "Argument Clinic" Sketch (ep. 29) where Mr. Vibrating (Cleese), a man presumably well paid to have arguments all day, argues only by the strictest definition of the term. Michael Palin, as his increasingly frustrated client, defines an argument as "a connected series of statements to establish a proposition," but Cleese maliciously contradicts whatever Palin says. Even when the bureaucrat is done and after Palin pays for a

full argument, Cleese maintains his contrary position of sheer contradiction. When Palin notices that although Cleese has said he is done, he
is still engaging the client, Cleese frustratingly asserts that he *is* done and
that maybe he is arguing now "in his spare time." Python's argument
clinic suggests a Kafkaesque world of bureaucracy (as eventually epitomized in Gilliam's masterpiece *Brazil*), where frustration is the norm and
getting any kind of service or even acknowledgment that you have a
case or cause in the first place is an inevitable exercise in sheer futility.

Python realized that, in the words of David Morgan, "the human
condition is, on the whole, pretty absurd" (Morgan 2005, 3). Python saw
that what they considered patently absurd (school, religion, the establishment in general), was consistently normalized, that what was considered normal was to them absurd. As Morgan also noted:

> Python was not about jokes; it was really about a state of mind. It
> was a way of looking at the world as a place where walking like a
> contortionist is not only considered normal but is rewarded with
> government funding; where people speak in anagrams; where
> highwaymen redistribute wealth in floral currencies; and where
> BBC newsreaders use arcane hand signals when delivering the day's
> events. (Morgan 2005, 3)

As we will discuss in the sections on philosophy and language, the
Pythons were constantly asking questions that could cause discomfort
and embarrassment. John Cleese has always been very vocal about how
incredibly obvious it was that much of the social construction of reality
is so evidently a custom that we reinforce by habit. This led to Python
choosing consistent targets and their "persistent lampooning of judges,
accountants, doctors, politicians, TV announcers, military officers, all
who claim, assume or aspire to institutionally established modes of authority, control and social status" (Neale 2008, 77).

To Cleese, "It's like so much of life, nobody actually stops to explain
what the purpose of it is" (Morgan 2005, 41). Sociologist Erving Goffman, in his book *The Presentation of Self in Everyday Life* (1959), wrote that

we in a sense go through life as actors on a stage, with normalized rituals in the front stage that we go along with because we are used to maintaining the appearance that everything we do is normal and has a legitimate purpose, even when the opposite is actually true. According to Cleese, for most people "[i]f you actually say to them, 'What's the purpose of your job?' they can't actually tell you. They've learned a certain number of actions, but they don't actually know what's underlying it all" (Pythons 2003, 41). Cleese is not simplistically suggesting that the emperor has no clothes but is asking: why do we give such importance to rituals and establishments that have no inherent value? The Pythons proposed in their own program not simply that life is silly but two additionally significant points: that the greatest danger for authority figures is humor (because they don't understand it) and that everyone needs to realize how much of a part we all play in keeping our false and meaningless sense of reality going. Python's true importance in many ways is that they ask us to not just laugh at the authority figures and systems that they demolish on-screen but also apply their absurdist line of questioning ourselves. As Cleese happily notes, "After watching Python, people couldn't take the world seriously for the rest of the evening, which is a great feeling and also entirely justifiable" (Pythons 2003, 350). Palin agreed: "Things were changing in the country, in music, fashion, all these tastes were suddenly up for grabs, and I think we wanted to change the way comedy was done" (Pythons 2003, 121). Python

> encompassed a much wider range of "thought" than had heretofore been the norm, including, as it did, references to Icelandic sagas, philosophers such as Jean-Paul Sartre, and relatively obscure historical events while persistently playing with the formats and forms of traditional variety and sketches, of popular culture and popular film and most notably of TV itself. (Neale 2008, 77)

The audience that Python appealed to was mostly young university-educated viewers who were "willing to make a cult of its absurdities and able to understand its references to appreciate the uses it made of media format and forms and to identify with its comic attacks on institutionalized authority" (Neale 2008, 77). Python took the medium of television and, as we will discuss, changed it into something simultaneously subversive and accessible. To their many fans, this was what television was *made* for and finally someone had gotten it right. Python can, perhaps, best be looked at as "capitalistic anarchists": while they opposed all forms of authority, they realized that the best revolutionary approach was to work from within the system, to both use the access mass media provided to reach a broader audience and to milk the flawed system for all it was worth. Python's anti-authoritarian tendencies remain timeless because they were not simply attacking the prevalent class-based British system; they were attacking the idea of authority itself. As Graham Chapman once noted, ". . . on the whole, we didn't emphasize impersonation of political characters of our time. Instead of picking on, say, a particular politician, we usually picked on politicians in general for a silly, pompous politician is timeless" (Chapman and Yoakum 1997, 25). Python in turn remains timeless, as timeless as pompous politicians and meaningless authority.

DISCLAIMERS

In this book, we will look at Python in terms of how they reimagined the world and highlighted the silliness of most of what (Anglophone) culture was taught to take seriously. The book is divided into seven (six, m'lord!) parts, each one taking its theme from a topic or series of interrelated topics that reoccur in Python frequently. Feel free to follow your own muse and start anywhere you want. In particular, the sixth part, "Python on Everything Else," uses shorter thematic pieces to look at some of the ways in which Python highlighted silliness in all corners of the world, from the Fish-Slapping Dance to the Montgolfier brothers to "girls with big tits." Those who bought the book just to see what we have to say about Sir Philip "Bleeding" Sidney or how the British view the French, will find them on pages 109 and 237 respectively, which ought to save you quite a bit of time when you think about it. Python, despite their rejection of linear thought, often was logically consistent, and even when they parodied the institutions that are traditionally dedicated to finding meaning in the human condition (art criticism, psychiatry, philosophy, lumberjacking), it was always parody with a purpose, even if that purpose itself was inherently silly.

Our ultimate goal in this book is *not* to try to tell you why Monty Python is funny. They just *are*—we'd no sooner try to explain all of their jokes than kill your kitten. The effort would be futile, in any event. As Michael Palin has said,

> . . . the joke is so many different things. In Python it isn't just the words; maybe seventy percent are the words and maybe ten percent are sort of look or gesture, something that just happened on that particular recording. There's the mystery of it. (Morgan 2005, 115)

Ignoring for the moment Palin's math, we agree: nailing down a joke is like nailing down Jell-O. It's kind of fun in the moment, but it's a very messy process and no one ever gets to enjoy the Jell-O again. And really: humoric analysis hasn't been considered a serious scientific pursuit since the Middle Ages, when phlegm and bile and choler were still in fashion. So we will leave some of the mystery, never fear.

Of course, there are worse things than comic analysis: comic self-analysis, for example. Terry Jones takes Palin's concern regarding the ineffability of comic creation one step further; for Jones, the self-analysis of humor is not only unproductive, it is counterproductive:

> As soon as you start to try and analyze, ask why it works, why it doesn't work, you can't do it anymore. The only reason for Python is to be *funny*. I suppose if you have a consistent outlook and a point of view, your attitudes come over even if you are writing nonsense, but there is certainly no conscious effort to put over a message. (Morgan 2005, 117)

Now, in our postmodern world, we needn't take the view of any particular author as gospel—who believes what authors say anyway? The author is dead!*

For example, simply because Stephenie Meyer *says* that her romantic tales of a conflicted vampire/innocent girl/pining werewolf (the hugely popular *Twilight* series, first published in 2003) is in no way influenced by Charlaine Harris' award-winning romantic tales of a conflicted vampire/innocent girl/pining werewolf (her *The Southern Vampire Mysteries* series, first published in 2001) doesn't mean it's true. And simply because the legendary fantasy author and literary critic J. R. R. Tolkien *says* he didn't have a world war allegory in mind while he was writing the *Lord of the Rings* doesn't mean that a comparison of the epic wars (on Earth and Middle-earth, real and sub-created) can't yield fruitful insight for modern readers.

And so it goes with Python. Whether Jones and company ever intended any "conscious effort to put over a message" in their comedy, their work belies an evident struggle with understanding the human condition—why else the various false endings in *Meaning of Life*? Why else the false ending of *Monty Python and the Holy Grail*? And what the fuck's up with the alien abduction scene in *Life of Brian*? I mean, really.

Michael Palin (an author, so don't listen to him!) noted that one "strand which I think is in a lot of Python humor . . . is human inadequacy" (Morgan 2005, 116). Following Palin's lead, the world's foremost Python scholar, Darl Larsen, has argued that Python's humor generally stems from a particular human inadequacy, one centered on the failure of human communication. As Larsen rightly notes, "There are very few examples in . . . [*Flying Circus*] of a successful communication or transaction" (301). We will play with that idea a bit as well in Part I: Theory; for now, we will simply add that some *MPFC* sketches seem to address both the joys *and* the limits of human communication—so perhaps

---

*"The Death of the Author" was a highly influential essay (1967) by French literary critic Roland Barthes, who argued that instead of focusing on intentionality and authorial biography, critics should interpret every work divorced from its individual creator. Such an approach gave rise to the panoply of interpretation that critics, readers, and highly opinionated bloggers continue to churn out to this day. So, thanks a lot, Barthes.

the Pythons held out some hope for human linguistic intercourse after all.

Other parts of this book will examine the roles of different media in Python's message and how their sketches both subverted and supported popular genres. And again, we are not without some authorial influence in this interpretation. Terry Gilliam once suggested:

> We were playing with the medium and shifting it around, in the way we were playing with television, and we get no points for that. I'm surprised because one can actually get one's academic intellectual teeth into this stuff. (Morgan 2005, 314)

We will try not to be too biting, but the potential for intellectual recognition of Python remains—with some notable exceptions—unexplored.

Elsewhere, we will discuss the Pythons' lasting influence on popular culture and popular culture's influence on them. In short, we will brush against the thighs of History, canoodle with Politicians, nuzzle Theory's cleavage, and make the beast with two backs with Pop Culture. (The seventies seem so long ago now, don't they? Sigh.) All this we do in service to the humor of Python and all they have taught us.

With these many caveats in mind, we will argue that, on the whole, the Pythons held a sometimes violently anti-authoritarian attitude, one that shows itself in their parody and satire. As noted, John Cleese, in particular, showed a particular talent for portraying "an Establishment character undermining the Establishment" (Morgan 2005, 77). Yet that's not to say that by being anti-establishment they were, ipso facto, funny. There have been plenty of severely unfunny revolutionaries throughout history who prove the contrary.* So Python's rebellion itself isn't funny, but their rebellion fueled their funny; in particular, it informs a great deal of their content (their targets, their settings, their situations). If you're already a Python fan, you may come to realize that their anti-authoritarian

---

*I mean, Che Guevara possessed almost no comic timing whatsoever and Karl Marx just butchered knock-knock jokes. A helluva mime, of course, but not so much with the comedy.

worldview subtly became your own. If you're not yet a fan, perhaps you should put this book down, quietly turn away, and start watching/listening/Googling the Python-verse. Then, once you've been indoctrinated, come back and take a further read. Unless you consider us puppets of the imperialist bourgeoisie, in which case feel free to burn your book at your leisure. (Purchasers of the *Executive Edition* of this tome can simply press the "immolate" button sewn into the dust jacket, of course—the smoke is cinnamon scented!)

And so, without trying to kill the joke that is Monty Python, we will poke around a bit and see what's under the hood. We'll try not to be too pedantic, but since one part of understanding anything in this big ol' world—whether comic or otherwise—is recognizing context and referent, we will try to fill in some of the knowledge gaps for some of the jokes (but certainly not all; if you want to better understand the individual referents in *Flying Circus,* Darl Larsen has already published an exhaustive compendium of factoids: read it). We will try to alert you to what factoids the erudite Pythons have already taught you, how their stream-of-consciousness surreal humor achieved what your patient, structured, and devoted high school teachers couldn't. Monty Python taught you shit—about philosophers and kings, footballers and trees, art and history, cross-dressing and comedy. And fish slapping. Oh, did they teach you about fish slapping.

This work is a tribute to a group who educated us about the way in which most of what we regard as fixed and authoritative is inherently not just a social construction but also quite laughable. In letting us feel that we can laugh at the world instead of mourning its inequity, that we can expose evil through the light of satire and can banish hatred by laughing at the idiocy of the bully, Python has taught us more than almost anything we ever learned in school—and between us, we've been in school for far too long. If we didn't learn everything we needed to know from Monty Python, we learned a lot, and this book is designed to share that with you.

We'll end this pre-emptive mea culpa with an unintended blessing culled from an interview with Michael Palin:

I think there's a danger in Pythons analyzing their own work. I think we shouldn't do it. Anyone else wants to do it, that's fine. I sort of feel that we produced the material, it's out there; once one tries to sort of analyze why we're *funny*, I think it's—I think it's *impossible* to answer for a start, and I also think once we unpick ourselves and give guidelines, in a sense it takes away from the audience their choice of how they react to Python. (Morgan 2005, 115)

So to be clear: we don't want to spoil the joke for anyone by over-analyzing the humor of Monty Python. But remember: we're not Pythons, so we're not verboten from doing so—we don't make the jokes, folks; we just like to think about them. Don't let what follows take away from your enjoyment or your personal judgment. Do use this book to think about whether Python has taught you, as they have taught us, everything we know. Of course, that advice is only for those of you who bought the regular version. We hear that there is a really cool *Executive Executive Edition* of this book with gold trim and all kinds of bells and whistles, a tome that is *guaranteed* to teach you everything you need to know by watching Monty Python, but as the kind folks at Thomas Dunne only send that edition out to über-rich customers and *New Yorker* reviewers, we're not really sure what's in it; if anyone does get a copy, please let the authors know.

"**All brontosauruses are thin on one end . . .**"

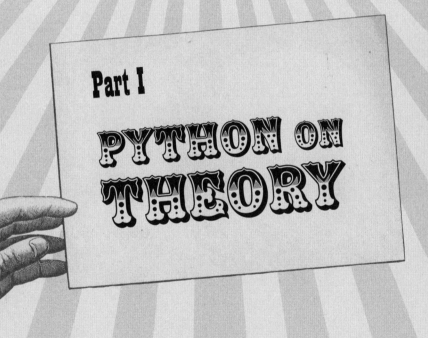

Part I

PYTHON ON THEORY

TAG UNDER: philosophy, linguistics, genre, names, profanity, the media, Surrealism, humor, atomic bomb, Semprini, and pornography.

This chapter, divided into numerous subsections, will look at the way in which Monty Python applied their rigorous training to philosophical and theoretical subjects. We will examine the many television and film references to subjects including politics, religion, linguistics, and even humor to give our readers a greater appreciation of how Python subversively used complex theories for cheap laughs. For example, there's a great deal going on in the cheap laugh elicited by the peasant in *Monty Python and the Holy Grail* who explains to King Arthur that a true political mandate comes from the people, as opposed to some "watery tart lobbing a scimitar at you!" The silliness of the exchange is funny in itself, but the underlying political theory that drives the humor makes the sketch more than simply funny—it's art.*

The Pythons themselves were certainly learned in various current theories (political, linguistic, comedic), but—if the *Flying Circus* sketch "Anne Elk" and her "Theory of the Brontosaurus" (ep. 31) is any indication—they may have held a skeptical view of theories in general. Or at least some of the ways in which any theory is accepted as a proven worldview.

Seated in the spartan conversation pit (*"the usual late-night lineup set"*) of the television show *Thrust: A Quite Controversial Look at the World Around*

---

* But that's a topic for another chapter. Maybe 5 . . . no, 3.

Us, the Presenter (Chapman) introduces his audience to his guest, Miss Anne Elk (Cleese in prim bespectacled Pepperpot mode). As the intro music swells, the two settle into interview postures. Behind them, a black-and-white image of a brontosaurus* hangs on an easel. Starting off the show with a serious directness, Chapman turns to Miss Elk and prompts: "You have a new theory about the brontosaurus." Yet, rather than present her theory, or offer an anecdote about how she came to her theory, or state why her theory is radical or innovative or how it will change human perception of the Jurassic Period (all typical talk-show "teaser" responses), Miss Elk instead either offers her host variations on "I have a theory; it is mine" . . . or she repeatedly clears her throat. Eventually, as Chapman's exasperation grows, Miss Elk delivers her groundbreaking theory:

> This theory goes as follows and begins now. All brontosauruses are thin at one end, much thicker in the middle and then thin again at the far end. That is my theory, it is mine, and belongs to me and I own it, and what it is too.

By so blandly running up against the responsorial expectations for such a "cutting-edge" show (note the provocative main title and the "quite controversial" postcolon title that opened the scene), Elk's revelation underwhelms Chapman, who responds with, "That's *it*, is it?" He then subsequently loses all interest in his guest, fields a phone call, checks his shoes, and wanders off.

Not content to amaze her audience with one incontrovertible theory (which is hers), Miss Elk follows Chapman's Presenter off the *Thrust* set, onto Bounder of Adventure's travel set (where Idle's tourist, Mr. Smoke-Too-Much, continues his earlier rant) as the Fire Brigade choir from the earlier "All-England Summarize Proust" sketch wanders on. Oblivious to the metatheatrical mashing going on around her, Miss Elk proudly utters her second theory:

---

*Now (and again) known as the apatosaurus. No, really: ask any ten-year-old.

"My second theory states that fire brigade choirs seldom sing songs about Marcel Proust." Upon which, as the stage prompts note, *"With only a half-beat pause the fire brigade start singing the Proust song."**

Faced with an explicit refutation of theory, the multiple sketches collide, give way to chaos, and—as a loony looks in—the episode fades out.

FACTOID BOX: Theory

Theories are testable and well-informed ideas about different scientific, pseudo-scientific, linguistic, religious, or social topics. Theories pose questions and contain valid hypotheses that can be tested. In the social science fields, there are many different methodological approaches to theory, but most approaches rely on quantitative, qualitative, historical, or textual analysis of some sort. As Kevin Williams put it, in most theoretical methods "theory can be tested through empirical investigation" or "can be secured through systematic and rigorous procedures of investigation" (2003, 2). While most theories cannot technically be "proven" beyond a shadow of a doubt, certain theories (evolution, gravity, the Mets losing this season) are so well accepted as to be regarded as fact instead of theory. In terms of archaeological theory, Anne Elk's "theory" about the brontosaurus may be accurate in some ways but is certainly not the kind of theory that would be acceptable as the conclusion to serious research. Ahem. Ahem.

---

* See the section on Literature in Part III: Art for more on the "All-England Summarize Proust Competition" . . . and Python's artful employment of *"a lady with enormous knockers."*

Such may very well be the response from most readers when presented with any part of any book titled "Python on Theory." Critical Theory—the jargon-laden, navel-gazing, mental masturbation of needlessly verbose overeducated white-collar intellectual types—is stereotypically a dour endeavor that sucks the life out of whatever it examines. Psychoanalytical Theory, Feminist Theory, Literary Theory, Marxist Theory, Stimulus-Response Theory, Economic Theory ... the list goes on and on, and every one of them is a snoozer. Yet unlike Anne Elk's theory (which proves to be absolutely empty and certainly not avant-garde), theory—even inherently humorless theory—can illuminate and be illuminated by the Pythons' oeuvre. This part of the book will sketch out how various modern critical theories—some quite cutting-edge when *Flying Circus* first aired—are echoed, presaged, or problematized by the erudite Pythons. If naught else, the Pythons taught theoretically minded viewers that sometimes a cigar isn't just a cigar—it's an exploding penguin on the telly.

PHILOSOPHY

"Half a bee, philosophically, must, ipso facto, half not be."

From the enumeration of philosophical luminaries in "The Philosophers Song" (usually presented in the live versions of the "Bruces" sketch) to the conversational rhetoric of the "Argument Clinic" sketch (ep. 29) to the existential lament over Eric the half a bee (on the *Monty Python's Previous LP* record) to the philosophers playing football (in *Monty Python's Fliegender Zirkus*) who, instead of actually playing football, largely ponder the idea of playing football, Python seemed virtually obsessed with philosophy. The concept of trying to understand the meaning of life was one of the underlying themes of Python (heck, they even structured a film around the question), as was the complexity of language and how language helped to maintain and create reality; note, for example, the chaplain of the boys' school who is admonished by the headmaster because he was "wrestling with Plato" (in the "Seven Brides for Seven Brothers" sketch, ep. 18).

Throughout their career, Python tackled the philosophical approach to "unearthing and explicating the meaning of life and what the ultimate human goods are" (McGinn 2012). They deconstructed the application of philosophy in real-life settings, realizing that we can look at philosophy as "a systematic reflection on the nature of reality and humanity's place in that reality"(McGinn 2012); and because Python looked at reality as a weirdly constructed set of situations adrift from logic and meaning, they were able to assert that using philosophy in a world that made no sense with no real mandate for authority could lead to all kinds of new absurdities. In a meaningless or chaotic world, philosophy offered no consolation but was perhaps reduced to, as Alfred North Whitehead wrote, "a series of footnotes to Plato" (Smith 2012). Granted, those notes were scribbled in crayon in the margins with unsteady, childlike penmanship, but you have to give the human race points for trying.

Philosophy, a concept that the Pythons doubtless studied in some depth while at university, was a key and consistent part of the Python deconstruction. The word "philosophy" derives from the ancient Greek "philos" and "sophia" and translates literally as "love of wisdom." The term "philosophy"—the "origin is sometimes attributed to Pythagoras" (McGinn 2012)—is one of the great bugaboos of academia, in that while everyone who attends college *studies* philosophy (in some form or another, whether in or out of the discipline proper), the idea of the philosopher (like the legendary Pythagoras, alone, walking about, presumably thinking great thoughts about the totality of human existence), remains a puzzling concept to most outside of the rarified field. Most people still have no real idea what exactly philosophers *do* for a living. Hell, most people tend to think of philosophy as in Python's football sketch, where great thinkers wander about scratching their heads and musing about difficult ideas. This is despite the fact that even the term "philosophy" itself has many different meanings outside of the academic discipline and applying "the label to any seeker persisted until around the 18th century" and is similar to the study of science in many ways because "the subject is systematic, rigorous, replete with technical vocabulary, often in conflict with common sense, capable of refutation, produces hypotheses, uses symbolic notation, is about the natural world, is institutionalized,

FACTOID BOX:
Spot the Drunken Football-Playing Philosopher!

The "Philosophers Football Match" was a heady game indeed! For the Greeks, the impressive lineup included: Socrates, Plato, Heraclitus, Empedocles of Acragas, Aristotle, Epicurus, Archimedes, Epictetus, Aristotle, Plotinus, "Chopper" Sophocles; and for the Germans: Kant, Schlegel, Marx (who came in the second half as a replacement for Wittgenstein), Hegel, Leibniz, Schopenhauer, Schelling, Beckenbauer,* Jaspers, Kant, Nietzsche, and Heidegger.

---

* Beckenbauer is the "ringer" on the German team, of course. Franz "Der Kaiser" Beckenbauer was not a philosopher by trade but the greatest German footballer of all time. He was also an active player in the 1960s and 1970s, which made him an instantly recognizable figure for the viewers of *Flying Circus*.

peer-reviewed, tenure grading, etc." (McGinn 2012). While we all engage in philosophical debates, perhaps what Python was really parodying was the professionalization of the field.

Python generally employs a more democratic approach, taking philosophy out of the academy and putting it back on the playing field, sometimes literally. (See also Part V: Sport.) While Python does name many philosophers in the football match, there is no sense that they are espousing any particular philosophy; instead Python treats the field as one more lofty subject to be bandied about in and out of context, ecumenically embraced as a whole. Why claim one philosophical precept as true when you can make fun of the whole lot of them?

The game—which ends when Archimedes has an idea and after shouting "Eureka!" scores an actual goal—is largely a long shot of the philosophers musing as they walk about the field. The sketch works because, as philosopher Julian Baggini, in an article about current philosophers re-enacting the match, quoted Terry Jones as saying that "football is a team activity, which philosophy, as a general rule, isn't" (2010). Hence, the brilliance of the match.

Even the Python sketches that do not cite specific philosophers by name suggest that specific philosophical concepts were being used to illustrate humorous points. In *Monty Python and the Holy Grail*, the idea of how the muck-addled peasants relate to the (relatively) clean and regal-looking King Arthur, clearly separated by a chasm, not just based on the fact that the King "hasn't got shit all over him" but also because the King has a hereditary and magical claim on the crown . . . a claim that is disputed by Palin's peasant who argues that real power does not come from the Lady of the Lake but from a mandate from the masses. The fact that even the usually patient King Arthur is soon verbally oppressing him ("Help, help, I'm being oppressed!" Palin cries) fits into the medieval worldview, where class and privilege were not just the ordinary unquestioned facts of life but the basis for a system that was designed to persevere, despite the seeming lack of a moral center in mankind.

One philosopher, Thomas Hobbes (who according to the Bruces' song was "fond of his drams"), can be used to sum up the philosophical world of *Holy Grail* where authority is arbitrary and even a most chivalrous knight (Lancelot) on a quest to rescue the maiden fair ends up killing most of a wedding party in his righteous wrath. As Jacques Barzun put it, "Hobbes saw man in the state of nature as an aggressor, man is wolf to man. Unless controlled, he and his fellows live life that is 'solitary, poor, nasty, brutish and short.'" From these premises, reason concludes that government must be strong, its laws emphatic and rigorously enforced to prevent outbreaks of wolfish nature against other men (2000, 267). Although Hobbes is often presumed to have been a royalist apologist, he does not specify a monarch and so his work but could also be interpreted as the "justification for an absolute parliament" (Barzun 2000, 267). Hobbes' view of the world—a place that needs a strong social contract because man must be protected from himself—*is* the medieval world of *Holy Grail,* where unprotected old women are viciously said, "Ni!" to by their passing strangers with impunity.

The Swiss philosopher Jean-Jacques Rousseau (sadly not mentioned in "The Philosophers Song"; one can only imagine what he must have drunk!) would also have seen the mistreatment of the "constitutional peasants" as an egregious breach of the social contract. Rousseau essentially reduced his explanation of the social contract to "each of us places in common his person and all his power under the supreme direction of the general will; and as one body we all receive each member as an indivisible part of the whole" (1975, 15). Sadly, as Rousseau lived in the eighteenth century, he was not able to advise Palin's medieval (and fictional, for that matter) peasant of his inalienable rights.

Logic is often one of the issues discussed in Python's explorations into philosophy. Even Chapman's autobiographical book, *A Liar's Autobiography,* itself suggests that all biographies, as well as all accounts of the apparent truth or reality of any situation, are actually very much open to personal interpretation (Chapman et al. 1980). One need only look to the brouhaha that ensued in 2006 when talk-show host Oprah Winfrey discovered that an autobiography she had placed on her influential "Oprah's Book Club" recommended reading list—*A Million Little Pieces*—turned out to be largely a fiction. Unfortunately for the author, James Frey (a recovering drug addict and, apparently, serial liar), the truth of his memoir was rather divergent from the historical reality corroborated by criminal records and public death certificates. (Oprah's wrath was awesome.) Although humans often seek empirical reality or personal truths, perhaps the best we can achieve is a sort of common agreement, a reality that "makes sense" to all involved. Especially to Oprah.

But Python also had their own internal version of logic. Things "happened" not because of causality or the autonomous nature of human beings but because the universe was random and chaotic. While the "Lumberjack" sketch (ep. 9) is best known for its iconic song (and that's okay!), it is also one of the sketches where Python plays upon the concept that reality is just an assumption that we all share. In the sketch the lumberjack (played by Palin) starts off as a barber who is frightened that he might cut a little bit more than hair from his customers. After the customer (Jones) finally realizes that the barber is only pretending to cut his hair (using a rather well-timed recording of a banal barbershop conservation), the barber reveals his true career plans and moves off the barbershop set to a more pastoral one, reminiscent of the woods of British Columbia. While this is yet another Pythonesque comment on the nature of television it is also an acknowledgment that we are all playing roles in an artificial world, that reality itself is as malleable as identity, and that we should not put too much faith in the constructed world that surrounds us.

To many, including real-life philosophers, this deconstruction of philosophy was one of the better representations of philosophy ever portrayed in television and movies. As Julian Baggini (editor of *The Philosophers' Magazine*) wrote about Python and philosophy

> . . . at the risk of getting silly, I'd go so far as to say that Python represents a coherent Anglo-Saxon take on existentialism. French thinkers such as Camus and Sartre recognized the absurdity of life, but it took the English Pythons to show that the right response was to laugh at it. (2010)

Baggini also points out that John Cleese thought that "comedy and deep thought could go hand in hand" (2010) and what the Pythons were doing, such as in the Pepperpots' quest to find Jean-Paul Sartre and ask him about the meaning of his books *Rues a Liberté* * (*Roads to Freedom*), indicates that we are all on a quest to find some kind of meaning in life. Python works towards that end by questioning whether there is inherent meaning in any institution and asking where presumptions of authority actually come from. Academic philosopher Alan Richardson has said,

---

* When they finally reach the apartment of "Mr. and Mrs. Jean-Paul Sartre (who apparently lives in the same building as Mr. and Mrs. Jean Genet)" they ask the offstage Sartre if "his famous trilogy, *Rues a Liberté*, is it an allegory for man's search for commitment." He merely answers, "Oui."

"The only difference between Monty Python and academic philosophy is that philosophy isn't funny" (Malamud 2011).

Python also continually dropped names the way an upper-class twit would at a cocktail party. Almost every sketch that deals with logic or philosophy brings up the names of various experts in the field, almost daring the viewer to keep up. In the "Bruces" sketch alone (ep. 22), the banned "great socialist thinkers would certainly include at least the structuralism school so popular in the 1960s and 1970s in Europe, including such luminaries as Ferdinand de Saussure, Claude Lévi-Strauss, Lacan, Foucault and Althusser" (Larsen 2008, 296). Larsen does not mention two who would have been very prominent on that list, Baudrillard and Derrida, who also dealt with the connection between language and reality, which in many ways was exactly what Python was trying to do when they examined philosophy.

LINGUISTIC THEORY
"Ee ecky thump."

Monty Python's exploration of language—of the uses and abuses of language in the name of humor, of lexical and syntactic ambiguity resulting in humor, of the limits of language as a communicative device—is perhaps the most ubiquitous element in their oeuvre and arguably the element that most identifies them as practitioners of "intellectual" humor and exposes their (un)common Oxbridge background. In particular, their comic abuse of traditional grammar, vocabulary, and pronunciation belies their mastery of conventional linguistics and linguistic theory. Granted, when their audience fails to "get" these jokes it can alienate them ("What the hell is so funny about saying that? *I* say that!"), but when the audience does laugh such linguistic humor can both reinforce and inform.

Larsen, commenting on "French Subtitled Film" (ep. 23) points to the current revolution in linguistic theory that the Pythons drew upon:

[Miscommunication] is a key element ... for the Pythons, and is based on the recent interest in semantics and semiotics, the growing awareness that meaning isn't just "there," it is imbued by and for society/culture, and that meaning can and does fluctuate depending on *context*. The separation of a word from its "meaning" allows for new meanings and even multiple meanings to be temporarily affixed to a word—there now exists the possibility of "wiggle room" in the world of language. Modernist authors like Joyce, Stein, Pound, Woolf, and Eliot pushed this separation, this interchangeability, and the Pythons came along at just the right time to explore that new ambiguity in the television format. (2008, 301)

Linguistic communication and miscommunication goes beyond individual words, of course: meaning is conveyed via singular morphemes as well as words, phrases, and idioms; meaning is conveyed through conversations (for what good is language if no one receives it?); meaning is conveyed through form and genre; and ultimately, as contemporary linguists were arguing at the time, meaning is reliant upon context. Here, then, is a sampling of how genre, conversations, and words (in particular, naming and word creation) are employed in Python.

GENRE
"Pantomime horse is a Secret Agent."

The Pythons are largely responsible for introducing the mash-up to television, and many of their most memorable mash-ups seem to have less to do with particular vocabulary use/abuse than with the questioning of generic constraints. However, inherent in the plethora of generic mash-ups depicted throughout the four seasons of *Flying Circus* is the validation of literary forms and viewer expectations or, in a wider sense, a validation of genre as effectively communicative. For example, *Measure for Measure* fails when performed underwater,* but

---

* As do *Hello, Dolly!* and Formula 2 racing.

Shakespeare's final comedy has traditionally succeeded onstage. *Wuthering Heights* fails as an exercise in semaphore but (presumably) succeeds as a novel. *Gentlemen Prefer Blondes* fails when presented via smoke signals but succeeds as a film. And so on.* Mode of presentation and genre—although so very often taken for granted—matter in these skits.

And, in one particularly effective, moving, and utterly ludicrous generic relocation in episode 22, *The Death of Mary Queen of Scots* (traditionally a tragedy) elicits far more humor than expected when enacted as a BBC Radio program, replete with an overabundance of (conventional radio) sound effects and pregnant pauses:

> Radio Announcer: And now we present the first episode of a new radio drama series, *The Death of Mary Queen of Scots*. Part one, the beginning.
>
> *Theme music: "Coronation Scot" as used in* Paul Temple *for years*
>
> Man's Voice: You are† Mary Queen of Scots?
>
> Woman's Voice: I am.‡
>
> *There now follows a series of noises indicating that Mary is getting the shit knocked out of her. Thumps, bangs, slaps, pneumatic drilling, sawing, flogging, shooting, all interlarded with Mary's screams. The two women [Pepperpots sitting at the radio] listen calmly. After a few seconds: fade as the signature tune, "Coronation Scot," is brought up loudly to denote ending of episode.*
>
> Radio Announcer: Episode two of *The Death of Mary Queen of Scots* can be heard on Radio 4 almost immediately.

---

*"Gunfight at the OK Corral in Morse Code" (ep. 15); "Stock Market Report by Exchange Telegraph" (ep. 27); "Julius Caesar on an Aldis Lamp" (ep.15); "M1 Interchange Built by *Paradise Lost* Characters" (ep. 35); "Housing Project Built by Eighteenth-Century Fictional Characters" (ep. 35). Or, in episode 3, Idle's children's storyteller is stymied by the rapid devolution of predictable nursery characters behaving crudely (where Old Nick the Sea Captain hangs "out down by the pier where men dressed like ladies," or where Rumpletweezer "sold contraceptives and . . . discipline? . . . naked? . . . with a melon!?")

†Pronounced "yoo arr" in low, thuggish (potentially Scottish) tones.

‡Pronounced in typically high-pitched Pepperpot falsetto.

"Well, what's on the telly?"
Two Pepperpots (Cleese and Chapman) explore lexical ambiguity in *Monty Python's Flying Circus.*

One of the women goes to the set and switches it over. As she goes back to her seat from the radio we hear the theme music again, fading out as the sounds of violence and screaming start again and continue unabated in vigor.

Man's Voice: I think she's dead.

Woman's Voice: No I'm not.

After a time, sounds of violence and screaming start again, rapidly fading under the tune of "Coronation Scot."

Announcer's Voice: That was episode two of *The Death of Mary Queen of Scots,* specially adapted for radio by Bernard Hollowood and Brian London.* And now, Radio 4 will explode.

(The radio explodes.)

---

* Possibly worth noting: in the American staging of the sketch, Hollowood (English writer/editor/cartoonist) and London (English boxer) are replaced with Gracie Fields (English actress/singer/comedienne) and Joe Frazier (American boxer).

Bereft of their radio, the two Pepperpots then turn to watch the television, which leads to the lexically ambiguous* question, "What's on the telly?"

The Death of Mary Queen of Scots thus serves as a violent—indeed, explosive—indictment of generic instability (a popular conceit in late-sixties avant-garde cinema) and a self-reflexive comment on passive audience expectation.[†]

Of course, if exploding radios and penguins do not call enough explicit attention to the suitability of performance modes, there remains the metatheatrical re-examination of generic incongruity in the re-enactments performed by the Batley Townswomen's Guild (portrayed, as usual, by the Pythons in drag). Skits include the "Batley Townswomen's Guild Presents the Battle of Pearl Harbour" (ep. 11) and the "Batley Townswomen's Guild Presents the First Heart Transplant" (ep. 22). In both re-enactments, regardless of the diversity of subject matter and genre, the Pepperpotted Pythons generally just wail on one another with their purses; as the script prompts for episode 11 notes, "the two sides set about each other with handbags etc., speeded up 50% just to give it a bit of edge"; and for episode 22 "The two groups of ladies rush at each other. They end up in the sea, rolling about and splashing, and thumping each other with handbags." In addition to the base slapstick violence presented, humor arises in the meta-meta narratives presented, of professional cross-dressing actors acting as amateur actresses acting (poorly) in various roles, all without any variety. But as before, underlying the nudge-nudge-wink-wink performativity elements is an implicit validation of generic expectations.[‡]

---

* That is, the word "on" as used in the context of television yields two possible meanings: what is "on air" (that is, what image is being emitted visually via the cathode tube of the television screen) and what is "on top" of the television set itself (in this case, an exploding penguin. You know, back when console television sets were essentially massive furniture pieces, not flat screens a half inch deep. Take a skinny penguin, nowadays . . .).

† See Larsen's (2008, 101) commentary on "Man Turns into Scotsman" (ep. 7): "incidental music referendum": diegetic and extra-diegetic conventionality.

‡ Likewise, see Larsen (2008, 104) on the "Science Fiction" sketch (ep. 7) regarding the "undermining [of] audience expectations of the genre."

And so, by comically employing early mash-ups,* the Pythons explore genre-specific meaning and audience expectation. But they also examine—and problematize—the expectations of everyday language employed in everyday situations, particularly in conversations between sellers and consumers, between those who have and those who want.

CONVERSATIONS
"Quite frankly I'm against people who give vent to their loquacity by extraneous bombastic circumlocution."

By indirectly asking the question, "When does language work?" the Pythons validate the established conventions of language while simultaneously alerting the viewer to the tenuous nature of linguistic convention. As the witty banter of many of their sketches amply shows, the Pythons were keenly interested in conversations—especially (but not exclusively) those that break down into miscommunication and confusion.

Compared to most other life-forms on the planet, humans communicate via a complex and highly articulated system of verbal signs; we are capable of linguistically transmitting information with astonishing speed, depth, and accuracy. We are also, of course, capable of utterly confusing, aggravating, and misleading one another with our words.[†] But generally speaking, humans who choose their words carefully are capable of connecting with their fellow humans on a level unknown in the animal kingdom.

Yet there are limits. Our reliance on oral and written communication also truncates human thought (has anyone ever *fully* expressed their "true

---

*This holds trebly true for the interstitials provided by Gilliam—every one is a deep mash-up, when you get down to it, and the gothic juxtaposition of the images results in much of their humor.

[†]The marvel of human communication is predicated upon clarity of voice and auditory reception, of course. See the Pythons' version of the Sermon on the Mount in *Life of Brian* for a particularly insightful example of interpretive closure and auditory misinterpretation. "Blessed are the cheesemakers" indeed.

love" to another?), breeds confusion ("When I nod my head, you hit it!"), and frustrates even expert users on a daily basis ("Did you know there's a word for when you can't quite remember a word? I forget what it is, but there is one."). The Python crew—like a great many other comedians . . . and some few tragedians—were highly aware of the limits of language, and through their very precise use of language they alert the rest of us to the very imprecise nature of language itself. As Python points out time and again, humans too often take language for granted . . . flawed and funny old thing that it is. Presque vu, s'il vous plaît.

Through a series of "what if?" scenarios posed throughout their sketches, Python explores the often-tenuous set of conversational expectations assumed "natural" by so many of us. Take, for example, the Four Conversational Maxims as articulated by Paul Grice in 1975.* Grice posited that a Cooperative Principle underlies all successful human interaction and urged every speaker to ". . . make your contribution such as it is required, at the stage at which it occurs, by the accepted purpose or direction of the talk exchange in which you are engaged." That is, in any "polite" (mutually agreed upon) conversation, the participants will attempt, to the best of their abilities, to "play nice"—they will not flout (intentionally contradict) the following four maxims/expectations:

Quality: a response should be, to the best of the speaker's
   knowledge, truthful.
Quantity: sufficient[†] information should be given.
Manner: the language used by each speaker should be clear,
   mutually accessible, and unambiguous.
Relevance: any response should be "to the point" or on topic.

---

*Paul, Grice (1975). "Logic and Conversation," in *Syntax and Semantics,* vol. 3: *Speech Acts,* ed. P. Cole and J. Morgan (New York: Academic Press, 1975), reprinted in *Studies in the Way of Words,* ed. H. P. Grice, pp. 22–40 (Cambridge, MA: Harvard University Press, 1989).
[†] Sufficiency determined by situational context. One's answer to "How are you?" will vary dramatically if the question is asked by a friend at a bar, a passerby in the hallway, or a doctor in an emergency room.

Now of course, in everyday conversations people invariably violate or flout these maxims for various reasons; we violate maxims to avoid unwanted conversations (Q: "Hey, baby, what's your sign?" A: "Yo no hablo inglés"); to point out our displeasure with certain topics (Q: "Don't you love me, Reginald?" A: "Wonderful weather we're having, don't you think, Cynthia?"); or simply because we have not paid sufficient attention (Q: "Are the pot pies done?" A: "Beef or turkey!"). The Pythons, of course, most regularly flout the conventions for humor. "The Cheese Shop" (ep. 33), for example, is one of their most famous sketches, and one of the lengthiest examples of someone successfully flouting the Maxim of Quality; truth, it seems, is in many ways like fermented milk—it gets sharper with age, often stinks, and is sometimes simply not available.

Cleese (as the upper-class, or at least learned, customer Mousebender) visits "Ye Olde Cheese Emporium" in search of "some cheesy comestibles" after a contemplative turn at the public library; Palin (as the working-class proprietor, Mr. Wensleydale) stands behind the remarkably clean—indeed, it is devoid of cheese—counter, apparently available to serve his customer while bouzouki music plays in the background. What ensues is a protracted Q&A regarding what cheese—if any—is available for purchase in the "finest [cheese shop] in the district." Mousebender gamely requests, by name, some fifty-plus cheeses, only to be repeatedly denied (with minor variations on "No") by Wensleydale, who nonetheless leads the increasingly exasperated Mousebender to believe that—as this is a cheese shop—there must be some cheese for purchase. In the end, Wensleydale confesses that he does not, in fact, have any cheese at all for sale; Mousebender then shoots him in the head.

In the end, the sketch is funny not simply because the shopkeeper lies repeatedly (the crescendo of increasing customer exasperation, the seemingly endless barrage of cheesy nomenclature, and that bloody bouzouki player are the humorous triple threat here). But our collective linguistic assumption that in any conversation—particularly one set in the context of sales, cheesy or otherwise—should be predicated upon the honest exchange of information enables the sketch to proceed at all. So deeply engrained is the Cooperative Principle that we—like Cleese's "peckish"* customer (the aptly named Mousebender)—give Palin's shop-keeper (the cheesily named Wensleydale) the "benefit of the doubt" for far longer than he deserves. As the finale approaches, of course, even Mousebender loses faith in the inherently optimistic sociolinguistic contract he assumed with Wensleydale: "No, that figures. It was pretty predictable really. It was an act of the purest optimism to pose the question in the first place." And so, for violating the basic tenets of linguistic sociability, Wensleydale deserves to be shot. And he is, which leads into the increasingly bloody episode of the next sketch, and the finest mash-up in all of Pythondom (according to noted expert in suchlike, Brian Cogan): Sam Peckinpah's *Salad Days*.

As Grice might suggest, polite society (and perhaps society in general) is predicated upon linguistic cooperation, upon commonly understood verbal conventions. Without those predictable linguistic conventions (as with generic expectations) humans cannot effectively communicate meaning, and without effective communication polite society breaks down: people get shot, for instance.

Akin to the "Cheese Shop" sketch, the "Argument Clinic" sketch (ep. 29) is at first based on the divergent expectations of the participants. Coming into room 12 (as directed by the receptionist), Palin's customer expects to engage in a five-minute argument, only to be assaulted by Chapman's abuse: "Don't give me that, you snotty-faced heap of parrot droppings!" However, once the error in conversational expectation has been identified by the participants ("Look! I came in here for an argument") the two conversants are able to communicate effectively ("Oh! I'm sorry, this is abuse.").

However, unlike in the "Cheese Shop" sketch, the participants in this sketch do not seem to be intentionally violating/flouting the Gricean Maxims ... or do they? Once he finds the correct room, Palin comes to a verbal impasse with Mr. Vibrating (Cleese), employee of the argument clinic as the two argue about what exactly an argument‡ is: one conver-

---

* See also: "esurient."†
† See also: "all hungry-like."
‡ Or at least what a "good argument" is.

sant argues simply by uttering simple contradictions ("No, it isn't!"), the other by employing what he considers "intellectual process." Since the two cannot agree whether an argument is essentially the utterance of "contrary position[s]" or "a connected series of statements to establish a definite proposition," their conversation seems doomed to fail and/or to continue indefinitely. Like the theatre of generic expectation that informs our appreciation of the literary arts—anyone reading *Paradise Lost* expecting to enjoy a light RomCom or reading *Twilight* expecting epic poetry will be disappointed (and likely very confused)—the theatre of conversational expectation is required for effective communication.

Yet before the limit of human patience is again breached (as in the "Cheese Shop" sketch), Cleese/Vibrating betrays his violation of the Gricean Maxims by claiming that—contrary to the evidence witnessed by the audience—Palin's customer has not paid for another five minutes of arguing. While Cleese's obviously false utterance (a violation of the Maxim of Quality) should be enough to halt the conversation—clearly, one of the participants is not playing fair—Palin's character is more interested in arguing that by continuing to contradict his assertions that he had indeed paid, Mr. Vibrating is in fact arguing according to Palin's own definition of "an argument" and therefore confirms through his continued engagement in the conversation that Palin had, indeed, paid. This would then, of course, also confirm Palin's view that argument is an intellectual process, as he has won the argument via the application of logic to known circumstance and knowledge.

Naturally, Mr. Vibrating does not agree with this conclusion, stating that "I could be arguing in my spare time"; he even baits Palin's frustrated customer with a final contrary salvo (ignored) before Palin exits to voice his displeasure in the Complaints Department . . . only to be *complained to*, rather than *listened to* . . . thus ending the sketch with a final broken theatre of conversational expectation, another bit of confounding linguistic ambiguity.

Ultimately, the protracted sketch—and the entire episode—dissolves in a series of embedded arrests based on accusations that the participants "did willfully take part in a strange sketch . . . of an unconventional nature with the intent to cause grievous mental confusion to the Great

British Public." Furthermore, the entire show is accused of "acts of self-conscious behaviour." And indeed they are, as all examinations of language require self-conscious behavior if said examinations are conducted via language. It's enough to cause grievous mental confusion to anyone, really.

PRAGMATICS
"Say no more!"

The extreme circumlocution (lit.: "speaking around") of the "Nudge Nudge" skit (ep. 3) likewise reveals the necessity of established conversational criteria—felicity conditions, to be precise. Here the Maxim of Manner is violated, or at least stretched, to the point that intended communication fails. Written by Eric Idle (as Jones metatheatrically notes during the episode: "I want to see a sketch of Eric's. Nudge Nudge."), the sketch revels in verbal rather than conceptual comedy—a typical divide among the Pythons, as they themselves recall: the Cambridge Pythons tended to produce verbal scripts, while the Oxfordians produced more conceptual humor. It is a master class in conversational failure predicated upon what linguists call pragmatics: the non-literal, non-verbal elements of human communication.

In the sketch, Idle's pubgoer attempts, in every way but directly, to ask his fellow patron (Jones) what it's like to have sex with a woman. Idle's character (Norman, according to the script) employs a great many euphemisms for "active sexual partner" ("Is your wife a . . . goer . . . eh? Know what I mean?"; "Your wife, is she, eh . . . is she a sport? Eh?"; "She's been around, eh?"; "Your wife interested in, er . . . photographs, eh? Know what I mean? Photographs, 'he asked him knowingly'"), all of which are not comprehended by the oblivious Jones, who has not been explicitly "cued in" by Idle. That is, Jones and Idle are not operating within the same set of conversational expectations. Nevertheless, Idle offers traditionally salacious non-verbal cues (nudging Jones with his elbow, leaning in conspiratorially, waggling his head, slapping his hands together); all the while, he metatheatrically underscores his non-verbal cues by verbally "narrating" his own performed action (Idle actually says, "Nudge nudge. Snap snap. Grin, grin, wink, wink, say no more," while nudging Jones, miming photography, winking, and grinning). The attention bestowed upon the pragmatic moments of communication (the traditionally non-literal, non-spoken secondary elements of human communication), normally so essential to the clarification of verbal speech, are useless here, as Jones' anonymous character (simply listed as "Him") innocently fails to "get it," fails to understand what Idle is insinuating.

The failing conversation only ends when Idle is forced to *explicitly* ask what he's been implying extra-linguistically throughout—"What's it [sex with a woman] like?"—an explicit utterance then punctuated by an atypically *"enormous artificial laugh on soundtrack."* Just as the Pythons ridicule traditional telegraph humor elsewhere—they generally eschew jokes with obvious punch lines*—they ridicule the need for explicit utterance here. Subtle communication reveals wit, erudition, and comprehension, not overt, *tah-dum-dum!* explicitly punctuated expression. Yet even when one chooses one's possessive words *very* carefully, confusion can arise. Insight too.

WORDS: ONOMASTICS AND NEOLOGISMS
"They call me . . . Tim?"

Onomastics—the study of names, their history, and meaning—has a long and storied place in world history, both fictional and non-fictional. Traditionally, names have been believed to hold power: know a person's true name and you hold power over them. Take, for example, the fairy tale about Rumpelstiltskin. As most of us know (but very likely have no recollection *how* we know), Rumpelstiltskin (the usual English transliteration of the original German *Rumpelstilzchen*: lit. "little rattle stilt"— hence imp-who-rattles posts, akin to a poltergeist) tells the tale of a

---

* See, for example, the running gags "But it's my only line!" and the use of captioned "And now the punch line" in various skits (as in ep. 3).

maiden who is ordered to spin straw into gold. Not knowing how to perform this mercantile magic, the maid is distraught until a "little man" enters and offers to spin the golden straw for her, if she offers up to him—in series—her necklace, her ring, and finally her child. To all this she agrees; she is happy with the bargain until Rumpelstiltskin calls upon her to deliver to him her firstborn child. Still, there is an escape clause: if she can guess his true name, she can keep the baby.

She first guesses "normal" names, like Kaspar, Melchior, Balzer—"all the names she knew." None are correct. She then asks the locals for unusual names, such as Beastrib, Muttoncalf, and Legstring—but none are correct. Finally (third time's a charm!), she is told by a messenger that he had witnessed a "comical little man" hopping about on one foot crowing about his rather remarkable name: Rumpelstiltskin. She proffers this name and thus guesses correctly; in his "anger . . . [Rumpelstiltskin] stomped his right foot so hard into the ground that he fell in up to his waist. Then with both hands he took hold of his left foot and ripped himself up the middle in two" (Grimm 2002).

Now, not only is this fairy tale a fine example of the power names have over supernatural creatures, it also teaches a fine psychosexual lesson: ladies, always get the name of the gentleman before you give up to him your necklace, your ring, or any other "hole-y" object of worth. Especially if his name is a euphemism for "penis."*

Other, more serious tales teach us the power of names. Take G-d, for example. In Christopher Marlowe's tragic play *Doctor Faustus*, the good doctor summons a devil to do his bidding in exchange for Faustus' immortal soul. And, although Faustus thinks that dribbly candles, secret sigils, and four cc's of rat's blood is essential to the summoning ritual, as the erudite doctor finds out:

---

*Good—you're down here in the footnote where it's safe. See, his name—in the English, anyway—suggests that he is literally "rumpled skin on a stick," you know: a real dick. Although he successfully took from the maiden two fine symbols of her womanhood (stick takes the circles), after his identity has been established he suffers self-emasculation—ripping off his own "leg" after pounding a hole in the earth—and is thus utterly destroyed. G'night!

Faustus:	Did not my conjuring raise thee? Speak.
Mephistophilis	That was the cause, but yet *per accidens*.
	For, when we hear one rack the name of God,
	Abjure the Scriptures and his Savior Christ,
	We fly in hope to get his glorious soul. (Marlowe, I. iii)

To anagrammatize (rearrange the letters in) his name is to turn against God; to turn against God is to summon the devil. Not for nothing is "Thou shalt not take the Lord thy God's name in vain" on the top ten list.

So names traditionally carry power. Some names also "carry" meaning within themselves—either as part of their construction (whether locative, occupational, or attributive) or due to associations with others who have carried those names (the idiotic American family who named their child Hitler, for example, or even Carla's son on *Cheers* who was named Benito Mussolini after his two grandfathers).

Think about your own names—your praenomen (first name), your nomen (middle name, if you have one), and your cognomen (last name). If you have multiple nomen or cognomen, analyze them all (that's what you get for having modern and/or divorced and/or pretentious parents). If you have an oft-used nickname (as the Anglo Saxons would say, *an eke nama*), think about that as well. In the end, what do you consider your "true" name to be, and how does it influence your self-perception or the perception of others? Exactly what roles do our names play in our lives?

Many a cognomen (and many a nomen nowadays) may be a patronymic or matronymic, express kinship (Jameson, Olafsdőtter, O'Mally), indicate a place (London, Hall), or denote an occupation (Smith, Wright). It may also be a diminutive or variant of an older, more common name (as Wilkins is a diminutive of Williams or as Harman is a variant of Hermann), or it may express some physical or moral characteristic (Longfellow, Moody). Where a name comes from (the locative or topographical aspect), what cultural significance it carries or once carried (religious, moral, political, ideological), and how it is constructed (whether affixed, clipped, blended, vowel shifted, misspelled) may also carry linguistic meaning. A praenomen and nomen may denote a physical characteristic, a time or location, a virtuous (or dubious) character trait, a topographical feature or location, a nationality, or an occupation. It may identify the bearer with a historical or mythological figure, a literary creation, an inanimate object, or even a brand name. If your name is Jason, perhaps you were named after the famous Greek hero Iason. If your middle name is Voorhees, perhaps not.

A name may also simply "mean something in a dictionary sense." For instance, if your name is Villalobos, your ancestors may have been raised by wolves (or you are a minor allegorical figure in a Tarantino film). If you have a name derived from an occupation (like Butch—derived from "butcher," one who slaughters animals for a living), check the occupational history of your family and see if there's a reason behind this appellation. If your cognomen is Smith (or Silvers, or Goldstein, for that matter) see if your family has a history in metallurgy. If your name is Violet Rose Farmer, perhaps it's time to look into a career as a horticulturist.

Go ahead: take a minute and ask your family why you are named as you are. Are you named after a favorite relative? a family friend? a particularly fertile month? Did your folks lose a bet? Were there other names "on the table" when you were born? What were your parents going to call you if you came out of the womb differently gendered? Is your name particularly feminine or masculine? Or is your name unisex? Why are some names traditionally male and others female, for that matter?

Are there any naming patterns in your family? Did your parents practice "common initialization" (Jeff's in-laws—Ken and Carol—did, yielding K-ristin, K-k-ate, and K-k-k-arin). Is there a William in every generation of your family? We once knew a guy named Such; since he was Polish we figured Such was just a Polish name, like Staś.* We later found out that his given name was William, but that his dad's name was

---

* A diminutive form of Stanislav.

also William, his grandfather was Bill, and his uncle was Billy. In an effort at clearing confusion at the dinner table, his mom started calling him "Such," as in "There's *such* a lot of Williams." True story, we swear.

On the other side of the equation, is your name rare or unconventional? Are your parents movie stars who felt the need to name you Apple, or Moxie Crimefighter? Is your unusual name patterned after a more conventional name, or can you explain how it was invented? If you have an exceptionally unique name (like Dinette; or Julie, but spelled *G-h-o-u-l-i-e*), think about suing your parents for retroactive child abuse.

Like these examples, some names in the Python-verse defy expected principles of onomastics. Take, for example, Raymond Luxury Yacht, whose name is "spelt Raymond Luxury Yacht, but is pronounced 'Throatwobbler Mangrove'" (ep. 19). Forget spelling "Jeffry" with only one *e* or—heaven forfend—*G-e-o-f-f-r-e-y*: the Pythons entirely upend the conventions of orthography and phonetics (which are, admittedly, a tad screwy in English, what with the whole "melting pot" phenomenon and linguistic borrowing) with the unpredictable spelling of Raymond Luxury Yacht's name. As in many cases, the Pythons recognize the acceptable variance of a human construct (in this case spelling/pronunciation practices) and introduce us to an extreme test case. Raymond Luxury Yacht/ Throatwobbler Mangrove—even in the Python-verse—is "a very silly man" and unworthy of our attention . . . after our attention has been drawn, of course.

More frequently, for the Pythons (as for many writers and artists), character names act as narrative shorthand, whether explicit or implicit. For example, Basil Exposition (in the *Austin Powers* films) is explicitly named—he's in charge of plot exposition, his name tells us what he does. The Pythons similarly introduce us to the explicitly named and highly argumentative Mrs. Premise and Mrs. Conclusion (ep. 27). Remus Lupin (from the *Harry Potter* franchise) is implicitly named, unless you know your classical mythology, in which case his name is a dead giveaway.* Likewise Darth Vader (the "dark father") is a veiled naming ("Luke!

---

*Remus (along with brother Romulus) was one of the founders of Rome—they were both suckled by a wolf. "Lupin" is derived from the Latin "lupus," meaning

I am your father!"), just as Mr. Hilter and his "Dickie old chum[s]" Ron Vibbentrop, Reginald Bimmler, and "that nice Mr. McGoering" are less than cleverly renamed Nazis plotting a "hike" to annex Poland (ep. 12). Less obvious are the names of Mrs. Thing and Mrs. Entity (ep. 21), who idly engage in empty conversation and non sequiturs (their names, like their conversations, signify nothing) before their conversation transitions to a flashback involving Beethhoven. So too might, the name Ernest Scribbler (as discussed in the section on humor later in this chapter) yield relevant informational fruit, but it takes some effort to prise the meaning from the referent.

Thus, to varying degrees, some characters possess names that may actually help us remember them. But what if there existed someone whose very name worked against his fame? What if someone had an anti-mnemonic?

Most Europeans—following the Roman practice—carry on average three names. There are, of course, exceptions. On the side of brevity, there are public figures who can subsist on only one appellation: Cher, Bono, Charo, Beyoncé, Eminem, Elvira, Madonna, and Prince (who—as of this writing—was back to using the pedestrian Roman alphabet!) . . . the list goes on. There are far fewer who err on the side of excess: the actress Uma Thurman named one of her daughters Rosalind Arusha Arkadina Altalune Florence Thurman-Busson, but they commonly call her simply "Luna." Pablo Picasso's full name was actually Pablo Diego José Francisco de Paula Juan Nepomuceno María de los Remedios Cipriano de la Santísima Trinidad Ruiz y Picasso. And then there was the British teenager who, in 2008, legally changed his name to Captain Fantastic Faster Than Superman Spiderman Batman Wolverine Hulk And The Flash Combined.[*]

Yet none of these can hold a candle to the "greatest name in German Baroque music": Johann Gambolputty de von Ausfern-schplenden-schlitter-crasscrenbon-fried-digger-dingle-dangle-dongle-dungle-

---

"wolf." So the mysterious changeling introduced in *The Prisoner of Azkaban* is literally "wolf suckled by wolf"—yep, he's a mystery alrighty.

[*]Color both the authors more jealous than Superman Spiderman Batman Wolverine Hulk and the Flash combined.

burstein-von-knacker-thrasher-apple-banger-horowitz-ticolensic-grander-knotty-spelltinkle-grandlich-grumblemeyer-spelterwasser-kurstlich-himbleeisen-bahnwagen-gutenabend-bitte-ein-nürnburger-bratwustle-gerspurten-mitz-weimache-luber-hundsfut-gumberaber-shönedanker-kalbsfleisch-mittler-aucher von Hautkopft of Ulm (ep. 6). As the host of *It's the Arts,* Figgis (Chapman) comes to realize that in his attempted profile of the almost great composer, it's almost impossible to hold anyone's attention long enough to discuss Johann . . . Ulm's impact on the world. Sadly, the name of Johann Gambolputty de von Ausfern-schplenden-schlitter-crasscrenbon-fried-digger-dingle-dangle-dongle-dungle-burstein-von-knacker-thrasher-apple-banger-horowitz-ticolensic-grander-knotty-spelltinkle-grandlich-grumblemeyer-spelterwasser-kurstlich-himbleeisen-bahnwagen-gutenabend- bitte-ein-nürnburger-bratwustle-gerspurten-mitz-weimache-luber-hundsfut-gumberaber-shönedanker-kalbsfleisch-mittler-aucher von Hautkopft of Ulm proves the test limit of additive naming.

But these exceptions to naming conventions are exceptions even in the world of Monty Python.[35] Many of their characters are oddly named, and their odd names play into their characterization or lead to comic consequences. Mr. Mousebender seeks cheese like a mouse; Mr. Wensleydale sells (sort of) the cheese for which he is named (sort of). The offensively named Mrs. Nigger-Baiter explodes off camera, her only offense her name (although her excessive baby talk was, admittedly, insufferable); the Wizard Tim carries a name entirely inappropriate for an Arthurian fantasy milieu, but which is suited to the gothic juxtapositions peppering *Monty Python and the Holy Grail;* the Spanish Inquisition is populated by an unexpected variety of names: in episode 15 of *MPFC,* Cardinal Ximénez (a Spanish historical figure closely associated with torture) is accompanied by Biggles (a name strongly associated with a fictional character from British children's literature) and Fang (a whole-cloth Python creation); their names set up conflicting expectations that undercut the seriousness of their almost fanatical devotion to the Pope

---

[35] A name itself with a complicated history. See Morgan (2005, 25–27) for conflicting origins of the group's name.

(not that they need any help there). Finally, some names—like those of Biggus Dickus and his wife, Incontinentia Buttocks (from *Life of Brian*)—are simply unfortunate, carrying such negatively charged associative meaning that their very mention elicits adolescent laughter.

A great many names—both in the Python-verse and in the real world—come with "baggage" attached. Yet some names have meaning foisted upon them. Such is the case of "Semprini"—a neologism the Pythons coin in the "Chemist" sketch (ep. 17). There a chemist (or pharmacist, for you Americans out there) calls out prescriptions for his customers, prescriptions for such potentially embarrassing conditions as "the pox ... a boil on the bum ... chest rash ... wind," before a voice-over announces, "It is not BBC policy to get easy laughs with words like "bum," "knickers," "botty," or "wee-wee." The BBC voice-over is then interrupted by an off-camera voice laughing at the announcement itself. Clearly, as the Pythons suggest, even those in the BBC censor's office find the "easy laughs" of mild profanity easy to laugh at.

After the laughter is hushed, a bowdlerized slide show of "words that are not to be used on this programme" is presented:

B*M
B*TTY
P*X
KN*CKERS
W**-W**
SEMPRINI

The list, and the attention directed at exactly what *cannot* be said, of course creates a delicious "eff-you" to the real BBC censors, who quite often forced the Pythons into the use of such unnatural phrases as "I don't care how excrementally runny it is!" and euphemistic expressions such as "Do you want to go upstairs?" in their televised shows.* For those

---

*By contrast, the Pythons' live performances (see *Live at the Hollywood Bowl*, for example) often dispense with the euphemisms and opt instead for taboo laughs: "I don't care how fucking runny it is!" and "... would you like a blow job?"

who may have missed the seventies, the Pythons' list of "words that are not to be used on this programme" surely echoes the more widely popular "Seven Words You Can Never Say on Television" rant performed by American stand-up comedian George Carlin.

First released on vinyl in 1972, Carlin's (now relatively tame) list included: "shit," "piss," "fuck," "cunt," "cocksucker," "motherfucker," and "tits" (Carlin 1972). Prior to Carlin's recording, Lenny Bruce had been arrested in 1969 for uttering (according to Bruce) the following nine words: "ass," "balls," "cocksucker," "cunt," "fuck," "motherfucker," "piss," "shit," and "tits." Episode 17 and "The Chemist Sketch" of *MPFC* aired on October 20, 1970. Whatever one makes of the chronology of these profane lists, there was clearly something in the rebellious air at the time on both sides of the Pond—a sense of frustration regarding linguistic censorship, if naught else.

As silly, profane, or tame as the Python's list of terms—"bum," "butty," "pox," "knickers," "wee-wee," "Semprini"—may now be, one word is clearly unlike the others: "Semprini." Now, part of the gag relies on the incongruity of a proper noun among the list of recognized "dirty words"—its listing defies audience expectation and thus elicits laughter.* Of course, the end of the sketch is punctuated by the Chemist, who resumes his interrupted pharmaceutical distribution by announcing, "Right, who's got a boil on his Semprini, then?" thus appropriating the seemingly inappropriate proper noun as a neologism suitable to a list of BBC-banned words. In short, the Pythons turn Semprini into an ass.

Did he (Alberto Fernando Riccardo Semprini—often known only as "Semprini"—a British pianist and BBC radio staple between 1957 and 1969[†]) deserve such treatment? Aside from his being a household name in England at the time (again, for the Americans in the audience, think Lawrence Welk), Semprini's only sin seems to have been as a face of the BBC (the true target of the sketch's criticism) and—as the sound of tradition and/or consumer complacency—the antithesis of the avant-garde

---

*Recall the placement of the footballer Beckenbauer on the German philosophy team.

[†]Factoid courtesy of Larsen (2008, 235).

The original cast of *Saturday Night Live* (clockwise from left): Chevy Chase, John Belushi, Gilda Radner, Garrett Morris, Dan Aykroyd, Jane Curtin, Laraine Newman. Since its inception in 1975, *SNL* has "Americanized" *MPFC*'s free-form sketch comedy format with varying success.

rebellious attitude espoused by the Pythons. Authority, convention, complacency: these are all "dirty words" in the Python-verse.

Following the Pythons, the cast of the original *Saturday Night Live*—who openly took their show's loose sketch format and general attitude from *Flying Circus*—further extended this kind of nominal extension in their skit "Lord and Lady Douchebag" (season 5, ep. 20, 1980). The *SNL* sketch sends up English nobility while referencing a host of popular nominal derivations, including Lord Worcestershire's sauce, Lord Salisbury's chopped steak, Lord Wilkinson's twin blades, and the Earl of Sandwich's, er, sandwich,* as well as name-dropping the informally dressed Lords Cardigan and Ascot; of course, the eponymous stars of the skit are the Lord and Lady Douchebag (Buck Henry and Gilda Radner), who seem rather reluctant to discuss a recent invention of theirs, which they've been, ahem, sitting on.

As the *SNL* sketch reveals, the attribution of nominal creation to real persons is not *solely* the domain of comedy writers; innumerable "real" humans have had their names become popularly generalized/particularized/nominalized—some willingly, others less so. Captains of industry and heads of companies often see their names proudly attached to their products (for example, Chevrolet/Chevy, named after GM co-founder Louis Chevrolet, or the well-intended Edsel, named after Henry Ford's son). Others see their names popularly attached to less desirable items or ideas; two fascinating examples include the American Civil War major general (Union Army) Joseph Hooker, who—as the apocryphal story goes—helped encourage the wartime employment of "ladies of negotiable affection," and the Victorian-era British plumber Thomas Crapper, who, like Hooker, found his name popularly attached to a typically unmentionable noun, in this case the WC.† And then . . . some names seem to have (arguably deserved) ignominy foisted upon them with malicious intent.

Take, for example, the case of "santorum." In a 2003 op-ed column for the *New York Times*, writer Dan Savage responded to the perceived homophobic rhetoric of then–Republican presidential candidate Rick Santorum by running a reader-response contest to neologize (some would say defecate upon) Santorum's good name. Soon after, Savage

---

*But *not* his Sandwich Islands; as the Earl of Sandwich (Bill Murray) notes, "I'm afraid nothing has ever been named after a member of my family."

† Americans, a WC=water closet, or toilet. Really, do try to pay attention!

announced the birth of a new noun, "santorum," which he defined as "that frothy mixture of lube and fecal matter that is sometimes the by-product of anal sex." Internet publicity, political word of mouth, and late-night monologues helped spread the notorious neologism from there; as of January 2012, "santorum" as a sexual term outstripped the Internet-search popularity of the term "santorum" denoting the politician.*

All things considered, the good name of A. F. R. Semprini remains relatively unstained, despite the Pythons' half-assed attempt at besmirchment.

Of course, neologisms can cut both ways. *The Oxford English Dictionary* (and nothing screams "bastion of the establishment" like this fine old dictionary) officially recognized the cultural influence of Monty Python in 1989, recording for all posterity the neologism "Pythonesque: <*adjective*> Of, pertaining to, or characteristic of *Monty Python's Flying Circus*, a popular British television comedy series of the 1970s, noted esp. for its absurdist or surrealistic humour."[†] During their "reunion interview" at Aspen in 1998 (an interview that included an urn containing—or so the surviving members averred—the soon-to-be-spilled ashes of Graham Chapman) Terry Jones lamented the Pythons' once avant-garde anti-establishment aspirations: ". . . the fact that 'Pythonesque' is now a word in the *Oxford English Dictionary* shows the extent to which we failed." Some few of us would disagree, but as we have noted, reality is often what you make of it.

WORDS: PHONAESTHETICS
"What a super-woody sort of phrase!"

When the Pythons are not making words and names take on new meaning, they are likely commenting upon the inherent qualities of words

---

* For more on the "deliberate coining" of "santorum," see *The New Partridge Dictionary of Slang and Unconventional Language* (x–xi).
† The *OED* notes the first recorded usage of the term in the *Guardian* newspaper, October 1975.

themselves. One fine example appears in the "Woody and Tinny Words" sketch (ep. 42), in which an upper-middle-class family voice their opinions regarding the pleasure (or displeasure) derived simply from saying and hearing various words. For fun, try to see which of the following words sound woody (confidence building!) and which sound tinny (dreadful):

> SET ONE: gorn, sausage, caribou, intercourse, pert, thighs, botty, erogenous, zone, concubine, loose women, ocelot, wasp, yowling
>
> SET TWO: newspaper, litterbin, tin, antelope, seemly, prodding, vacuum, leap, bound, vole, recidivist, tit, Simkins*

The euphony or cacophony of words (what the Oxbridge scholars in Python—and probably Gilliam, too, why not?—would have known as phonaesthetics, the study of positive and negative sounds in human speech) may lead users to project certain connotations upon individual words (Crystal 1995, 8–12). Such phonaesthetic connotative projection devolves, in this skit, into a practically visible form of mental masturbation, wherein the father (Chapman) must be doused with a bucket of water to calm down after cogitating upon too many "woody-sounding" words. As he sagely notes, ". . . it's a funny thing . . . all the naughty words sound woody." It's a theory not entirely without justification (the understanding of how linguistic connotations are often derived from sounds, not the masturbatory powers of individual words! Bloody pervert.).[†]

---

* Answer key: set one = woody: set two = tinny
† Although see the partial-Python film *A Fish Called Wanda* for a lithe example of xenolinguistic eroticism. *Grazie*, Jamie Lee Curtis, *spasibo*!

POLITICAL THEORY (Part One): COMMUNISM AND MARXISM

"There will certainly be some car door slamming in the streets of Kensington tonight!"

While Python's right-wing caricatures (including the upper-class twit of the year competition) are hilarious and in some cases almost too obvious, Python also doled out equal time to critique not only the historical figures on the left but also the veneration and near sainthood that socialists and communists held for figures such as Marx and Lenin. In the "Communist Quiz" (ep. 25) sketch, Marx, Lenin, Mao, and Che Guevara are introduced with appropriate gravitas and an explanation of their roles in the history of communism, then subjected to trivia questions about British football and rock and roll (surprisingly, Mao does know that "Great Balls of Fire" is Jerry Lee Lewis' biggest number one hit, a fact that does not get him to the final round, alas).

The irony of the four architects of one of the most powerful and controversial political movements of the last few hundred years appearing on a game show called *World Forum* was not lost on Python, who frequently parodied not just democratic perceptions of authority and power but revolutionary movements as well. But then again, the game show, a quintessential symbol of capitalism, is also subverted by the inclusion of the communist thinkers on it; in short, the mash-up in this skit functions as a double deconstruction in which each element subverts the other. Perhaps the game show, where upward mobility is represented by prizes (including the grand prize, a "lovely lounge suite"), is itself a version of the Marxist class struggle writ large.

As Engels wrote in the introduction to *The Communist Manifesto*, "All history has been a history of class struggles, of struggles between exploited and exploiting, between dominated and dominating classes at various stages of social development" (Marx and Engels 1985, 57). Just as the Marxist-based proletariat has to compete in a rigged game of economic and spiritual exploitation, so too—in this sketch—do the founders of communism. Marx had written "... let the ruling classes tremble at a Communistic revolution. The proletarians have nothing to lose but their chains. They have a world to win. WORKING MEN OF ALL COUNTRIES, UNITE!" (Marx and Engels 1985, 120–121). Marx, however, unlike the other historical revolutionaries, was not hobbled by his chains on the game show but because of his inadequate knowledge of which teams had previously won the English football cup.

Marx, "a disciple of Hegel and already a marked man in Germany and France for his revolutionary temper" when he met Engels (Barzun 2000, 549), would seem an unlikely participant in a game show. His most famous short work, *The Communist Manifesto*, "combined an analysis of industrial society with a review of European history and a list of ten legislative reforms ... with a call upon workers everywhere to unite in overthrowing the existing order" (Barzun 2000, 549). But as workers could not rise up immediately under the current conditions, they would for the moment have to work within the system until the revolutionary vanguard was ready to lead them. Perhaps participating on the game show is a way for Marx to use the game show's illusions of upward mobility to demonstrate how class conflict could truly be resolved through communism. But perhaps not.

When Marx is competing in the final round with questions on the topic of "workers' control of factories" (which is strange when you think about it, as only Mao had answered any questions correctly in the first round—the game, like society, is clearly rigged), Marx is first asked, "The development of the industrial proletariat is conditioned by what other development?" Marx naturally knows the answer to this question, as he had previously written in *The Communist Manifesto*, that "the history of all hitherto existing society is the history of class struggles" (Marx and Engels 1985, 79) and that "the proletariat goes through various stages of development. With its birth begins its struggle with the bourgeoisie" (88). And so when Karl is asked by the host, "The struggle of class against class is a *what* struggle? A *what* struggle?" Marx's answer is straight from the pages of *The Communist Manifesto* as well: "A political struggle" (90). Marx seems ready to win the lounge suite, but at the last moment the show reverts back to football questions (despite the fact that Marx had clearly picked "Workers' Control of Factories" as his topic; the connection to British football may be a little tenuous). Marx loses the game show not only because he doesn't know about football victories that happened in England long after his death but also because he is competing within the same system that he had already declared to be an organization that needed to be overthrown, not joined. As Marx himself wrote:

> The development of Modern Industry, therefore, cuts from under its feet the very foundation on which the bourgeoisie produces and appropriates products. What the bourgeoisie, therefore, produces, above all, is its own gravediggers. Its fall and the victory of the proletariat are equally inevitable. (94)

By competing on the game show, Marx had already dug his own (admittedly posthumous) grave. And he didn't even get the lounge suite, which seemed to be even more distressing.

Python's commentary on class issues is perhaps best epitomized by the confused highwayman Dennis Moore. In the "Dennis Moore" sketch in episode 37, Moore (Cleese) rides the highways, stopping carriage passengers and robbing them of their lupins to give to a poor and sick family. When the family eventually convinces him that lupins are not alleviating their suffering,* Moore then robs the rich until they too are poor and the formerly poor family is now so wealthy that they disparage the silver spoons he recently stole for them, asking him instead to "steal something nice like some Venetian silver." It is only when Dennis Moore hears his own non-diegetic theme song (now stating that "He steals from the poor and gives to the rich/Stupid bitch!") that he realizes: "Blimey, this redistribution of wealth is trickier than I thought." Indeed, as Karl Marx had found out on the game show, replacing an entrenched authority is a tricky business.

---

*Lupins are, as far as this sketch is concerned, ornamental flowering plants, sometimes called blue bonnets. They are, incidentally, the state flower of Texas.

MEDIA THEORY
"Turn off the telly! You know it's bad for your eyes!"

As we will discuss in the section on televisuality and the BBC, Python was acutely aware of the possibilities of the televisual medium (and later film, CD-ROMS, video games, and even apps for tablets and phones). They came into the first series with a natural appetite for deconstruction and found that the environment of the BBC was fertile ground in which to foment discord. But it was not just their natural deconstructive bent that was working in terms of reimagining television; during the four years of their television series, Monty Python were as astute at media criticism as almost anyone outside of Marshall McLuhan. The Pythons could look at the institutions of television (as mentioned in the introduction and Part II: Python on History) and see how incredibly artificial and silly they were. As Michael Palin was to remark in his diary over a decade later, "All technological advances bring built in dissatisfaction" (2006, 98). If Python could deconstruct the medium of television to demonstrate how ridiculous it was, they could also deconstruct the message.

One brilliant but hardly subtle Gilliam-animated segment (ep. 33) depicts a television set repeatedly attacking the eyes of a viewer who is watching the news; off camera, his wife warns him that he should stop watching the telly as "you know it's bad for your eyes!" Python's genius for understanding the way in which television worked revealed that this simplistic approach to media criticism is inadequate; television may very well have been "bad for your eyes" but it was primarily the *forms* and conventions (disseminated optically) normalized by television that were bad for the viewer, physical effects aside. Gilliam himself realized this during his run on the television show and remarked later that

television is a deadening medium if you allow it to be (and most people do). I find the minute I switch on the television, I just sit there for hours once it starts. There's always something to watch and it's easier than going out and *doing* things. And so maybe it's just that I'm fighting against my ease of seduction, the ease with which TV seduces me. (Morgan 2005, 200)

While it is unclear if Python had read seminal media ecologist Marshall McLuhan by the time they were making the first season, they certainly were echoing his views on the nature of television. McLuhan's famous and mostly misunderstood aphorism that "the medium is the message"; this means (among many others things) that the content of television is by no means the most important aspect of television, but what kind of new mediated environments it favors. As McLuhan wrote, "... the medium is the message means, in terms of the electronic age, that a totally new environment has been created" (1964, ix). For those watchdogs who thought the point of media criticism was to watch for any slips of nudity or cursing, McLuhan patiently explained that this was actually a distraction in understanding television and that "the content of a medium is like the juicy piece of meat carried by the burglar to distract the watchdog of the mind" (32). Python's critics, who also concentrated on content over form, missed the message of television, one that—as Python pointed out—was patently absurd. Python opposed most television for not just its rank stupidity (its content) but also how it seemingly taught mindless obedience to the existing power structures (its form). The radically unpredictable form of *MPFC* thus served as a corrective antidote to the prevailing conformist dirges of most television shows.

In his seminal book, *Amusing Ourselves to Death,* author Neil Postman (writing almost a decade and a half after Python) bemoaned the fact that the rational linear mind of the previous print-based culture was rapidly devolving into a television-based mind-set, one that was non-linear, irrational, and prone to choose amusement over serious discourse or engagement. To Postman, television had it own set of truths and "the epistemology created by television not only is inferior to print-based epistemology, but is dangerous and absurdist" (1985, 27). Meanwhile, Python was also dangerous and absurdist, but in a good way. Python aimed to wake the audience as well as entertain them, whereas, according to Postman, most television—whether sitcoms, the news, or educational programming—still had one primary focus: to entertain. As

FACTOID BOX: Media Ecology

Media Ecology is a field of media studies inspired by McLuhan and others, such as Harold Innis, Walter Ong, and Jacques Ellul. It does not look at media in terms of effects but in terms of how new mediated environments are related to advances in technology. Outside of McLuhan, the most widely read proponent was the late Neil Postman, author of *Amusing Ourselves to Death*, a book that inspired a generation of new media scholars, as well as a Roger Waters solo record, *Amused to Death* (1992).

Postman observed, "... entertainment is the supra-ideology of all discourse on television. No matter what is depicted or from what point of view, the overarching presumption is that it is there for our amusement and pleasure" (87). While it could be argued that there were (and still are) more rationally based news and education programs on in Britain than in the United States (*MPFC* certainly among them), it could also be argued that, other than *MPFC*, there was nothing in what was then called "light entertainment" that required too much thought on the part of viewers at home. Postman argued that this is not merely the result of lazy programmers or hackneyed writers but that "it's in the nature of the medium that it must suppress the content of ideas in order to accommodate the requirements of visual interest; that is to say, to accommodate the values of show business" (92). By its nature, television works against the ideas of serious and rational thought. And as Marci Landy has noted, Python was "acutely conscious of television as perpetrator of misinformation" (2006, 30).

In part, this is why Python was able to succeed in mocking the conventions of television while others failed: Python recognized, from the start, how incredibly silly and pointless most of the self-limited conventions of television were and they were determined to find those limits and stretch them as much as possible.* As Landy wrote in her book on Python, the shows were a "self conscious reference to the medium of television" (35). They existed outside of the usual conventions of television, which typically created an illusion of a fourth wall (that you are simply watching someone in a living room, not on a set), that events are fixed in terms of linear time and space (conflicts are resolved within established—and often advertised—segments), and move according to a set of rules that govern this strange world. Python would occasionally employ a linear sense of time or space but denied its viewers—for the most part—any sense of closure in their sketches, which were silently punctuated by the conspicuous lack of traditional punch lines.

One of the main ways that Python demonstrated the inherent silliness of television was through ridiculing the ritualistic and meaningless nature of television news. In many cases, Python used either the interview format or a nightly news parody (sometimes with real BBC announcers) to show that despite the BBC's self-affirming mandate to be educational and informative, it nonetheless presented a fragmented, non-linear view of reality.

In his two books that explicitly tackle the nature of television and news broadcasts, Neil Postman (along with former newsman Steve Powers in the second book) analyzed the way that television news serves less as an actual indicator of important events and serves more as a stylistic exercise in meaningless facts and figures jumbled up and presented with enough razzmatazz to serve as entertainment. As Postman wrote, in televised news "we are presented not only with fragmented news, but news without context, without consequences, without values, without essential seriousness; that is to say, news as pure entertainment" (1985, 100). While most think of television news as perhaps the most basic and transparent forms of communication available ("We report, You decide"), in actuality television news is almost as surrealistic and silly as the best Python sketches. According to Postman, "embedded in the surrealistic frame of television news is a theory of anti-communication,

---

* Even as far as an Owl might allow.

featuring a type of discourse that abandons logic, reason, sequence and rules of contradiction" (105).

Take, for example, the extended Python sketch in which the news is presented over and over again, first for parrots, then for gibbons, and finally for wombats (ep. 20). The news does not cover any events that are actually world changing, just events that are designed to appeal to a specific demographic (in this case various animals), and goes out of its way to emphasize, for example, that "no parrots were involved in an accident on the M1 today" and that "a spokesman for parrots said he was glad no parrots were involved." When Python returns to a broadcast of *Today in Parliament* (in what the narrator calls "Parliamentary News for Humans") the report deviates into gossip and slander:

> From the back benches there were opposition shouts of "postcards for sale" and a healthy cry of "who likes a sailor then?" from the Minister without Portfolio. Replying, the Shadow Minister said, he could no longer deny the rumours but he and the dachshund were very happy; and, in any case, he argued, rhubarb was cheap and what was the harm in a sauna bath?

News is whatever the viewer—human or otherwise—deems "important" to his/her/itself.

This ties into Postman and Powers' argument about how the goal of news is not to depict reality as we know it but instead to show us spectacles meant to entertain. "All news shows, in a sense, are recreations in that what we hear and see in them are attempts to represent actual events and are not the events themselves" (Postman and Powers 1992, 97). The structures and conventions of news lead to a surreal situation where "we know that we are in the presence of a symbolic event, a form of theater in which the events of the day are to be dramatized" (109). Because of the nature of the medium, "there is rarely any attempt to explain issues in depth, or place events in their proper context" (110) and "the story order is constructed to hold and build the viewership rather than place events in context or explain issues in depth" (112). The news for birds, or simply the way in which even the perception that the Queen might be watching the broadcast leads to situations where real life is perceived through the lens of television, thus demonstrates how bafflingly strange television news can be. "A television news show reveals the world as a series of unrelated fragmentary moments. It does not—and cannot be expected to—offer a sense of coherence or meaning" (114). And as Postman and Powers go on to conclude,

> ... we are saying that television tends to turn its news into a form of entertainment, in part, because so much information is available that news has lost its relevance and meaning; that is, Americans are no longer clear about what news is worth remembering or how any of it is connected to anything else. (155)

This is precisely how the Pythons viewed television. Although they also saw it as fertile ground for their own experiments, they realized that it was made for mindless entertainment and that they could best satirize television by making its conventions more apparent. Python realized that their brand of deconstructive absurdist television could challenge the perceived power structures inherent even in television. According to Michael Palin, "People in positions of power don't like comedy because 'it's essentially subversive'" (Morgan 2005, 237). Gilliam, although one of the principal architects of their attacks on television, was ultimately uncertain of what effect, if any, they actually had, noting that "we were playing with the medium and shifting it around, in the way we were playing with television, and we get no points for that. I'm surprised because one can actually get one's academic intellectual teeth into this stuff" (Morgan 2005, 314). Cleese also acknowledged this and bemoaned that "we were playing games with convention which no one had ever done before, and it was very startling the first time you do it. But once people get used to a convention being broken, it's not startling at all, and then there's nothing left" (Morgan 2005, 314).

MPFC was perhaps the most surrealistic comedy show ever on television. It did not follow linear conventions yet had its own internal logic where bizarre juxtapositions and references to the medium of television

FACTOID BOX: Surrealism

Surrealism began as a literary movement in the 1910s/1920s (essentially an experiment in unbounded and purely imaginative "free-writing") but soon became a nigh-ubiquitous intellectual, psychological, artistic, and political movement. More or less out of vogue by World War II, surrealism remained a touchstone of non-conformity, free expression, and—as seen in the verbal non sequiturs of *MPFC* and the interstitial art of Terry Gilliam—evocative gothic juxtaposition.

became the norm. As Morgan noted, the show did not possess conventional linear plot, but "what it did have were odd and surrealistic juxtapositions, a penchant for twisted violence, and a belief that the human condition is, on the whole, pretty absurd" (3). Python members initially did not come from the traditional perspectives of Luis Buñuel or the Cabaret Voltaire, but they did have the influence of *The Goon Show* with its own brand of surrealistic slapstick. Even Gilliam was inspired by the parodic nature of underground comic books and *MAD* magazine, where the rules of linear comics were also abandoned with glee. In retrospect, the always well-read Palin could look back and note in his diary that when he "[r]ead of Buñuel and the surrealists in Paris in the late '20's and '30's" he noticed "[s]imilarities with the Pythons. Bourgeois against the bourgeoisie" (2009, 313). While the Pythons may not have called themselves surrealists, they certainly followed the pattern (or lack of any pattern) of surrealism, as Python sketches consisted of "refusing narrative closure; stopping a sketch in midstream; interrupting a skit . . . and especially mixing genres such as situation comedy and melodrama and animation and news" (Landy 2006, 47).

POLITICAL THEORY (Part Two): THE BRITISH CLASS SYSTEM

"I know these views aren't popular, but I have never courted popularity."

One of the primary targets for Python's humor was always the pompous absurdity of the British class system. While this may seem ironic, as most of Python came from comfortably well-to-do British households and went to the finest schools in England (Gilliam's wasn't that bad at all either), they nevertheless used the lens of their education and their tendency towards the absurdist to attack the British class system with unusual relish. While the "Upper-Class Twit of the Year" competition's targets are fairly obvious, most of the Pythons' worldview on the television show and the movies was based upon a resentment of the assumed privileges of class. Even parts of *Life of Brian,* which seems as far away from the British class system as anything the Pythons ever did, can be read as a political allegory in which the Romans are surrogates for the declining British Empire (a comparison that has been made—more than once—throughout history). As Palin pointed out, the Roman occupation of Judea was relatable since "you've got the whole of British imperialism, which was something which we were all brought up on" (Morgan 2005, 226). The idea of living in an empire that was in decline was something the five British Pythons had been keenly aware of since their earliest days. The aftermath of the Second World War and Indian independence in 1947 made it clear that if the sun was not exactly setting on the British Empire, the empire it shone upon was remarkably smaller than it had been previously. Michael Palin noted that in the late fifties and early sixties: "[t]he whole idea of empire seemed suddenly absurd, and it was all being given away. The severe, stern face of conservative Britain seemed to be gone, and into this slight limbo afterwards came the young comedians" (Johnson 1999, 74).

All of a sudden, what had once been representations of normalcy and sanity were shown to the Pythons to be quite the opposite. As Christopher Hitchens noted about the Pythons:

The great achievement of John Cleese and of the Pythons in general, is to take the British at their most bland and conformist (in pet shops, offering hospitality, donning bowler hats for a day at the office) and then to tear off the false whiskers and show the heaving morass of giggling, cackling lunacy that churns beneath. (2008)

Another author who singled out Cleese notes how he "epitomized the figure of the Englishman who was neat and primly mannered and at the same time, bat-shit crazy . . . going down with the ship that was the British Empire and setting off a great blaze of animated pyrotechnics on the way out" (Malamud 2011). The empire was gone, but while the Pythons realized this, the establishment seemed blind to this little fact, making them even riper for satire than usual.

A typical target of Python humor is the face of the establishment, whether the stockbroker, the chartered accountant, or the ubiquitous policeman voicing his trademark, "All right, what's all this then?"* Palin was astounded at how many police officers were fans of the show. As Palin said:

> . . . we used to do the most obvious attacks on the police, suggesting bribery and corruption and all sorts of veniality, and they thought it was absolutely wonderful. It just shows that satire doesn't really change people at all. They never believe that they're the target, they always think it's somebody else. (Johnson 1999, 76)

As in any society, the police with their uniforms and billy clubs were obvious representations of upper-class authority figures. But Python also concentrated on another sort of uniformed "authority": the upper-class twits in their bowlers, black suits, and umbrellas who populated London at that time.

---

*Python featured police officers trying to plant evidence, raiding suspect chocolate factories and Tudor smut peddlers, picking up strangers, and using magic wands in order to fight crime. Sounds like campus security at Hogwarts, really.

In part of a "Vox Pops" sketch in episode 5, Cleese appears as a "man on the street" stockbroker who gives his views of how to deal with class unrest, saying

> that they should attack the lower classes, first with bombs and rockets to destroy their homes, and then when they run helpless into the street, er, mowing them down with machine guns. Er, and then, of course, releasing the vultures. I know these views aren't popular, but I have never courted popularity.

These views, presumably, were also those attributed to a favorite target of Cleese, the upper-class twits who so confounded him with their privilege, rank, and assumptions of superiority (not to mention their constant car door slamming late at night and early in the morning that kept him in a state of sleepless fury). This led to one of Python's most brilliant sketches, the "Upper-Class Twit of the Year Competition" (ep. 12). Cleese lived near Sloane Square, where there were quite a few "Sloane Rangers"; as Graham Chapman remembered, "there was a wine bar just over the road from John's called the Loose Box, where there were a lot of these chinless wonders with names like Nigel. They would just make braying noises and generally behave like the twits in the sketch" (Johnson 1999, 74). In the sketch itself, the sporting events (see also Part V: Sport) include "waking the neighbor," "insulting the waiter," "kicking the beggar," "walking a straight line without falling over," and eventually, and most likely to the immense satisfaction of Cleese, killing themselves (although many proved less than adept at this final task). As the three medal winners' bodies are displayed, Cleese (naturally) as the breathless announcer giddily cries that "there will certainly be some car door slamming in the streets of Kensington tonight!"

This mistrust and even contempt for authority was shared not only by the five British Pythons; it was also a key part of the ever contrarian worldview of their token American, Terry Gilliam. What Gilliam really learned in school was "hatred for society, and wealth, and powerful people who I've never learned to deal with subsequently" (Morgan 2005, 20). But even Gilliam, famous for his battles with the other Pythons—and later, with the major American studios for creative and artistic control—was able to marvel at the way that the British Pythons could use humor to channel rage over the presumption of class and privilege. Gilliam observed:

> To me, Brits have always been able to laugh at themselves better than Americans can. And I thought that Americans always have been better at laughing at the other. For me, the Brits are a people that, you know, at the beginning of the last century had the biggest empire the world has ever known, and within a very short time it was gone. So how do you deal with that loss or that failure or whatever? By being self-deprecating. Laugh at yourself because you've fucked up, basically. Or you've lost the will or the drive to commandeer the world. And so, okay, you step back and just laugh at things. And I thought that was very important. I've always thought that America was very weak on irony, which the British have in heaps. That's the main thing with Python, we were making jokes about anti-authority. That's the kind of thing that translated immediately. Where you can take a pompous authority figure and you make him look like a fool. Everybody loves that. (Marsh 2012)

Gilliam represented a feeling among the Pythons that authority was there to be mocked, nothing else, and, when examined critically, perceived authority looked fairly ridiculous. While clad in the tropes of traditional British authority, even the judges' robes concealed women's underwear.

In the "Working-Class Playwright" sketch in episode 2, the conflict between the playwright and his mine-worker son is not just an inversion of the "angry young man" plays and novels of John Osborne and other radical British playwrights of the sixties; it also centers on class as the crux of the conflict between the son, home from the mines, and his famous playwright father. Their relationship is troubled by the fact that

Idle's character, Ken, has rejected the world of privilege and culture that his father revels in. As one critic noted, ". . . through a reversal of generational and work roles, the sketch inverts and undermines clichés associated with social class" (Landy 2006, 82).

Ken complains that the father is limited by his (far from provincial) prejudices. As Idle's Ken yells at him, "There's more to life than culture . . . there's dirt and sweat and good honest labor!" This was largely in response to the father's earlier tirade, where he imperiously told Ken:

> What do you know about getting up at five o'clock in t'morning to fly to Paris . . . back at the Old Vic for drinks at twelve, sweating the day through press interviews, television interviews and getting back here at ten to wrestle with the problem of a homosexual nymphomaniac drug-addict involved in the ritual murder of a well known Scottish footballer? That's a full working day, lad, and don't you forget it!

This reference to the angry-young-man generation was also, according to Larsen, perhaps a jibe at Chapman, who never tired of making fun of his own habits, but as Larsen also suggests, the father's life routine seems an amalgam of David Storey's *This Sporting Life* as well as the works of Harold Pinter and John Osborne (Larsen 2008, 29). The sketch is also "an inversion of the stereotypical representations of social class, characteristic of novels such as D. H. Lawrence's *Sons and Lovers*, that highlights the deep social and cultural differences between an artistic son and his miner father" (Landy 2006, 82). Working-class playwright indeed!

Overall, Python used their natural anti-authoritarian principles to highlight the inherent silliness in the British class system. Their critique, while unique to certain historical and social norms in Great Britain, makes sense when applied to the contemporary culture of America as well. Perhaps one reason that Python became so popular with their eventual American audience was that Americans were already used to socially critical comedy. From underground comics to Lenny Bruce and

George Carlin, America already had cutting-edge comedy that challenged perceived notions of authority. The Pythons upped the ante exponentially, of course, and were greeted in the United States as comic heroes during (and after) the Hollywood Bowl shows.* Python used theory not to make elaborate academic points (although the shows can certainly be interpreted as such) but to try and tear away the façade behind the giggling lunacy of everyday reality—and that lunatic reality was seemingly universal.

HUMOR

"This man is Ernest Scribbler . . . writer of jokes. In a few moments, he will have written the funniest joke in the world . . . and, as a consequence, he will die . . . laughing."

Thus a pseudo-historical stentorian voice-over introduces us to the final sketch of the first episode of *Monty Python's Flying Circus* and Ernest Scribbler (Palin), a man who laughs himself to death. In retrospect, this gallows humor announced to Python's viewers a recurring conceit that would resonate throughout the rest of *Flying Circus*: the self-reflexive examination of writing comedy.

The "Funniest Joke in the World" sketch (ep. 1) traces the "[s]udden . . . violent . . . comedy" of Scribbler's joke, from his own death (and that of his mother, a local coroner, and a Scotland Yard inspector) to the British military's acquisition of the "Killer Joke" for use against the Nazis in 1944. As the army colonel (played, as ever, by a straightlaced Chapman) explains:

All through the winter of '43 we had translators working, in joke-proof conditions, to try and produce a German version of the joke. They worked on one word each for safety. One of them saw two words of the joke and spent several weeks in hospital. But

---

* See *Monty Python Live!* (33–39) for all the post–Hollywood Bowl hedonistic gossip.

apart from that things went pretty quickly, and we soon had the joke by January, in a form which our troops couldn't understand but which the Germans could.

Once the joke was deployed, as Idle's voice-over calmly tells us, "[t]he German casualties were appalling."

The remainder of the skit cuts between stock footage (of Hitler, Churchill, and sundry military personnel culled from Pathé newsreels) and slightly twisted re-enactments of conventional war movie tropes (interrogations, battlefield encounters, civilians huddled about radios), wherein Devastating Humor replaces the WWII Arms Race. And, although it remains unstated in the sketch, behind all the arms metaphors looms the specter of the Manhattan Project.

As the sketch continues, the Nazis remain unable to counter with a lethal joke of their own (failed jests include Hitler attempting to tell a "my dog's got no nose / how does he smell" jape and a radio broadcast—in broken German—of the old "assaulted peanuts" pun), and so Germany falls to Britain's superior comic might. Finally, Idle's voice-over notes, "[i]n 1945 Peace broke out. It was the end of the Joke." Patriotic music swells and the final skit of the inaugural *Flying Circus* episode somberly ends with a slow pan skywards from a monument inscribed: "To the unknown Joke."

In addition to employing their soon-to-be-signature comic juxtaposition here (in this case Humor versus/as War, writ large), the Pythons rather boldly end their first episode* with a self-reflexive treatise on the nature and power of comic creation itself. By replacing martial might with comedic prowess in this revisionist WWII history, the Pythons not only "save England" but also elevate artistic creation to levels of cultural reverence normally reserved for war heroes (comparing the unknown joke to unknown soldiers) and levels of power usually reserved for WMD.

---

*"Whither Canada" was actually the second episode shot but the first aired. "Sex & Violence" was apparently shot first—see Larsen (2008, 4).

And, as we will see in other sketches—such as the Thomas Hardy–venerating "Novel-Writing" skit from the *Matching Tie and Handkerchief* album—Python would even dare to compare literary creation to football* (arguably more relevant in 1969 Britain than any past war effort). Although no one in their right mind would suggest that the Pythons inspired the hip-hop bravado of rappers in the 1980s (would they!?), the hubristic elements shared by both are remarkable.

The "Funniest Joke in the World" skit initially works because most of the wartime conventions co-opted in the name of humor are perfectly legible to those without an Oxbridge education; any WW II film involving a "name, rank, and serial number" interrogation would provide a viewer enough background to "get" the "name, rank, and why did the chicken cross the road?" exchange between Cleese (silently accompanied by Chapman, who is metatheatrically labeled "A Gestapo Officer") and Palin's chair-bound British officer; one need not know the entirety of the articles in the Geneva Convention† to "get" the joke here. Likewise, the general application of humor in place of violence (the reading of the joke by advancing British soldiers amidst the explosions and gunfire of conventional warfare; Palin's captured British officer averring that he "can stand physical pain, you know" but apparently breaking down when tickled with a comically large feather) is simple enough to elicit an incongruity chuckle or two. And, of course, the dubbing of "stock" Hitler rants continues to provide a laugh even today, if the nigh-ubiquitous Internet meme "Downfall" (aka "Hitler Reacts to . . ." or "Hitler Finds Out . . .") is any indication ("Downfall / Hitler Reacts" 2011).

However, there are also specific referents that may be lost to modern, post–WW II viewers, such as the depiction of a failed German attempt at radio-humor retaliation—dubbed the "German V-Joke"—which recalls

---

* See Part III: Python on Art.
† "Article 17: Every prisoner of war, when questioned on the subject, is bound to give only his surname, first name and rank, date of birth, and army, regimental, personal or serial number, or failing this, equivalent information" (Office of the High Commissioner for Human Rights 2012).

"Why did Kanye do that? He is so heartless!"
The viral "Hitler Reacts" meme, drawn from *Der Untergang* (*The Downfall*).

"the infamous Nazi 'V' rocket base in northeast Germany" where German atomic and rocket technology flourished, until bombed by the Allies in 1943 (Larsen 2008, 13). The failure of the syntactically ineffective pun, delivered in comically broken German/English ("Der ver zwei peanuts, valking down der Strasse, and von vas ... assaulted! ... peanut. Ho-ho-ho."), delivers an exemplar of a bad "telegraph joke" (too pat, too coy, too predictable—the type of humor the Pythons repeatedly ridicule in the series),[52] but it gains some small sophistication if the viewer is aware of the German technological failures at Peenemunde; as Larsen wryly notes, "... the German V-Joke falls flat (misses its target)" just as the German V-rockets similarly missed "significant targets" during the war (18).*

_____

* See Larsen on "The Idiot in Society" (ep. 20), "nobody does that anymore": the Pythons were keenly associated with "the move away from the traditional ... gag-rich, set-up-and-rimshot-payoff ... school of television comedy". (276)
* It is of course worth noting that the British Killer Joke—as shouted to deadly effect throughout the skit—is likewise Germanesque gibberish: "Wenn ist das Nunstuck git und Slotermeyer? Ja! ... Beiherhund das Oder die Flipperwaldt gersput!"

In addition to the German V-rockets, another WWII technological "marvel" looms large behind the high-powered humor of the "Funniest Joke in the World" sketch: the atomic bomb. In particular, the detailed description of how the British military weaponized Scribbler's joke seems to directly recall many of the procedures surrounding the Manhattan Project—the American-led weaponizing of atomic energy that ultimately (if controversially) led to the end of the war.

The bulk of those involved in the Manhattan Project—like those in the Joke Brigade described by Chapman's Colonel—operated in relative isolation, crafting parts of an unknown whole, unaware of what exactly they were working on, sworn to secrecy, under penalty of heavy fine should they break their silence. For both sets of highly educated scientists/humorists, their effort results in a global impact.

The Atomic Parallel Parable occurs in many media, of course, although it is not typically employed for humorous purposes. One need only look to the early Godzilla franchise (*not* Matthew Broderick!) or to Alan Moore's *Watchmen* series (*not* the film!) for examples of how the "atom bomb"—as giant radioactive dinosaur or giant naked blue man—could profoundly affect the world. In short, the parallel modes of production suggest the Manhattan Project partially inspired the Pythons writing this sketch . . . yet there are other indicators that the atom bomb was on their minds as well. The script prompts for the sketch and the naming of the Killer Joke's creator likewise help inform the viewer of the nuclear context from which the sketch sprang.

The *Flying Circus* script prompts—the rehearsal notes for the actors written by their fellow Pythons—that follow the death of Scribbler are surprisingly deep:

> The scribbler's mother (Eric) enters. She sees him dead, she gives a little cry of horror over his body, weeping. Brokenly she notices the piece of paper in his hand and (thinking it is a suicide note—for he has not been doing well for the last thirteen years) picks it up and reads it between her sobs. Immediately she breaks into hysterical laughter, leaps three feet into the air, and falls down dead without more ado. (Python 1989a, 10)

As Darl Larsen observes:

> It is intriguing to read just how much non-visual, even non-essential information is included in these scripts meant for performance.... These moments are a fascinating conceit on the writers' part, since the tidbits (1) do not end up on screen, and (2) would be completely lost without actually reading the performance texts. They often read as almost inside jokes—only available to and decipherable by other Pythons. (2008, 17)

In this case, the scene is silent (save for the giggling of Idle as she reads), and so (without the benefit of caption or voice-over) viewers must glean the motivation for Scribbler's mother's reaction solely through Idle's over-the-top Pepperpot performance. Why then the detailed performance notes indicating that Scribbler had contemplated suicide?

Idle does admirable work in following the prompts here; granted, his death leap may not be "three feet in the air," but he does a fine job approximating a Bugs Bunny–style death here—as does a Nazi Cleese, who later cartoonishly dies laughing to a barely suppressed Woody Woodpecker–esque "Ha-ha-ha-*haa*-ha!" Clearly, the cast's cartoony overacting underscores the unrealistic fantasy world portrayed in the sketch, one where wars are won with words, not weapons. However, even if the audience reads beyond the pratfalls into Idle's forlorn reaction that Ernest had been suicidal, the scripted prompt that Mrs. Scribbler's son had "not been doing well for the last thirteen years" seems utterly lost and, à la Larsen, appears to be "non-essential" information. So why thirteen? Was it simply chosen as an unlucky number, or might it carry additional numerological relevance?

Perhaps significantly, it was thirteen years between the postulation of an atomic bomb by Leó Szilárd (September 1932) and the devastatingly effective deployment of Little Boy over Hiroshima (August 1945). Thirteen years between Leó's theoretical inspiration and the creation of a working bomb. Thirteen years between Ernest's thoughts of suicide and the writing of the Killer Joke. Both gestation periods produced world-changing weapons of mass destruction/comedy. Does a viewer of Python need to know this shit? Certainly not. But it may be that the Pythons were running a silent gag in the background, a gag that may help us recognize the satiric weight of a sometimes cartoonishly silly sketch. In retrospect, if one reads Terry Jones' later *War on the War on Terror*—a collection of essays written in response to the responses following 9/11— one can see the political and historical erudition of the Pythons in general. They would not, in other words, have been unaware that the Killer Joke would resonate metaphorically as the Killer Bomb. Indeed, they would have relied upon their astute viewers to catch the "hidden" allegory themselves.

Finally, there is the creator of the unintentionally deadly Joke himself: Ernest Scribbler. Names inevitably carry meaning in Python; among their many uses, names provoke incongruous humor (as with the far too mundanely named "Wizard Tim" in *MP&HG*) or provide immediate insight into a character's character (as with the fully defined "Sir Not-Appearing-in-This-Film"—likewise from *MP&HG*—and the barely disguised "Mr. Hilter" from *FC*, ep. 12). Even at a base linguistic level, Ernest Scribbler's last name provides a quick oxymoronic backdrop against which the Python's oxymoronic project (Tragedy won by Comedy) is set: by definition, a scribbler writes nonsense to no purpose, while one writing in earnest does so seriously and with purpose. Yet—as with much of the humor in this sketch—this name carries potential secondary (and typically learned) meaning that further underscores the depth of the Pythons' wit as well. Larsen suggests that Ernest's surname is "an allusion to the Scriblerus Club, the ur-Python learned literary troupe" (15) that included such eighteenth-century British literary luminaries as Alexander Pope, Jonathan Swift, John Arbuthnot, John Gay, and Thomas Parnell; coupled with Scribbler's "serious" first name, this evocative (and trés Oxfordian) reference would certainly reinforce the satirical importance of the project at hand (and the series as a whole). If the Pythons were hubristic enough to suggest that Humor is more powerful than War, then surely they would not have hesitated to compare themselves (as the writers of "the funniest joke in the world") to the most well-educated clique of comedy writers in English history.

And yet, while there are certainly learned and literary underpinnings possible in the naming of Ernest Scribbler, within the context of WMD and WWII, the name Ernest Scribbler may indirectly evoke a third option: Albert Einstein, the popularly recognized Father of Atomic Energy.

Einstein, as everyone knows, brought to the world the "theory of relativity" and the very catchy formula $E=mc^2$. That Albert Einstein is popularly associated with atomic power (having submitted, with Leó Szilárd, the "Einstein Letter" in 1939 urging FDR to weaponize atomic energy), the name "Ernest Scribbler" takes on particularized historical resonance. Einstein was himself something of a doodler (indeed, one might even call him an "earnest scribbler") with a sense of humor, and we can see in this seemingly simple name the further juxtaposition of literary/fictive (the Scriblerus Club) and scientific/actual (Einstein) creation.

So how powerful is humor in the Python-verse? According to the lead cover story in the *New York Times* of August 6, 1945:

> The White House and War Department announced today that an atomic bomb, possessing more power than 20,000 tons of TNT, a destructive force equal to the load of 2,000 B-29's and more than 2,000 times the blast power of what previously was the world's most devastating bomb, had been dropped on Japan.

If the Killer Joke was "sixty thousand times as powerful as Britain's great prewar joke" and Little Boy was two thousand times more powerful than any prewar bomb, then the Joke would have been thirty times more powerful than the first employed atomic bomb. No wonder the war ended a year early according to Python reckoning.*

---

* And so, far from bombing, the first episode of *Flying Circus* ends with a bang. There: we said it. It had to happen. Mea culpa.

GILLIAM: THE ODD MAN OUT

Hello, and welcome to the *interstitials!*

Since the bulk of this treatise (fairly or unfairly) privileges the words spoken and silly walks perpetrated by the Pythons on-screen, it seemed that the least we could do was devote some small space—crammed, we think appropriately, between the "proper" English chapters—to the maverick American responsible for the unique visual aesthetic of Monty Python: Terence Vance Gilliam.

Terry Gilliam was born in Minnesota, went to Occidental College in Los Angeles (where he studied physics and politics), worked for the Harvey Kurtzman* magazine *Help!* (where he produced a short photo-comic—*fumetti*—with John Cleese), briefly doodled about Europe, joined an American advertising agency, moved to London, illustrated a few segments for the Jones/Palin/Idle show, *Do Not Adjust Your Set*, and thus, in a very haphazard way, was on the radar when *Monty Python's Flying Circus* was first being assembled. The rest, as they say, is (fractured and satiric) history.

While the British Pythons all joined *Flying Circus* as part of pre-existing creative blocs (Chapman and Cleese; Palin and Jones . . . plus Idle), Gilliam wandered in solo, and with very little exception that's how it stayed. The Brits wrote sketches in pairs (although Idle sometimes flew solo, especially on musical numbers), then came together to discuss, refine, and enact them; meanwhile, Gilliam illustrated his cut-and-paste interstitial cartoon sequences in virtual isolation and without any extensive creative oversight. As the following sampling of script notes suggests, so long as Gilliam's animated sequences linked, *in some vague way,* the often-disparate live sketches, the other Pythons generally left him to his own devices:

> "Titles begin with words 'Monty Python's Flying Circus.' Various
>   bizarre things happen." (ep. 1)

---

* Kurtzman was a seminal figure in American cartooning, responsible for introducing both *MAD* magazine and *Little Annie Fanny* to the world. The comic-book industry's Harvey Awards are named in his honor.

"Ends with cut-out animation of sedan chair; matching shot
links into next film." (ep. 4)

"By the miracle of money we swing into a fantastically expensive
opening animation sequence, produced by one of America's
very own drop-outs." (ep. 7)

"Animation sketch leading to a booth in a quite expensive
looking office shop, Italian style." (ep. 19)

"Animation: perhaps even mixed with stock film—as the
fevered mind of Gilliam takes it—sheep armed to the teeth,
executing dangerous raids, Bill Cassidy and the Sundance
Sheep, sheep with machine gun out of its arse, etc." (ep. 20)

"Animation sketch." (ep. 19)

While we talk of the Pythons as deconstructionists throughout this
book, Terry Gilliam took deconstruction literally. Gilliam's animation
was literally cut out from art books, catalogues, vintage photographs,
and other cultural detritus, then reassembled in ways that, like the verbal gymnastics performed by the other Pythons, challenged perceived
notions of storytelling and narrative construction. Just as the English
Pythons reconstructed language in order to demonstrate the utter silliness behind perceived constructions of authority, Gilliam demonstrated
that the visual signifiers of authority were also ripe for deconstruction.
In the world of Gilliam, for example, a policeman was not merely revealed to be a mindless instrument of authority for a phallogocentric
system that made no sense but could be made to literally take his uni-
form off to reveal a very feminine physique hidden within. Gilliam, unbound by the financial constrictions of set, lighting, cast, et cetera, could
create elaborate special effects through an (albeit intensive and backbreak-
ing) work schedule of cutting and pasting animations together. But beyond strictly financial limits, as Gilliam himself noted, "You can do things
to animated people you just can't do to real ones" (*Almost the Truth*).

Ultimately, despite the seeming creative distance between the surrealistically witty sketches of the Oxbridge Pythons and the surrealistically witty animations of the Occidental Python, Gilliam's laboriously rendered cut-and-paste stop-action animations worked seamlessly with the live-action sequences, ultimately producing the device through which a show bent on deconstructing traditional television structures could be simultaneously disjointed *and* cohesive. His art in many ways defines Monty Python, and for viewers of the initial series his opening sequence silently shouted that they were about to experience something unlike anything else on television.

The fart noises were simply a bonus.

"Tonight I want to examine the whole question of eighteenth-century social legislation—its relevance to the hierarchical structure of post-Renaissance society, and its impact on the future of parochial organization in an expanding agrarian economy. But first a bit of fun."

Part II

PYTHON ON HISTORY

TAG UNDER: historicity, the Inquisition, witchcraft, Enlightenment, so-called the Queen, pantomime, class, anachronism, and pornography.

erforming historical sketches was natural for Python. It was clearly a genre that they were used to sending up. They had all worked on material of this sort on *At Last the 1948 Show*, *The Complete and Utter History of Britain*, and/or *Do Not Adjust Your Set*. Their shared backgrounds at Oxford and Cambridge had made this almost inevitable (Gilliam had also been a political science major back at Occidental College) and as Michael Palin remembered:

> Terry and I were both interested in history—Terry because he read medieval English and was very interested in Chaucer and all that, and me because I'd done three years of a history degree at Oxford. I was brim-full of all this useless information! (Morgan 2005, 148)

This "useless information" would prove to be invaluable for both Palin and Jones prior to *MPFC*, desperate to complete new and challenging material quickly in order to get airtime for their material (and equally important when working for David Frost: to get paid!), so they naturally drew on their school backgrounds. Eric Idle concurred that history was one of the key obsessions of most members of Python, saying:

> I think history played a big part in Python. Terry did history, Mike did history, I did history up to A-Level. When people say it's

undergraduate humor, I think they're wrong. It's post-graduate humor. By the time we're writing Python, we've all been through Cambridge or Oxford. (Pythons 2003, 85)

The British Python members, as well as Gilliam, had long been fascinated with history and their comedic sense was tempered by a new mind-set that said that history was fair game for comedic revision. Why not take their natural sense of the absurd and apply it to the sacrosanct world of beloved historical legends?

Python knew, better than most, that history was not reliable. This is not to say that they believed that there is no empirical idea of truth (see the philosophy section for a look at *that* question) but that history, even recent history, is open to revision and reassessment. Python came of age during a time and place where both literature and history, subjects that had been analyzed with rigor for years, were now being revised as the new criticism was working its way into academia. In addition, deconstructionism, the French literary movement that began in the sixties and was literally embodied by the unrest in France in 1968, and the Situationist movement both mirrored and embodied Python's view of the impermanence of facts. But, this was technically not a recent phenomenon. Python knew well, as Joyce Appleby, Lynn Hunt, and Margaret Jacob wrote: "In the decades since World War II, the old intellectual absolutisms have been dethroned: science, scientific history, and history in the service of nationalism" (1994, 4). This led to a new impulse to study history with rigor and objectivity and to reject supposed fixed accounts of historical events. While Appleby et al. trace this back to the way in which political expediency helped increase a general skepticism about absolute truth, this impulse also went back to the new rationality of the Enlightenment and its rejection of fixed religious or political notions of history. As Diderot stated, ". . . all things must be examined, all must be winnowed and sifted without exception without sparing anyone's sensibilities" (Baker, Boyer, and Kirshner 1987, 84). The legacy of the Enlightenment had started a new trend in Western mainstream thought, where authority could be openly questioned. As Appleby et al. mentioned, "The philosophies of the enlightenment had sought truth with a purpose, the reform of existing institutions" (1994, 41). While this did not affect all parts of the academy, and indeed the British educational system was still very rigid and restricted centuries after the Enlightenment, the new historians of the twentieth century, from the progressives to the social historian of the 1960s, had begun to revive the Enlightenment-era ideals of challenging fixed notions of historical certainty. As a result, skepticism became a hallmark of historians as "interdeterminacy about human processes seems more believable today than the determinacy of inexorable progress" (Appleby, Hunt, and Jacob 1994, 159). New social historians from the sixties onwards "fostered the argument that history could never be objective" and most accepted versions of history served as a reinforcement of the dominant ideology (Appleby, Hunt, and Jacob 1994, 200).

For years, the emphasis by historians had been on a standardized view of history, or "standard historical occurrences," as historian Lawrence Levine wrote. According to Levine, historians are aware that "our understanding of these standard historical occurrences inevitably varies from generation to generation, because they perceive that, of necessity, we view them through the prism of a changing present" (1993, 4). The new historiography was no longer about great men and royal dynasties and epoch-changing battles but about regular people living everyday lives, people who were "rather actors in their own right, who, to a larger extent than we previously imagined, were able to build a culture, create alternatives, affect the situation they found themselves in, and influence the people they found themselves among" (Levine 1993, 7). If history was not simply an objective set of facts agreed upon by consensus but instead was open to multiple interpretations, including ones that challenged the dominant belief systems, then history was ripe for comedic revision.

Monty Python led the comedic vanguard in a Trojan horse* of antiauthoritarianism and was more sympathetic to the new and often-radical social movements than most British (or any) comedians on television at that time. The English members had grown up listening to the stream of

---

* Or possibly a badger.

consciousness antics of *The Goon Show* and had absorbed the lesson that comedy could not only tackle any subject, it could handle many subjects at the same time* and highlight how ridiculous most things were when examined closely. While they may have come from different economic backgrounds, Python's members all shared one thing in common: a contempt for authority figures, whether from the government, religion, the law, or anything else that smacked of the establishment, and they possessed a sufficient knowledge of historical events to use them to make larger points. Many of the Pythons had also addressed history in their previous television work before forming Python, particularly Palin and Jones, who had previously worked on a program (*The Complete and Utter History of Britain*) wherein historical British events were presented as if modern news media had covered them. As Palin wrote in his diary, the show was

> a fusion of the academic side of our upbringing and the comedy side: how you look at the world and make sense of it by turning it on its head. The two things came together. Suddenly, it was a very easy idea that we should treat history as if it had always been covered by modern media and communications, so you could have cameras at the Battle of Hastings, and so on and so on. (2006, 121)

This new approach to history continues on throughout *MPFC* as well as their subsequent movies. Not so much that media was always explicitly used as the lens through which to examine history, but that looking at history and trying to make sense of it by turning it on its head was a Python staple from the start. The past was just as ripe for silliness as the present.

The Pythons also realized that they did not need to be true to history in order to represent it.† But this meant that Python also had the freedom to look at history not as though it were some distant, vague,

---

*Python thus championed both multitasking and mash-ups—it's almost as if they invented the interweb!

†Although it is worth noting that *Holy Grail* was lauded for its verisimilitude, including jarringly realistic scenes of medieval squalor (which Gilliam would lovingly recreate with even more authentic filth in *Jabberwocky*).

FACTOID BOX: *The Complete and Utter History of Britain*

TCUHB, a six-episode BBC television series that Palin and Jones created and wrote in 1969 (before joining Monty Python), tackled famous incidents in British history as if they were being covered by modern news media today. An example: the victorious French being interviewed in the locker room after the Battle of Hastings (making the obvious link between sports and battle). Unfortunately, most of the series is now lost because of the BBC's unfortunate habit of "wiping" their tapes after usage. (Rather ironic to consider how much of "real" history is lost to us via authority "wiping" as well.) While Palin and Jones were ultimately disappointed with the execution of the program, it did lay the groundwork for their later historical deconstructions in *MPFC*.

unknowable past but as a continuous present, one populated with anachronisms and historical figures that in many ways reflected modern attitudes and ways of thinking. This was not as far from the mark as it seemed; to consider the vanities, pretension and ridiculous nature of historical moments such as the Spanish Inquisition and the British Empire was a bold move on the Pythons' part that took them away from being mere re-creationists and instead led them to engage in a wholesale deconstruction of the very idea of history. According to Michael Palin (referring to *Holy Grail*),

Once you put in that sort of historical perspective, and play the game which Terry and I had done ages ago on *The Complete and Utter History of Britain*—ascribing modern characteristics to historical figures, taking them out of a stained glass window and making them less wooden, bringing them to life—then it all seemed to have a logic of its own and was a real pleasure to write. (Pythons, 297)

Python did not confine themselves merely to British history; they incorporated figures from numerous mythologies and legends, as well as important historical characters, primarily from Europe (as in Cardinal Richelieu, Mr. "Hilter" and his entourage of "National Bocialists," the Montgolfier brothers, et al.), but also veered far from Europe with characterizations of historical characters such as Attila the Hun, Genghis Khan, Lenin, Marx, and the ever redoubtable Chairman Mao. Although Python rarely touched on America in the original series, as they became more involved with American culture (especially after Cleese and Chapman lived in America for extended periods of time), Monty Python did see the comedic potential in U.S. history. One idea for a movie that the troupe toyed with was a Python history of America, which would have been "[a] totally fabricated history using facts and when we want them—rather on the lines of GC's *A Liar's Autobiography*" (Palin 2009, 349). While this film was, sadly, never made, it does illustrate the Pythons' potential to critically and comedically examine almost any topic in human history—even something as inconsequential as the (former) Colonies.

This revisionist use of history was tied into Python's contempt for perceived authority: no figure (except perhaps for Jesus, despite what the critical attacks on *Life of Brian* may have indicated) was exempt from Python's criticism. Python was a product of their times, and they shared many of their generation's emerging attitudes towards a traditional view of history. As Appleby et al. noted:

The post-war generation has questioned fixed categories previously endorsed as rational by all thoughtful men and has denaturalized social behavior once presumed to be encoded in the very structure of humanness. (4)

Python grew up in a time when challenging authority was *becoming* the norm for their generation. The Python ethos did not merely use history as fodder for general silliness, although they certainly did so every time they approached historical topics. Rather, the Pythons' natural mistrust of authority made them especially careful to not show any reverence for history AT ALL. While the young Python members were getting stellar educations, it did not make them any less critical. By realizing that they could approach history in a fresh way they opened up the floodgates for new material. As John Cleese said, "There was a tremendous liberation, this energizing feeling when you break through stuff you feel constricted by and you suddenly sense all the possibilities around" (Pythons 2003, 136).

Although your present authors laud the Pythons' erudition, the Pythons were not walking *Encyclopedia Britannicas*. As Graham Chapman summed it up in one of his autobiographies:

> Much has been made about the apparent "intellectualism" of Monty Python. Well, we're certainly not a dumb bunch—I mean we've got a historian (Terry Jones), a "word addict" (Idle), a lawyer (Cleese) and a medical doctor (me), but I don't think there's a great deal of depth behind the intellectual content of something like the "All England Summarize Proust" sketch. I mean, obviously we had *heard* of the "big" literary and philosopher names and knew some rudimentary stuff about them, but certainly the person(s) who wrote that sketch didn't know everything that Proust had written or said. They probably knew enough to get them an O-level pass or work his name in a crossword. (Chapman and Yoakum 1977, 44)

However well-informed they may (or may not) have been, the Pythons' anarchistic tendency gave them the freedom to do what they wanted, but for the first two years of *MPFC* a lack of oversight by the BBC let them create a format that also deconstructed television. When approaching even local history, Python was naturally irreverent towards heroes, particularly the most beloved icons of British culture: the Royal Family.

The royals, in their own way, were becoming to many in Britain the representative of all things passing. (It is no coincidence that only a few years later the Sex Pistols released their scathing single "God Save the Queen" on the year of the Queen's Silver Jubilee.)* In a decade geared towards youth culture, the most typical modern approach to the Royal Family was to look at them as quaint and anachronistic. Python took it a few steps further. In the "Royal Episode" (ep. 26), Python informs their audience at the start of the program that there is a good chance that at a certain point the Queen herself would be watching. When (after several false alarms) the moment finally comes during the "Insurance" sketch the entire cast leaps to their feet as the British national anthem plays. As the announcer Palin intones with great solemnity, "And we've just heard that Her Majesty the Queen just tuned into this programme and so she is now watching this royal sketch here in this royal set. The actor on the left is wearing the great grey suit of the BBC wardrobe department and the other actor is . . . about to deliver the first great royal joke here this royal evening." At this point the camera pans across the set and the narrator continues, "Over to the right you can see the royal cameraman, and behind . . . Oh, we've just heard she's switched over. She's watching the News at Ten." As we hear "cries of disappointment" the program then inserts a shot of the real News at Ten anchorman Reggie Bosanquet, whose reading of a news report (linked to an earlier sketch where miners walk off the job due to conflicting views of "the name of the section between the triglyphs in the frieze section of a classic Doric entablature" and want concessions such as "thirteen reasons why Henry III was a bad king") is interrupted by the national anthem heralding that the Queen is now watching the episode. Bosanquet leaps to attention, but continues to read a news report that links to the next sketch.

By conflating a possible "visit" via television with all the pomp and ceremony of an actual royal visit (the BBC announcer's breathless and fatuous description of what the actors on the floor are wearing and calling the next joke a "royal joke," et cetera) Python mocks not just the notion

---

*The original "God Save the Queen" is from 1745, and is the de facto national anthem of the U.K. A good many aging punks would argue that the 1977 version is now the de facto anthem, of course.

FACTOID BOX: Pantomime

A Python staple, the pantomime horse is a "significant figure in English pantomime tradition" (Larsen 2008, 391).

Pantomime (or simply "panto") is a theatrical tradition of short, costumed silly plays, ostensibly for children, that became popular in Early Modern England following the Italian commedia dell'arte tradition. Action in pantomimes is often driven by slapstick, characters are simply "types" (including the popular clown Harlequin), and plots are often drawn from traditional fairy tales. Even today, "pantomimes are regularly performed at Christmas time in the UK, both live and on TV." (Larsen, 391) Nothing quite like it in the Americas, really.

that the program could know if and when the Queen was watching but also mocks the inherent silliness in the pomp and pageantry of the royal visitations. This ties into the natural anarchistic tendencies of Monty Python. Not that some members did not have some sympathy for the Royal Family, but even so, the royals were in the end yet another anachronistic symbol of mindless authority. The Royal Family were (and are) ridiculous authority figures because they no longer play the authoritative roles they had played for most of British history. While the Queen (and the rest of the Royal Family) technically retains some vestige of nominal power to this day, she is primarily a figurehead who is in many ways as starchy as her doppelgänger in Madame Tussauds. From Tussauds it is a quick step to the grand English tradition of the pantomime, and another Python staple, the pantomime Princess Margaret, who later went on tour with Python, watching from a royal box as they performed.

In Python, the pantomime horse first appears in the context of a firm downsizing. A manager (Cleese) tells two pantomime horses, Trigger and Champion, who have been working for the firm for three years, that due to budget constraints one of them will have to be let go (ep. 30). When they protest, the manager tells them that "one of our management consultants actually queried the necessity for us to employ a pantomime horse at all!" The only solution for the horses is to fight to the death. The scene then shifts to a nature documentary about Darwinian notions of survival of the fittest and as we see them fight, a Germanic narrator (Cleese) tells us that "this time one of the pantomime horses concedes defeat, and so lives to fight another day." The (presumably winning) pantomime horse returns later in the episode (now named Dobbins) lying in a canoe with Carol Cleveland. As they relax and share a drink, the pantomime horse spins around and fires at a group of Russian pantomime horses, before jumping into his sports car with Cleveland and racing after the Russian pantomime horses. As the announcer of the film *Pantomime Horse Is a Secret Agent*, John Cleese breathlessly narrates the chase, which ends with a fight between the pantomime horse and the pantomime Princess Margaret, who are quickly joined by the Duke of Kent and Jacques Cousteau (among others). After the credits have finished rolling, the nature film narrator (also Cleese in voice-over) tells us that the English pantomime horse wins and so is assured of a place in British history and a steady job in a merchant bank. Unfortunately, before his pension rights are assured, he catches bronchitis and dies, another victim of the need to finish these shows on time.

Even in as oddly metatheatrical a sketch as "Pantomime Horse," the final jest reflects back to the Pythons themselves, those self-described "kooky funsters" who, apparently, struggled with their own deadlines.

The reoccurring pantomime Princess Margaret was most likely parodied because of her "well-documented appearances in Windsor Palace pantomimes as a child, where she played Aladdin, for example, during the war" (Larsen 2008, 392). In the "Biggles Dictates a Letter" sketch (ep. 33), Princess Margaret is referred to as a "pantomimetic royal person," which also refers back to her early appearances in pantomime (Larsen 2008, 428). She also opens episode 39, described as "HRH the Dummy Princess Margaret" who hosts "the British showbiz awards." Python friend Kim "Howard" Johnson summed up her running gag nicely by saying that "in pantomime there is usually a pantomime horse or cat or cow," so instead Python naturally went for a pantomime Princess Margaret (Johnson 1999, 139).

Despite the Pythons' repeated gentle mocking of the Royal Family, it seems as though at least some of the Windsors shared similar interests. Prince Charles in particular was an avid fan of the Pythons' primary influence, *The Goon Show*. As Charles once said:

> . . . it has always been one of my profoundest regrets that I was not born ten years earlier than 1948, since I would have had the pure unabounded joy of listening avidly to the Goons. I only discovered Goon-type humor appealed to me with a hysterical totality just as the shows were drawing to a close. (Hamilton 2003, 107)

Similar sense of humor or not, it seems clear that Python recognized something many outside of England failed to recognize: in an age when the Royal Family has only symbolic authority (if even that) they are nothing less than a pure anachronism and, when one considers it (the pomp, the costumes, the Queen's wave, et cetera), quite a bit silly. As Lord Hattersley, a Labour peer, lamented in 1988, ". . . the institution of monarchy is inherently silly. And it obliges everything it touches to do silly things" (Hamilton 2003, 173). Python merely confirmed the notion of many fans: watching adults play dress up is always a bit amusing. Even the famously "unamused" Queen Victoria may have let a chuckle slip out from below her frown while watching numerous versions of her royal personage running out of the gate in the "Queen Victoria Handicap" in episode 43.

Queen Victoria (1819–1901) also appears in the "Michael Ellis" episode of the fourth season (ep. 41), where she interrupts the drunken poetry reading about ants to announce a new direction in British poetry, one away from poems (or "prams," as a probably drunk in real life Graham Chapman as the drunken hostess calls them) about ants. As the Queen (Palin), accompanied by her deceased husband, Albert (in a coffin), proclaims:

My late husband and we are increasingly concerned by developments in literary style [*developing a German accent*] that have taken
place here in Germany ... er England. There seems to be an increasing tendency for ze ent ... the ent ... the ant ... to become
the dominant ... *was is der deutsches Entwicklungsbund.* ...

As the befuddled and apparently German Victoria cannot find the word,
the attendant corrects her that it is "theme" and Victoria proceeds to
proclaim that from now on, ants are "verboten" and that British poetry
will concentrate now on "skylarks, daffodils, nightingales, light brigades,
and ... *was ist das schreckliche Gepong ... es schmecke wie en Scheisshaus ...
und so weiter.** Well, we must away now or we shall be late for the races.
God bless you *alles.*"

The fact that Queen Victoria would proclaim a new direction in British poetry is a bit off the mark. However, this doesn't mean that Queen
Victoria wasn't a patron of the arts. She, and especially her consort, Albert (along with Henry Cole), started the Royal Society for Arts in 1847.
"In 1847, Henry Cole and the prince worked together in mounting a series of exhibitions; the first attracted 20,000, visitors, the second in 1848
attracted 70,000, the third in 1849, over 100,000" (Woodham-Smith
1972, 400). While Queen Victoria did not explicitly demand new direc-
tions in the arts, her regime was certainly friendly to arts, science, and
industry. Apparently, even if she did not personally oversee new direc-
tions in British poetry, she had good reason to demonstrate at least some
anxiety about poetry. In March 1882, minor poet Roderick McLean attempted to assassinate the Queen after she did not reply kindly to a
poem he had sent to her royal personage. He was later sent to Broad-
moor Asylum, where he lived out his days. Although it is unclear what
was so incredibly vexing about the Queen ignoring a poem, shooting at
Queen Victoria was apparently becoming a national sport in England at
the time: McLean was the eighth assassin to try to shoot Victoria over a

---

* It seems to translate as "what is the terrible gepong ... it tastes like a shit house ...
and so on," carrying on in the grand Python tradition of mangling other languages
for comedic purposes.

forty-year period. Apparently the Queen was so taken by several school-boys who disarmed McLean with their umbrellas that she remarked that it is was worth being shot at, "to see how much one is loved" (Hibbert 2000, 427). Apparently, every now and then "we" *were* amused.

The Python version of Victoria adopts a rather thick and increasingly bewildered German accent, a gag that likely references the fact that her mother was Princess Victoria of Saxe-Coburg-Saalfeld, who had married into the British Royal Family; this gag is also somewhat off the mark. Despite rumors, German was not Queen Victoria's native language, nor the one she was most adept in. She did spend time learning German (among other languages) in her youth and later learned Urdu in her dotage; she became passably fluent in German by her twenties. In fact, her German tutor reported that she had acquired a German accent "particularly remarkable for its softness and distinctiveness" and that "she knew most German words in common use . . . and understood the leading rules of the German language. . . ." Even though there was much speculation that she was always fluent in German and that she had learned it from her mother, she also denied these claims and wrote that while young she did not "speak German with fluency" (Woodham-Smith 1972, 104). Even later while penning letters to her future husband, Albert, she had to write in a mixture of English and broken German. As Cecil Woodham-Smith concludes, ". . . the truth seems to be that the princess studied German as she studied French and Italian as a lesson, but did not use it as a second mother tongue" (105). Of course, by the time she was married to Prince Albert, the royal consort, her German would have been much improved and likely used on a daily basis.

Her parting line of "we must away now or we shall be late for the races" refers to the later episode 43, where a horse race, the Queen Victoria Handicap, is shown. This exciting race consists of "eight identically dressed Queen Victorias who go bustling off up the field." The announcer (Idle) breathlessly calls the race, noting "Queen Victoria still the back marker as they approach the halfway mark, but making ground now, suddenly pass Queen Victoria with Queen Victoria, Queen Victoria and Queen Victoria still well placed as they approach the first fence."

As the announcer shifts back to the studio, we then see a succession of sports announcers dressed as Queen Victoria talking about the European Cup. The Queen Victoria Handicap capitalizes upon the ambiguity potential in the name of the race (a handicapping of participatory Victorias rather than a handicap in her honor), as well as the idea of the royal "we," which is taken to its ridiculous and logical extreme. Queen Victoria, one of the most iconic figures in British history, is in some ways the silliest, as even those of us who grew up in America knew her as a dowdy, seemingly eternal widow, perpetual scowl on her face, using the so-called majestic plural to describe herself. She was one of the best-known representations of British royalty outside of England, even though it was highly unlikely that she would have actually used the majestic plural on a regular basis. By Victoria's time, the word had mostly fallen out of style and had become something of a joke. As Ben Zimmer noted in a 2010 *New York Times* article on the use of the word "we":

> The roots of these adverse reactions lie in the haughtiness of the majestic plural, or royal *we*, shared by languages of Western Europe since the days of ancient Roman emperors. British sovereigns have historically referred to themselves in the plural, but by the time of Queen Victoria, it was already a figure of fun. Victoria, of course, is remembered for the chilly line, "We are not amused"— her reaction, according to Sir Arthur Helps, the clerk of the privy council, to his telling of a joke to the ladies in waiting at a royal dinner party.

While most scholars believe the line itself to be apocryphal and that Queen Victoria actually had quite a healthy sense of humor (Hibbert 2000, 471), Queen Victoria and the Victorian Age inspired by her example may still be regarded as the antithesis of everything Python stood for: pompous, monotonously serious, staid, sober, and, above all, proper royal authority. Obvious class references are also (as usual) being mocked by Python. As Zimmer notes, the royal and editorial "we" are examples of the exclusive "we," meaning that the person being addressed is not included in the scope of the pronoun. Thus the use of the royal plural in the sketch further illustrates not only Python's view of the relevance of the Royal Family and how silly the institution was/is but also how most institutions of this sort are only social constructs, elaborate historical façades that have as much real authority behind them as any pantomime Princess Margaret.

With Python deconstructing the current Royal Family, it was natural that they would also take apart the nobles and landed gentry in British history. Palin and Jones had already parodied the conventions of British history in their series *A Brief and Utter History of Britain*, and in *MPFC* historical characters could pop up at any minute. Although historical continuity and linearity were completely optional in Python, historical figures taken out of context were often revealed to be normal people complete with eccentricities and sometimes self-awareness of the futility of their "historically significant" actions. The Spanish Inquisition (as analyzed in the next section) may seem completely foreign to us today, but, by transplanting it into Victorian England, Python stressed how alien and ridiculous it should have been in *any* setting. In the sketch, when Cardinal Ximénez (Palin) messes up his lines, he insists that they re-enter and redo the lines over and over again, as futile an endeavor as trying to rationalize the Spanish Inquisition's obsession with heresy. Eventually Ximénez is forced to give up and hands his lines over to Cardinal Biggles (Jones), who nervously tries to read the lines in a deliberately strained, stagey tone; meanwhile, Cardinal Fang (Gilliam) vamps melodramatically in the background. Thus the deadly serious and once-feared inquisition is revealed as a farce. Python portrays historical figures not as revered and august personages but as bit players in a grand and meaningless game where rules are arbitrary and all manifestations of authority are inherently ridiculous.

When filming *Holy Grail*, Python wanted to be able to strike a balance between unreality and reality, creating an "accurate" Middle Ages but with modern people (the historian, the police, the illustrator) standing out as anachronisms. As Gilliam mentioned:

> . . . we approached *Grail* as seriously as Pasolini did. We were watching the Pasolini films a lot at the time because he more than

anybody seemed to be able to capture a place and a period in a simple but really effective way. (Morgan 2005, 51)

With Pasolini in mind, "the Pythons were not only able to redefine the limits of narrative structure (basically by ignoring them!), but also to take innovative and unconventional styles of filming . . . and apply them to comedy" (Morgan 2005, 145). Even the crew noticed that Python paid attention to historical details, creating a world that worked because they took the premise, if not the characters and their actions seriously. As Howard Atherton, a camera operator on *Holy Grail*, has said, "they were quite serious when they were doing comedy; they're very intellectual about the whole process[. . .] they wanted to make it look like a film and not like television" (Morgan 2005, 160–161). This was a manifestation of not only the troupe's professional pride but also their nearly academic understanding that in order to parody history research and a keen awareness are needed to hit the right notes—verisimilitude breeds identification, identification allows for critique.

This attention to historical detail applies to their other films as well. In *Life of Brian*, when the People's Judean Front are arguing, "What did the Romans ever do for us?" they bring up, among many things, the legendary Pax Romana, or long Roman peace. As Michael Grant notes, the Pax Romana Augustus lasted circa 27 B.C. to A.D. 180 and

> the enormously far-reaching work of reorganization and rehabilitations which he undertook in every branch of his vast empire created a new Roman peace, in which all but the humblest classes benefited from improved communications and flourishing commerce. (1997, 15)

Yet, when the Pax is floated as one of the many things the Romans actually have given them, the character Reg simply shouts, "Shut up!" Even the line of prophets and wannabe messiahs each shouting their own version of religious dogma would have been familiar to the Romans of the time; as Jérôme Carcopino argued in his book *Daily Life in Ancient Rome*, most Romans, who knew something about Judaism, would have had little knowledge of the new religion of Christianity because, when "seen from the outside and from a little distance, the two religions were at first easily confused with each other" (1968, 136). Python's attention to detail served them well in constructing realistic, well-researched scenarios to completely bollocks up. This applied not only to historical settings but also to some of the "great men" in history as well.

HISTORICAL FIGURES (Part One): SIR PHILIP SIDNEY
"Now, my good wife. Whilst I rest, read to me a while from Shakespeare's *Gay Boys in Bondage*."

One of the Pythons' greatest achievements was to take historical figures out of context and place them in increasingly absurd situations, ones where they could only bob and weave while caught in a maelstrom of absurdity. One figure, perhaps unfamiliar to American viewers at least, was the renowned British author, poet, and political figure Sir Philip Sidney. Sidney (1554–1586) was a much-beloved British historical figure, one who does not easily compare to any in U.S. history. To Palin, he was a "complete Renaissance man and along with Charles Darwin and the founders of *Private Eye*, among the most famous old boys" (53). Sir Philip Sidney figures in Python not only because he was a Renaissance man but also because his story was one of enormous potential cut dramatically short. According to historian Alan Stewart, "Philip Sidney has shone through four centuries as England's hero, its shepherd-knight, its greatest courtier poet" (2000, 7). Sidney's hyper-glamorized life, both during his short career and posthumously, was the stuff of legends. Like most Renaissance men, he had apparently done more before breakfast than most people accomplish in their entire lives. To Stewart, Sidney was "[a] man of real stature, magnetic charisma and immense political potential, who was recognized, loved and prized in his own lifetime" (8). This evaluation is borne out by historical record. Sidney was a French baron at seventeen, juggled marriage proposals from two Princesses, received a military posting as the governor of the Low Countries port of Flushing, and wrote (among other literary and critical works) *Arcadia, Astrophil and Stella*, and *The Defence of Poesie*. He was an "acknowledged leader of men" and "at the time of his death he was being openly spoken as the next leader of the Low Countries" (Stewart 200, 6). Yet because of royal disfavor he was "forced to live a double life: of fame and praise abroad, and of comparative—and deliberate—neglect at home" (7).

Sidney, like many of history's heroes, was more mythic than human, more lauded after death than in life, and more popular conception than historical reality. Even in his death throes, Sir Philip Sidney was superhuman; he died not because of an overwhelming attack or inevitable subterfuge but of his own chivalry. He likely died of a badly infected wound gone gangrenous, but even "the wounding of Sidney is the stuff of myth; allegedly, seeing that his fellow-in-arms sir William Pelham lacked tight armor (cuisses), Philip had taken off his own as a sign of solidarity" (Stewart 2000, 312). Sir Philip, the epitome of Elizabethan chivalry, was gallant to the bitter end, dying with great dignity, throwing off this mortal coil the way a true gentleman should, surrounded by his friends, uttering quotable remarks to the last breath. As Stewart points out, the legends around Sir Philip's death smell the most of hyperbole: "Most famous of all is the story told by Granville of how Philip declined a drink of water, giving it instead to a common wounded soldier" (313).

Stewart and many other historians now regard such stories as apocryphal, but when the Bodleian Library put up a frieze in the seventeenth century "memorializing the world's greatest authors, the portrait of Sir Philip Sidney headed the modern greats, just as Homer had headed the ancients" (Stewart 2000, 2). After Sidney's death, legend grew and "[t]ogether the funeral, the publication of Sidney's works and the writings of his life create the figure who became the epitome of Elizabethan chivalry" (Stewart 2000, 5). Sidney was thus as much a creation of public relations as any contemporary pop or sports star. In reality, "much of his adult life was spent in the country, strapped for cash, penning what he himself spoke up as literary trifles, none of which he actually published" (3). In some ways, the real Sir Philip Sidney resembled fictional Python poet Ewan McTeagle ("I'm absolutely skint") more than the self-sacrificing epitome of Elizabethan chivalry.

Python re-creates a surrealistic Sir Philip in episode 36, which opens in an employment office for Edwardian characters ("Tudor Job Agency—Jobs a Specialty"), an office soon revealed to be a front secretly selling pornography. Suddenly the scene is interrupted by Palin in Tudor garb, introducing himself as Superintendent Gaskell, who has arrived for a raid with the unseen and apparently absent Sergeant Maddox. When Gaskell is addressed repeatedly as Sir Philip Sidney, he replies indignantly that "I'm not a bloody Tudor at all. I'm Gaskell of the Vice Squad and this is Sergeant Maddox." But of course Maddox is no longer there, and Gaskell/Sidney desperately tries to maintain his composure as the customers leave the store, even trying to go through all of the names of "the men down in 'F' Division at Acton," but even this cannot stop his identity from sliding further into that of a woefully displaced historical character.

Upon leaving the shop, Gaskell/Sidney is astounded to find that he is now in a Victorian garden, where he comforts a weeping girl and is recognized once again as Sir Philip Sidney by the father (Jones). At this point, Gaskell slides further into his Sir Philip Sidney persona, accepting the identity more as his own, although his "sharp-tongued wit" now largely is confined to telling stories of vice-department raids in a vaguely Edwardian tone. Sir Philip's life is ever busy and he is soon called upon to respond to a Spanish landing in England, whereupon he discovers two Spanish soldiers unloading cases of pornography (although they claim that they are merely transporting Lope de Vega's latest play, *Toledo Tit Parade*, which is "very visual"). They fight Sidney but are soundly defeated by the Renaissance man.

Sir Philip returns in triumph to his home in London, where his wife (Carol Cleveland) reads him a new play, William Shakespeare's *Gay Boys in Bondage*. Sir Sidney is naïvely pleased by the turgid prose, clearly (to his wife and the audience) a work of pornography rather than literature. But so comfortable is Superintendent Gaskell in the role of Sir Philip Sidney that he accepts the situation as normal, although it is strange he does not recognize pornography, as he had recently helped the empire by confiscating "six thousand copies of *Tits and Bums*" and "four thousand copies of *Shower Sheila*" porn magazines from the Spanish ship recently landed on the English coast. He is content not only with his home and wife in Edwardian England but also in the myth of Sir Philip Sidney. Like Traditional History, Gaskell has chosen to believe the legend over the truth, and this itself is further turned on its head by the arrival of the long-lost Sergeant Maddox, who bursts into the room with other police officers and recognizes Gaskell not as Gaskell but as Sir Philip Sidney. Despite Gaskell's protestations that he is a fellow officer, Maddox responds that not only does he recognize him as Sir Philip Sidney, but "sad I am to see you caught up in this morass of filth." Like the real Sir Philip Sidney, Gaskell has learned too late the perils of interdeterminacy, that leading two lives, one a myth and the other grounded in reality, can lead to death (in the case of the real Sir Philip Sidney) or incarceration (in the case of Gaskell).

But what about those gay boys in bondage mentioned earlier (and subsequently seen in a Gilliam animation at a theatre with a banner reading: "The Aldwych Theatre. The Royal Shakespeare Company presents *Gay Boys in Bondage* by William Shakespeare")? How likely was it that Sir Philip Sidney's wife would be reading a pornographic book? Pornography, which your authors assume has existed throughout recorded history, was not unknown during the time of Sir Philip Sidney. As with VHS tapes and DVDs, pornography had become a key part of popularizing the then new technology: the printing press. One book, *I Modi* by the Italian artist Marcantonio Raimondi, an illustrated work with sixteen different sexual positions shown, was published in 1524, and despite Raimondi's imprisonment by Pope Clement VII and all copies being destroyed, a second edition in 1527 with additional poems (along with images) was a success, until it too was seized and largely destroyed (Lawner 1989). Even during Sir Philip Sidney's time, there remained the eternal struggle between merchants of smut, whether in a Tudor employment agency or via Spanish vessel, as there would also be the equivalent of a vice squad officer attempting to shut them down, whether he was a present-day police officer or the much-mythologized Sir Philip Sidney himself.

HISTORICAL FIGURES (Part Two): CARDINAL "SO-CALLED" RICHELIEU
"I sure did that thing."

Cardinal Richelieu, one of the most famous figures in French political history, incongruously appears for the first time in Python in a British courtroom as a character witness in a trial for a parking offense (episode 3). The counsel calls Cardinal Richelieu as a character witness following the (now-deceased) Arthur Aldridge, who, when one thinks about it, had not been a very helpful witness at all in the sketch. Richelieu (Palin) appears and through some friendly questions from the counsel we are introduced to the epochal accomplishments of the red-garbed clergyman.

> Counsel: Er, are you Cardinal Armand du Plessis de Richelieu, First Minister of Louis XIII?
> Cardinal: Oui.
> Counsel: Cardinal, would it be fair to say that you not only built up the centralized monarchy in France, but also perpetuated the religious schism in Europe?
> Cardinal: (*modestly*) That's what they say.
> Counsel: Did you persecute the Huguenots?
> Cardinal: Oui.
> Counsel: And did you take even sterner measures against the great Catholic nobles who made common cause with foreign foes in defence of their feudal independence?
> Cardinal: I sure did that thing.

The cardinal goes on to be a seemingly acceptable character witness for Harold Larch, who is valiantly fighting a parking ticket, but only after the counsel further elaborates the cardinal's many achievements:

> Counsel: Speaking as a Cardinal of the Roman Catholic Church, as First Minister of Louis XIII, and as one of the architects of

the modern world already—would you say that Harold Larch
is a man of good character?
Cardinal: Listen. Harry is a very wonderful human being.

Of course, this is not the real Cardinal Richelieu, as Inspector Dim of
the Yard (Chapman) bursts in to cross-examine the Cardinal "so-called"
Richelieu, tricking him into admitting that, in fact, the real cardinal had
died in December 1642, unmasking Palin as "Ron Higgins, professional
Cardinal Richelieu impersonator." However real the cardinal in the case
may have been, the facts carefully unveiled on the stand are essentially
true and in some ways actually underestimate the importance of Richelieu in terms of world history. But see how cleverly Python sneaks in
factoids? So subtle. Unlike ...

According to Jacques Barzun, the regime of Louis XIII was one that
could be considered an "absolute monarchy with a centralized rule and
bureaucracy that answered not to regional leaders, but to the monarch"
(2000, 241). Barzun notes that Louis XIII's networks of "henchmen and
spies" helped maintain and consolidate his power and ". . . under his rule
the nation solidified—foreign powers were kept at arm's length, the dis-
sident Huguenots restricted to specified towns and nobles cowered by
conspicuous and unexampled executions as lawbreakers" (2000, 241).

Despite his spiritual role as a cardinal, Richelieu was ever a pragmatist and, during the Thirty Years' War, Richelieu, "belying the national
interest to lie on the Protestants' side, allied himself to Lutheran Sweden"
(Barzun 2000, 248). Cardinal Richelieu, who was "always the pragmatist
rather than a reformer . . . eschewed grand designs in favor of a method—a
method of making things work, avoiding confrontation" (Horne 2004,
128). According to Alistair Horne, Richelieu's early programs operated on
three prongs: to "crush Huguenot power, to humble France's great lords
and to thwart Austrian Designs" (128–129). Richelieu essentially functioned as the head of state and this worked out quite well for his liege,
Louis XIII; as Horne put it, ". . . but for the advent of one of history's greatest politicians, Cardinal Richelieu, Louis XIII's reign might have been a
calamity for France" (126) and "for France, this was to prove a marriage
almost made in heaven. For the monarchy, it was to transform an unat-

tractive accidental princeling into a great king" (128). To Horne, "Richelieu had assigned the boy the role of playing second fiddle in France, and first in Europe" (128). But despite Richelieu's many contributions to France's political power, he also concentrated on the arts and culture. In the end, "Richelieu's greatest cultural legacy to France lay not in brick and mortar, however, but in the creation of the Academe Francaise to defend and enhance the purity of the French language" (Horne 2004, 133). It is still unclear to this day as to how good a friend he was to Harry Larch.*
Richelieu's costume, if not character, was put to further use for the Pythons; with some slight alterations from the BBC wardrobe department, it functioned quite well as the robe of another sort of cardinal, one from one of the most horrific times in religious history, the Spanish Inquisition.†

THE SPANISH INQUISITION
"Our chief weapon is surprise . . . surprise and fear . . . fear and surprise . . . our two weapons are fear and surprise . . . and ruthless efficiency."

Actually, quite a few people *did* expect the Spanish Inquisition; chief among them were Isabella of Castile and Ferdinand of Aragon, who persuaded Pope Sixtus IV to start the whole bloody thing in the first place. As historian Joseph Perez tells us:

> . . . between 1478 and 1502, Isabella of Castile and Ferdinand of Aragon took three complimentary decisions. They persuaded the Pope to create the Inquisition; they expelled the Jews; and they forced the Muslims of the kingdom of Castile to convert to Catholicism. All these measures were designed to achieve the same end: the establishment of a united faith. (2005, 1)

---

*The Larch . . . the Larch.
†But you expected that, didn't you?

This had been coming for quite some time. Originally in Spain (a divided country, then only recently loosely united) Judaism had been tolerated for years, albeit under the same restrictions and ghettoization common in the rest of Europe at the time. Yet as the fourteenth century moved aside for the fifteenth, Spain was wracked with huge economic, political, and health-related crises that challenged the majority Catholic faith. The Black Death had claimed untold numbers, as had wars and disease promulgated via rudimentary sanitation. As Perez suggests, such devastation led to a rise in religious devotion and the creation of a newly penitent atmosphere, which was typical of a world where many felt that their own apparent lack of piety had led to a vengeful God's wrath being rained down upon them. Sadly, history shows us that time and time again such worldviews often lead to attacks on the nearest scapegoat, in this case the Jews. In Spain, the "presence of a 'deicide people' among the Christians was considered to be scandalous, and on all sides, people turned against the Jews" (Perez 2005, 5).

In the anti-Jewish hysteria of the time, Isabella and Ferdinand, alarmed by reports that Conversos, or Jews who had been forcibly converted to Catholicism were secretly practicing Jewish rites, petitioned Pope Sixtus IV to establish an inquisition to rid Spain of the heresy that the royals were convinced existed in every town and city. Reluctantly and with trepidation, on November 1, 1478, the Pope authorized this officially in a papal bull titled *Exigit Sinceras Devotionis*. This decree authorized the Spanish rulers to appoint inquisitors in their kingdom. This was controversial even at court, where high-level advisors such as Cardinal Mendoza, the Archbishop of Seville, had pleaded with the royals that the problem was not so much heresy as it was a common lack of full indoctrination in the Catholic faith; Mendoza instead advised an emphasis be added reminding the faithful of their catechism and religious training. His warnings were not heeded, as the King worried that many forced converts were backsliding to Judaism (many undoubtedly were, and can you blame them?), and after two years of relative inactivity, in 1480 Ferdinand and Isabella appointed the first inquisitors, starting an office that would not officially be closed until 1834.

Python's "Spanish Inquisition" sketch, which combines world history, the British class system, and a love of wordplay, deals not only with the Spanish Inquisition but also with the surrealism that the Pythons were increasingly incorporating into sketches. While most Python fans remember the dramatic entrance into the manor house and the gleefully exaggerated performances of Palin, Jones, and a benign, giggly Gilliam (in a rare high-profile role), the sketch pokes fun at British social customs but also allows viewers to laugh at one of the most horrific times in Western history. As the Pythons would also do with communism, Attila the Hun, and the Nazis (National Bocialism), they took the inherent fanaticism and sense of dread evoked by the Inquisition and essentially encouraged us to laugh at the situation and to question how such episodes could have ever taken place in human history at all. By parodying the Spanish Inquisition, Python shows us how absurd authority remains, not just in the distant past, but also in the present day.

SI: MAJOR PLAYERS
Biggles Combs His Hair

While many Python fans, erudite as they are,* may have read about the Spanish Inquisition, it may have only resonated in a vague, half-remembered way from high school. Those who were watching Python as it aired chronologically may have been confused by Palin's outfit from an earlier episode and wondered why a "so-called" Cardinal Richelieu (actually a famous Cardinal Richelieu imitator) was bursting into the room, but despite the resilience of Hazel Pethig and the resources of the BBC wardrobe department, the costumes that three Pythons wear in the "Spanish Inquisition" sketch (ep. 15) are more or less historically accurate: it's how fashionable members of the inquisition would dress. While most would assume that Palin is meant to resemble Tomás de Torquemada, the most feared of all the Grand Inquisitors (next to Cardinal Lucero), Palin's character is actually the *third* most-feared of all

---

* Yes you are! You are!
  Who's a good boy then?

the inquisitors. The fact that Palin announces himself as Cardinal Ximé-nez no doubt refers to one of the most feared inquisitors after Torque-mada, Cardinal Ximénez de Cisneros. Cisneros was primarily active in Spain during the years 1499–1517, where he proved an intractable en-emy of the Muslims in both Spain and northern Africa. It was Cisneros who was responsible for the forced conversion of many of the Muslim inhabitants of Granada and the burning of all Arabic literature (save that of medicine) that he came across. Along with Cardinal Lucero and Car-dinal Torquemada, Cisneros was one of the most infamous and persis-tent leaders of the inquisition.

Diego Rodriguez Lucero

Lucero was an inquisitor in Cordova between 1499 and 1508, until he was imprisoned for his excesses. To historian Toby Green, "the reverend inquisitor Lucero was evidently a hawk rather than a dove. His motto was, 'give me a Jew, I'll give you him burnt'" (2007, 66). Eventually Lucero's reputation for outright cruelty led to him being removed from his (cruelty-free!?) position. After he was dismissed, he was succeeded by Cardinal Ximénez de Cisneros, who apparently was more palatable but whose "belief in spiritual renewal was married to rabid extremism" (Green 2007, 114).

Cardinal Fang

After careful etymological and genealogical research, your humble au-thors could not find *any* evidence of a Cardinal Fang in the historical rec-ords of the Inquisition. This is, we believe, primarily because the character has never existed outside of this sketch. While many of the names of the inquisitors are lost to us, all historical accounts agree on the categorical absence of the so-called Cardinal Fang. However, this may not be just a throwaway gag; it could also be an insider's reference to Gilliam's high school humor magazine (also named *Fang*) or an oblique reference to the oddly named (and overtly fictitious) husband ridiculed in many of the routines of American comedienne Phyllis Diller (popular in the 1950s and '60s for her boundary-breaking stand-up). Or it could simply be that the concept of a Cardinal Fang is, in and of itself, quite funny. Biting humor, even.

(Cardinal) Biggles

Biggles (James Bigglesworth) is not your typical Spanish inquisitor but instead "a demented fictional character" and wartime flying ace in both the Second and First World Wars; further, during those rare, blasted interludes of peace, Biggles served as a sergeant in the Special Air Police. Biggles was first featured in a novel by W. E. Johns in 1932 and went on to become a seminal figure in children's and young adult books until Johns' death in 1968. By 1968, Biggles had appeared in at least ninety-six books, with several other releases after his death. Biggles, who never seemed to settle down and was a right butch cha, served mostly with his boon comrades Algy and Ginger. Biggles appears a few times in the Python-verse, once as a cardinal named in the "Spanish Inquisition" sketch. On *Monty Python's Contractual Obligation Album*, Biggles is mentioned during the bookstore skit, in one of the fictional fictions called *Biggles Combs His Hair* (no doubt referring to how mundane the series had become after several decades). Biggles, as played by Graham Chapman, also appears in another *MPFC* sketch, "Biggles Dictates a Letter" (ep. 33), where he tries to dictate a letter to King Haakon despite the insistently saucy come-ons of his sultry secretary (Nicki Howorth), who strangely refers to him as "Señor Biggles," despite his protests and denunciations of her as a "harlot" "loopy brothel inmate," "paramour," "concubine," "*fille de joie*," and "naughty lady of the night." Despite the pair's banter the sketch also plays upon Chapman's open homosexuality; he plays Biggles as a violent homophobe who shoots dead his longtime friend Algy (Palin), after Algy cheerfully outs himself at Biggles' request. Oddly, Biggles/Chapman lets his more obviously gay companion, Ginger (Gilliam, described as "a terrible poof in camp flying gear, sequins, [and] eye makeup"), live. Clearly, Python-Biggles is no longer the quaint wartime hero and boys' role model portrayed in the oft-bowdlerized books of the fifties.

Outside of the traditional Python oeuvre, Michael Palin read at least one Biggles book for a series of books on tape, and Biggles, Ginger, and Algy also are featured in some fairly salacious situations in Graham Chapman's *A Liar's Autobiography* (Chapman et al. 1980). Among the many titles in the official Biggles series are *Biggles Flies West*, *Biggles Flies South*, *Biggles Cuts It Fine*, *Biggles Makes Ends Meet*, *Biggles and the Leopards of Zinn*, *Biggles Takes It Rough* (perhaps the book Chapman refers to?), *Biggles in the Underworld*, and, of course, *Biggles Combs His Hair* (no: not really). Palin was asked to write a script for a Biggles film in 1981, and because the last script was "strong on adventure but lacked humor" Palin replied that it was "just like the Biggles stories" (2009, 71). Biggles became a reoccurring theme for Palin, who once performed a solo piece for a charity show about "Biggles, Algy and Ginger trying to get tickets for a Bruce Springsteen concert" (Palin 2009, 414) and later wrote another short piece "Biggles and the Groupies" (Palin 2009, 417). Chapman wrote that "Biggles is very much the archetypal Englishman ... and the star of a lot of books primarily for boys—they were quite sexist about it"; he also remarked about shooting Ginger that "he probably shot him because he was very English. He wouldn't understand anything about anything at all, but knows when he's being fair" (Johnson 1999, 144).

Tomás de Torquemada

Torquemada (1420–1498) can be regarded as a sort of a "Sir Not-Appearing-in-the-Sketch," but his presence looms large not only over Python but over every historical interpretation of the inquisition. Torquemada was among the first five inquisitors appointed by Pope Sixtus IV and became Grand Inquisitor in October 1483; his appointment gave him the power to appoint inquisitors and generally set the overall tone of violence and secrecy that would define the inquisition historically. Torquemada was, by many accounts, a devout and modest Catholic, who was "renowned for his austerity: he never ate meat, wore clothing only of linen and refused all honors"; but despite this modesty, it still was "Torquemada who structured the Spanish Inquisition, making it a strongly centralized institutional and producing its first code of procedure" (Perez 2005, 29). Essentially, Torquemada was the man who singly set the level of brutality that others such as Lucero and Cisneros followed.

Torquemada was of the Dominican order, but contrary to the Dominican tradition,* "his reputation for transience and rigor is well justified. Spurred on by him, the inquisition proved appallingly severe and murderous" (Perez 2005, 105). Torquemada also convinced the King and Queen to finally expel the remaining Spanish Jews in order to sever the Conversos from living links to their neighbors and relatives still practicing Judaism. Torquemada was also key in implementing the punishment of heretics, and the vast majority of those condemned to death died under his reign. According to Perez, Torquemada's inquisition changed the very nature of Spanish life, where "the development of the inquisition implied that loyalty to the state required adhering to the new militancy; a piece of aggression that had once been conceived in political expediency had ended up dismantling a way of life" (41). While Torquemada was Grand Inquisitor, eighty-eight hundred prisoners were burned at the stake and over nine thousand punished in other ways. Apparently Mel Brooks (as Torquemada in *History of the World, Part I*) was right: you "can't Torquemada anything."

SI: TORTURE
"The Comfy Chair?"

The Spanish Inquisition did use torture, but it wasn't their only tool for gathering information (Palin, as Cardinal Ximénez, insists that their chief weapons are fear, surprise, and an almost fanatical devotion to the Pope); the elements of fear and surprise were utilized often enough to convince people that confessing was the best way to avoid being imprisoned indefinitely . . . and subsequently having to bear the cost of their own prosecution. When someone was detained by the inquisition, it was usually because a "friend" or neighbor had secretly denounced him or her. During their imprisonment, which in some cases lasted several

---

* *Pace*, Molloy, *pace*.

years, the accused was not confronted with any charges but instead asked to explain why they may have been captured and constantly urged to confess the specific heresy that they had committed. The burden of proof was on the imprisoned, and the assumption was that they were guilty until proven innocent. While there was a lawyer provided for the victims under many circumstances, the lawyer's main purpose was to convince the accused to confess just to get the whole thing over. Those found guilty were then paraded in the show trial of the public auto-da-fé and then burned at the stake. If the victim was rich or influential or could pay a bribe, they were often strangled before being burned—a small mercy.

If the accused did not confess during their captivity, they were often subjected to torture. This was not particularly unusual for the time period, and some historians now believe that the inquisition practiced *less* torture than many civilian courts of the time, "because it reckoned the procedure to be fallible and inefficient" (Perez 2005, 147). Before torturing the victim, a doctor was usually summoned to make sure that the alleged heretic was strong enough to be tortured, and the torturer was not allowed to spill blood or cause permanent injury. Mutilation was also expressly forbidden under the surprisingly explicit guidelines for torturing an alleged heretic.

For the first 150 years of the inquisition, torture was considered an acceptable, if sometimes-unreliable, tool used to make a heretic confess their crimes. Historian Toby Green points out:

> . . . there was never any question about it being deemed incompatible with civilized society, or even counter-productive. In medieval Castile and Portugal, torture was in daily use by the criminal courts and so its employment by the Spanish and then Portuguese inquisitions was not remarkable. (2007, 68)

However, one should remember that torture was only one tool among many others that the inquisition could use to induce confessions. As Palin's Cardinal Ximénez points out, fear was also one of their key weapons, and Green backs this notion, noting that "the relentless injustice of the system . . . created fear among prisoners" (2007, 82). You could be taken at any time, under any circumstances, at the behest of even the most laughable accusation, imprisoned for as long as they deemed necessary, and then most likely would be tortured and executed in a horrible manner.

As for the torture itself, there were centrally two methods employed: what we would now call waterboarding and the pulleys (a variation on the rack). While there were many improvements to the rack over the subsequent years, the easiest and most efficient (and probably least expensive) type of torture was a makeshift rack, where the victim was suspended by a pulley with ropes on their wrists and weights attached to their feet and then, if the victim was still not confessing their heresy, the rack itself was used and "the prisoner's wrists and ankles were bound together by rope that were then twisted tighter by means of a lever" (Perez 2005, 148). This happened to roughly 90 percent of those tortured, and it is assumed that many confessions were extracted by this means. As Python demonstrated, getting the correct form of rack was the key and that "soft cushions" were generally not all that useful in extracting confessions.* A comfy chair might extract a confession, but really it was not that efficient if there was something good to read handy and providing the victim had sufficient illumination to read said book.

SI: AUTO-DA-FÉ
"Auto-da-fé, what's an auto-da-fé?"

The auto-da-fé, although unmentioned in the Pythons' Inquisition sketch, is no doubt familiar to fans of Mel Brooks. An auto-da-fé was a public trial where numerous victims accused of heresy were ceremonially judged and then handed over to the secular authorities for punishment, typically being burned alive at the stake. As mentioned earlier, those who chose to confess at the last minute and repent their sins were given the mercy of having their necks broken before being consigned to the

---

* Nope, not even with "all the stuffing up in one end."

"Auto-da-fé? What's an auto-da-fé?"
Mel Brooks as the choral inquisitor Torquemada in *The History of the World, Part I.*

flames, certainly a less painful way to die, if not all that pleasant in the moment. The purpose of the auto-da-fé was twofold: to deliver the heretics to their horrible fate and also to show the public the terrible price for those who broke with Catholic doctrine. The first auto-da-fé took place in Seville in 1481 and set the standard that would be followed afterwards.

While the Python sketch indicated that one of the key elements of the Spanish Inquisition was their almost fanatical devotion to the Pope, in the earliest days of the inquisition the Pope actually *opposed* the inquisition and tried to scale back its notorious abuses of power. Pope Sixtus IV was horrified by the excesses of the new inquisition, which denied appeals of convicted heretics (including priests and bishops) to Rome. Sixtus demanded that this appeal system be reinstituted immediately, but was vigorously opposed by Ferdinand. Eventually, when Sixtus IV died in 1484, his successor, Innocent VIII, dropped the matter under diplomatic pressure.

As Perez points out, the auto-da-fé "was not to save a heretic's soul, but to ensure the public good and strike terror into the people" (15). The ceremony included a public confession, after which the civil authorities executed the prisoner. Most of these occurred on a Sunday in public, and the local town was invited to watch. Many presumably came not just for the spectacle or because the weather was nice but so that they would be seen in public vigorously endorsing the inquisition's methods and thus demonstrate their own upstanding moral character.

WITCHCRAFT
"She turned me into a newt!"

Python's version of the inquisition is typical of their approach to all forms of human authority: to point out what Hannah Arendt called "the banality of evil," the inherent silliness that lies behind all types of perceived authority. Python put the inquisition into a Victorian setting to show how absurd it was under any circumstances. As Adam Gopnick wrote in an article in *The New Yorker* on the Spanish Inquisition (and of course Python comes up), "Monty Python could take it as a figure of fun because Enlightenment ideals of tolerance make us feel safe from it" (2012, 75). That is, because we are so far removed from the age when matters of faith were considered important enough to die for (um, that last sentence was written a bit optimistically . . .) we feel safe and that "one ought . . . to feel guilty about laughing at the old Python sketch, but it's hard not to feel a bit giddy watching it. How did we become this free to laugh at fanaticism?" (75). We can laugh because Python lets us know that the best weapon against authority figures is to point out how patently absurd they are inside and out.

One curious thing about the Spanish Inquisition, considering how adept they were at arresting heretics, was that for a good part of the inquisition the main goal was to catch lapsing Conversos, while largely ignoring other deviations from the faith. While the Reformation did eventually catch the inquisition's notice and many Lutherans and other denominations were persecuted, witches were largely left alone. While those who embraced the Protestant faith and other heretical deviations from Catholicism were hunted down mercilessly, witches were considered to be either hysterics or women deceived into thinking they were witches. While medieval Europe was not kind to witches (whether they weighed the same as a duck or not), under the inquisition's selectively watchful eye they could go about their business, as long as they did not openly attack the papacy or turn someone into a newt.

As in many Python sketches, the inherent surrealism of inquisitorial practices is taken for granted. In the protracted sketch, which recurs throughout the episode, all the characters are aware that they are not real people; they are playing characters and must make the best of their situation. After Palin's Ximénez cannot get his lines right, he passes them on to Jones' Biggles, who also cannot quite explain clearly their chief weapons. Even during the torture session, when confronted by Biggles holding up a kitchen rack Ximénez has no choice but to go on, pleading, "Oh, go on, just pretend for God's sake!" At that point the sketch is interrupted by a BBC representative who asks Chapman's Reg to participate in a link. Eventually the Spanish Inquisition reappears, this time as part of a movie about the Spanish Inquisition, only to utilize the amazingly ineffective cushions and the dreaded comfy chair. Palin's Ximénez has charged Lady Mountback (Cleveland) with four counts of heresy (heresy by thought, word, deed, and action—four very real counts that the inquisition would have used), but their only recourse is to shout at her to confess. The Spanish Inquisition reappears one more time at the end of the episode desperately trying to reach a courtroom (via bus) where the line "no one expects the Spanish Inquisition" has been uttered, but because they are fictional characters and the credits are already rolling they do not make it there in time. As they fly into the courtroom they meta-theatrically comment on the rolling credits until the show ends with Palin's Ximénez shouting, "No one expects the Spanish—oh, bugger!" just as "The End" appears. To Python the Spanish Inquisition is grist for the (now not working) mill and the characters are going though the motions, enacting rituals that have no real meaning, that make no sense to a rational, modern (post-Enlightenment) human being. By taking the Spanish Inquisition apart, Python has defanged Cardinal Fang and one of history's most profound horrors. Authority—particularly authority that seeks to use violence to enact its will—is demonstrated as inherently ridiculous, thus showing us that all human authority is only as meaningful as we make it.

HISTORICAL FIGURES (Part Three): MARY, QUEEN OF SCOTS
"I think she's dead."

Mary, Queen of Scots was a sometimes-sympathetic character in the context of her times but is nowadays best known for her particularly rushed trial and brutal death. In his book *Mary Queen of Scotland and the Isles,* Stefan Zweig, writing in the florid prose still acceptable in historical works of the time (1935), summarizes the particularly gruesome death of Mary Stuart, condemned to death by her own sister in 1587 after almost nineteen years in captivity. At the start of the execution, Mary displayed some of the royal temperament, first forgiving the executioner and his assistant, then putting her own head on the block while praying in Latin, "In te, Domine, confido, ne confundar in aeternum." This dignified control was then shattered as "the first blow fell awry, striking the back of the head instead of the neck," causing Mary to groan, no doubt in horrific agony. The executioner tried once again, and as Zweig writes, "at the second stroke, the axe sank deep into the neck and the blood spurted out copiously. Not until a third blow was given did the neck depart from the trunk" (Zweig 1935, 352–353). This gruesome but not atypical execution (it was customary to bribe or tip the executioner to ensure a speedy death; in this case her cousin Elizabeth may have wanted to send a message to her allies and supporters) seems to be natural fodder for a Python sketch, reminiscent not only of the "Sam Peckinpah's *Salad Days*" sketch but also in the lingering dismemberment of the Black Knight in *MP&HG*. But Mary's death is done off camera as a radio play (a particularly coy play on the title of many a BBC miniseries about historical events and the apparent violence); a horrendous beating, strangulations, gunshots, et cetera, imitate the format of radio (and of Python's beloved Goons), where the auditory violence is even more hideous and funny, as it takes place largely in the listener's imagination. The reality of Mary's horrible death is apparently not suitable for on-camera dramatization, even by the Pythons. At the conclusion of her execution, one final indignity awaited; as Mary's head was held up by her hair, what was in reality a wig slipped off and "the head dropped on the ground. It rolled like a ball across the scaffold, and when the executioner stooped to receive it, the onlookers could discern that it was that of an old woman, with close-cropped and grizzled hair" (1935, 352–353) . . . an unnerving sight for those quietly murmuring, "God save the Queen," at the spectacle of the horrifically murdered old woman. Just as Python pointed out the essential "banality of evil" in showing how completely ridiculous notions such as the Spanish Inquisition and "National Bocialism" are out of historical context, we cannot forget that in their respective time periods these were not a source of laughter but of (to some) approval and collaboration and (to others) terror and perhaps even abject obedience. Python's deconstruction of the way in which ideologies, ideas, and people who would, in a perfect world, have been ostracized as ridiculous and dangerous instead in reality caused more than their fair share of human misery. These are not isolated incidents but an inherent part of human nature, one that must be confronted and controlled.

In his book *Civilization and Its Discontents,* Sigmund Freud argued that one reason that we needed a civilization based upon not arbitrary rules but a strong social contract (echoing Locke, Hobbes, Rousseau, and others), is because humans are prone to taking notions (which Python would regard as silly), such as rigid class systems and absolute authority, and making them seem normal. To Freud one of our major problems (other than the vagaries of nature and the frailty of the human body) was "the inadequacy of the regulations which adjust the mutual relationships of human beings in the family, the state and society" (2002, 37). Freud goes on to conclude that "this contention holds that what we call our civilization is largely responsible for our misery, and that we should be much happier if we gave it up and returned to primitive conditions" (38). While Freud did not echo the familiar misreading of Rousseau that we should return to nature,* he believed that a root cause of anxiety and neurosis was the pressure cooker known as society. Freud saw the inherent frustration caused by the ways in which we are forced to conform to social norms that ran against our individual desires; Python pointed out that those very norms themselves, the systems of authority, class, and privilege that we put in place and then take for granted, are as necessary as a well-funded Ministry of Silly Walks.

What marked the Pythons not just as creative comedians but as bold original thinkers was the fact that in their historical work they "documented" the opposite of perceived thought. That having a Royal Family made as much sense as hiring a pantomime horse at a corporation. They looked at the brutality of historical figures in terms of not how normal someone like Attila the Hun was but what a ridiculous and sad aberration. A part of Python's brilliance lies in their needed reminder that the first step in opposing ideas that are patently ridiculous is to point that fact out *in public*. Once people realize that they do not have to be part of the herd and "go along with the joke," then truth, and perhaps even freedom, is possible.

---

* Rousseau was not actually arguing for a literal return to nature. Rather, he argued for a different version of the idea of the social contract. To Rousseau, "the social order is a sacred right which serves for the basis of all others" (1975, 6). Rousseau essentially reduced his explanation of the social contract to how "each of us places in common his person and all his power under the supreme direction of the general will; and as one body we all receive each member as an indivisible part of the whole" (15).

GILLIAM: THE FOOT

Okay, the foot. Everyone knows the foot. But what do you know *about* the foot, eh?

Gilliam culled the famous "Python Foot" from an isolated part of a painting called *Venus, Cupid, Folly and Time* (1546) by artist Agnolo Bronzino (1503–1572) and made it central to the series' surreal agenda. Gilliam's own book on animation (*Animations of Mortality*) is itself a classic example of the Python sensibility. For example, Gilliam praises Bronzino, "who painted with supreme classical elegance, bringing out the abstract nature of form with a glossy marble-like sense of purity that only Ingres was to capture some three centuries later." Yet in the text, the next picture is an isolated close-up of the foot, as Gilliam continues his thought on the artist: ". . . or was he just an old wop painter who did feet for animations?" (Gilliam and Cowell 1978). Gilliam is of course referring to Jean-Auguste-Dominique Ingres ". . . a leading neo-classical painter, [who] was also deeply influenced by Raphael" (*New York Public Library Desk Reference* 2002, 228); however the original question (gratuitous ethnic slur aside) is not an either/or question, but under Python logic it can easily make sense that Bronzino is not only one of the great masters of his time but is the contributor to one of the silliest pieces of animation ever included in an opening-credits sequence. Basically this is a win-win situation for the (horribly maligned) artist and the audience.

But there is far more to Terry Gilliam's simply complex art than an enormously destructive heavenly foot. While we comment quite a bit about Python and Gilliam's debt to postmodernism and their contribution to the "mash-up" elsewhere in this book, we'd like to briefly stress the many other aspects of Gilliam's artistry here. First of all, Gilliam was an artist in mixed media long before he joined the crew of *Flying Circus*. And, just as Ray Harryhausen is single-handedly responsible for bringing stop-action animation to the masses (and thus influencing the next generation of filmmakers, including Tim Burton), so is Gilliam responsible for bringing the cut-and-paste aesthetic to the current generation.

For all the self-deprecation and distance Gilliam has sometimes set

"Piede ala Bronzino"
Terry Gilliam's oft-used foot-based interstitial animation for *Monty Python's Flying Circus.*

between his current life as an angry, quirky director and his past life as an angry, quirky illustrator, his artistic legacy can be clearly seen in *South Park.* As Trey Parker and Matt Stone have laughingly confessed (*Monty Python Conquers America*), their comic sensibility owes a great deal to Monty Python and their animation for *South Park* owes a great deal—perhaps everything—to Terry Gilliam:

> Trey: I mean, there's not even a line. It's just, that's it. It's just
>   Terry Gilliam.
> Matt: It's plagiarism.
> Trey: Terry Gilliam did that.
> Matt: Let's just animate it like that.
> Trey: Let's just plagiarize Terry Gilliam and make millions of
>   dollars. That's basically what we did.

Gilliam's sprawling cut-and-paste creations work because they compel the viewer to gaze upon barely controlled chaos. His twisted and subversive style can be glimpsed even early on, and the sixties counterculture movement (combatting what Gilliam saw as American complacency) is a major influence throughout his work. While the Pythons have worked with other visual artists, Gilliam's work is associated with the overall Python style not simply because he happened to design the credits and interstitials for *Flying Circus*; just as the differing but equally surreal Oxbridge senses of humor looked to the absurd for inspiration, Gilliam's sense of artistic chaos was inherently Pythonesque even before he joined Monty Python. Just as the other Pythons deconstructed through language the seeming safety and comfort of British institutions (don't trust what they say), Gilliam pointed out how equally absurd it was to take institutions such as the worlds of art, design, and film seriously (don't trust what you see). Gilliam subverted traditional artworks because, like Pollock and Johns, he understood the mechanics as well as the theory of artistic production. Monty Python worked holistically because Gilliam was tilting at windmills alongside the other Pythons. That his windmills were the old masters and vintage photographs representing staid, reliable British life just made his work all the more subversive.

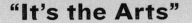

"It's the Arts"

Part III

PYTHON ON ART

TAG UNDER: art, painting, authors, hip, poetry, prose, drama, Englishness, splat-stick, literacy, cinema, Broadway, musicals, medievalism, and pornography.

ART

"I'd like to talk to you tonight about the place of the nude in my bed . . . um . . . in the history of my bed . . . of *art*, of *art*, I'm sorry. The place of the nude in the history of tart . . . call girl . . . I'm sorry. I'll start again. . . . Bum . . . oh, what a giveaway."

As with their generally deconstructive notions towards linearity and form, when the Pythons commented on art they didn't just take art pieces out of context (the museum, the gallery, et cetera) but also questioned the traditional perspectives regarding how art itself is created and perceived. In the first episode of *Flying Circus* to air, "Whither Canada," Python deconstructs the idea of art criticism itself. In the "Picasso/Cycling Race" sketch, various famous artists (largely painters) compete in a cycling race while simultaneously completing new artworks, all the while being judged not by art critics or curators but by sports commentators. The banality of the situation and the rote criticism used by sport commentators is ripe fruit for Python (see also Part V: Python on Sport) but also serves as a barometer for how the same kind of metaphors can be employed in criticism of any type. However, the metaphor of art as a race is tenable because competition is inherent in any art form, especially for art students and "lay" appreciators of art, who first learn about art through the lens of what art historians and art critics deem is acceptable as art and what is not.

Python members probably had their own opinions on this question as well. Larsen suggests that Python possessed workable knowledge of the great masters and, as in this sketch, highlighted the work of twentieth-century artists who would have been influential in shaping their own worldview. The

> laundry list of twentieth-century artists competing in this race is significant, as these artists would have been shaking up the world of art, design, advertising, architecture, and even morality and culture as the Pythons were growing up and shaping their own sensibilities. (2008, 10)

One suspects that the more artistically aware viewers of *MPFC* would have similarly identified—and thus gotten some small frisson of art-nerd acknowledgment—the bulk of the painters who whizzed by on their bicycles in this sketch.

In fact, the artistic revolutions of the twentieth century were so radical in comparison to the past that Mircea Eliade could write that then-current disciplines such as music, poetry, and art "have undergone such radical transformations that it has been possible to speak of a 'destruction of the language of art'" (1975, 72). The Pythons were well aware of this and understood that when an accepted way of creating art has changed there will be a need to create a new type of critical language to describe that art.

Python looks at the idea of creation in the context of how competitive the art world is and in terms of how the dynamics of the creative process work and how subsequent movements in art helped to comment upon and shape culture. By turning art into a literal race, Python comments not only upon "the competitive environment created and nurtured by the mass culture art world of the period" (Larsen 2008, 10) but also on how the banal, repetitive world of televisual commentary reduces any kind of serious discourse to silliness. This also reflected Python's ability to play "with the plasticity of their medium—they understood well the manipulative elements—making demands of both the medium and the audience as they took their Modernist-*cum*-Postmodernist television presentation and re-presentation to new limits" (Larsen 2008, 9). In the first few minutes of the first episode, Python is already asking the audience to let go of their traditional views: not just to reconsider the medium of television and how the framing mechanisms inherent in the use of the medium lead to conventions ripe for parody but also to reconsider the nature of creation, artistic ability, the nature of art, and the way in which we regard painting much as we regard sports: some are "better"— more capable as artists and athletes—than others according to a critical (and implied empirical) standpoint. Python shows us that even applying critical judgment to the vanguard of the main artistic movement of the twentieth century was in itself a sort of competition, one that ignored the idea that art could truly be revolutionary; instead art becomes just another spectacle that can be viewed listlessly, categorized easily, and consumed as entertainment.

ART CRITICISM
"I don't know much about art, but I know what I like."

In addition to Gilliam's animations, Python made many overt references to art during the course of the series. In one sketch, "The Art Critic" (ep. 4), two middle-aged Pepperpots, Janet (Cleese) and Marge (Chapman), are visiting an art gallery with their ill-behaved, bratty children. Marge reports that her son Ralph has been "nothing but trouble all morning" and, indeed, this is spectacularly true: of Janet's Kevin as well: "He's just been in the Florentine room and smeared tomato ketchup all over Raphael's Baby Jesus." After swatting at Kevin, she yells at him to "put that Baroque masterpiece down!" Kevin had also spent part of the morning going berserk in "an exhibition of early eighteenth-century Dresden pottery" and taking "out his black aerosol and squirt[ing] Vermeer's *Lady at a Window*." Janet's friend Marge has a similar problem with her equally ill-tempered son, Ralph, who had also been wreaking havoc in the gallery, smashing "every exhibit but one in the Danish Contemporary Sculpture

Exhibition." The mothers, who commiserate that this behavior is at least "not as bad as spitting," end up looking forlornly at Turner's now-ruined *Fighting Temeraire* before they both opt to eat the painting, one remarking that before then she had "never really liked Turner" before then ending with a rare (for Python anyway) punch line from Janet: "I don't know much about art, but I know what I like."*

After a quick cut to "a book lined study" an art critic with—as the script says—"a mouthful of Utrillo" (Palin) notes that his recently concluded meal has included not just the French master but also a Rubens ("with all those cherries") and a Vermeer (which he has spilled "all down my shirt!"). His wife (Katya Wyeth) then enters the room to bring in a pitcher of water and puns: "'Watteau', Dear?" In a repeated Python reference to the artificial nature of televised humor, Palin's art critic is outraged at this "terrible joke," leaving his wife to bemoan: "But it's my only line!"† This is echoed in a scene a few minutes later when the Colonel (Chapman) stops another sketch and links us to *"a man sitting at a desk"* (Gilliam), who also announces, "This is my only line" (technically not accurate, since after the audience groans at the jest Gilliam defensively replies, "Well, it's my only line").

The "Art Critic" sketch is a wry comment on the disposability of art and (as one of the sketches where Python frontloads the sketch with a formidable array of the greats of the art world, only to end with a bad pun) is a send-up of art galleries, ill-behaved children, and how we "consume" art. Larsen notes that this sketch violates the so-called natural distance "imposed by museums and galleries, allowing the characters" to actually taste the art, bringing to bear a sense that heretofore had no bearing on the art form or its appreciation" (2008, 62). The sketch also questions the perceived authority inherent in choosing what makes a painting a work of art or not. Marge and Janet can consume art, realiz-

---

*The Pope (Cleese) would utter the same line—albeit under different circumstances—following his argument with Michelangelo regarding *The Penultimate Supper*; to be discussed shortly.

†This line is itself a running gag throughout the series, more often uttered by a Glamour Stooge than a male Python (but note the immediate exception, above).

ing that they are not experts but simply "know what [they] like," while the critic is presented as an avid consumer of art as a concept/object he can dissect critically, thanks to a skill set honed through specialized training and a critical eye. Python demonstrates that both gallery visitors and critics consume art in much the same way. We privilege everything— art, sport, culture, potential sex partners—based on presumed pedigree and perceived approval of authority. While Marge and Janet only bring their children to the art gallery in order to entertain their obnoxious brats, a critic can comment (with his mouth full of Utrillo) that "I think Utrillo's brushwork is fantastic . . . but he doesn't always agree with me . . . [belches]. Not after a Rubens anyway. . . ." Even if the critic is a *better* consumer of art, he still ingests it rather than truly appreciates it. As a critic he cannot help but compare and contrast the two giants of the art world as he eats them; he literally devours great art as one might symbolically devour an exhibition or museum full of great works. In the end, art appreciation is reduced to comparative analysis, wherein art—as in the "Picasso/Cycling Race" sketch—is a competition.

Palin's art critic returned in episode 8: "Full Frontal Nudity," where he attempts to discuss the place of the nude in the history of art but keeps uttering Freudian slips about "the place of the nude in my bed," "in the history of tart . . . call-girl . . . I'm sorry. I'll start again. . . . Bum . . . oh what a giveaway." His introduction is cut off by the reappearance of his wife (Katya Wyeth, again), who again makes "a terrible joke" with the usual rejoinder: "But it's my only line!" Despite her protestations, the scene transitions away with a caption noting "but there let us leave the art critic to strangle his wife and move on to pastures new." Ultimately the sex-obsessed art critic is unable to deliver his commentary about the place of the nude in the history of art and when presented with a viable partner, engages in violence rather than sex. The critic as authority is thus taken down a notch.

Following the lead of the Great Masters (Python), Dan Aykroyd—of *Saturday Night Live* fame—as the Chicagoan E. Buzz Miller (of the public-access program "E. Buzz Miller's Art Classics": season 3, ep. 8, 1977) shows a similar appreciation for classy art, albeit with a less shamefaced or violent twist. Seated alongside a giggly and tarted-up Laraine Newman (as "Miss Christie Christina . . . of the Coach and Pole Bar"), Aykroyd introduces the audience to the *Venus of Urbino,* which was painted, as he says, "in 1538 by a guy in Venice—and . . . this is for real—his name is spelled *T-i-t-i-a-n: Tit-*ian! Honest ta God." Once Miller and Miss Christie Christina stop tittering, he continues his artistic appraisal: "He's a very famous, respected artist and this is a bona fide art treasure, and I don't think that anybody can disagree that this is a really nice painting of a broad onna couch." The rest of Buzz's reviews similarly involve other "classy" painted nudes, his delight in nipple slips, and Miss Christina's breathy giggles.

One feels that E. Buzz Miller, Janet, and Marge share a common critical mode—if not aesthetic value—with the Pope (Cleese) from the *"Penultimate Supper"* sketch (*Live at the Hollywood Bowl*). After arguing with Michelangelo (Idle) over his manifold creative additions to the commissioned *Last Supper* painting—additions that include a kangaroo, twenty-eight disciples, and three Christs—the Pope concludes his critique by saying, "Look! I'm the bloody Pope, I am! I may not know much about art, but I know what I like!" Whether Pepperpot or Pope, art appreciation is hardly a science to be mastered.

But back to, ahem, Titian . . .

Palin's art critic returns in episode 25, this time with Idle's fellow art critic, walking though a gallery commenting on the merits of the various "Italian Masters of the Renaissance." Their exchange is particularly reminiscent of acceptable art criticism.

> "First Critic: Aren't they marvelous? The strength and
>   boldness . . . life and power in those colours.
> Second Critic: This must be Titian's masterpiece.
> First Critic: Oh indeed—if only for the composition alone.
>   The strength of those foreground figures . . . . the firmness of
>   the line . . .
> Second critic: Yes, the confidence of a master at the height of
>   his powers.

The critics' reverie, which seems to be a parody of art criticism at its most banal, is of course then interrupted in typical Python fashion by a general walkout strike of characters in the paintings over working conditions. As "the man from 'The Hay Wain by Constable'" explains, it started with the Impressionists, "with the *Dejeuner sur l'Herbe* lot, evidently they were moved away from above the radiator or something. Anyway, the Impressionists are all out. Gainsborough's *Blue Boy*'s brought out the eighteenth-century English portraits, the Flemish School's solid, and the German woodcuts are at a meeting now." With that, the Renaissance school joins them and soon the walkout of the paintings is being discussed on the radio, with the helpful offer that "Sir Kenneth Clark" (the noted art critic and perennial host of many programs dedicated to the arts) has "said he will talk to any painting if it can help bring a speedy end to the strike." Naturally, the character-less paintings lack an audience and auctions at Sotheby's are seriously affected. Finally, famous statues end up going on strike in support of the paintings, with one obvious abstention, the armless Venus de Milo.*

While this sketch certainly parodies labor conditions, it also criticizes how art is valued as commerce and suggests that art itself understands how it is doomed to be grouped by style or time period. Python takes the idea that art can be formally grouped into great schools and then asks the wonderfully illogical logical questions: If we group them together, might they also function as a group? And if a group, could they not demand better working conditions? In the Python-verse, art is a truly immersive experience, one that interacts with its public and makes conscious decisions to demand better working conditions. Python took art out of the realm of the specialist and finally brought to life an idea so many teachers have tried to get through to their classes for centuries: art is not something to be confined to galleries but is a living, breathing

---

* The authors would love to insert here a witty reference for the Harry Potter crowd regarding the mobility of characters in Hogwarts paintings, but we'd hate to pander. Again.

series of works that can be interacted with in daily life. That is, of course, unless they are on strike.

In his book *Art & Physics: Parallel Visions in Space, Time, and Light*, Leonard Schlain points out that "throughout history, the artist produces symbols and icons that in retrospect prove to have been an avant-garde for the thought patterns of a scientific age not yet born" (1991, 19). Although Schlain was making connections to how the development in perspective and vision were paralleled by developments in scientific inquiry, it can also be said that art—especially from the Impressionists to the present—provided a symbol system that led not to the traditional unities of time and space but to disunity and deconstruction. Susanne K. Langer, one of the foremost critical theorists of the twentieth century on art and symbolism, wrote about how the way in which we settle on rational critiques on the function and form of art is an inherently flawed construction as well. When non-"experts" try to talk critically about art, they are already relying on a standardized and illogical set of assumptions about art and how they should be viewing it critically. As Langer opined, ". . . the first naïve comment is apt to be that it is, or is not, *quite accurate*, next that the subject is, or is not, worthy of being represented; and then, probably, that the work is pleasant or unpleasant" (1979, 250). These fallacies, which treat art as a product, talk about everything outside of the work of art and then try to apply moral judgment when none is needed. To Langer "the artistic import is what painters, sculptors and poets express through their depiction of objects and events" and the import of artistic expression is "the verbally ineffable, yet not inexpressible law of vital experience, the pattern or affective and sentient being. This is the 'content' of what we see as beautiful form and this formal element is the artist's 'idea' which is conveyed by every great work" (257). Being trapped by art critic jargon prevents the individual from truly experiencing the work of art: ". . . there are no degrees of literal truth, only artistic truth, which is all significance, expressiveness, articulateness, has degrees; therefore works of art may be good or bad, and each one must be judged by our experience of its revelations" (Langer 1979, 263). So perhaps Janet and the Pope weren't so silly after all.

PERFORMANCE ART
"Numbskulls and boobies from all over the country have been arriving to go through their strange paces before a large paying crowd."

Python also tackled the more recent and more difficult to categorize work of performance art in episode 37, where Eric Idle (as an announcer) goes over the performance pieces in "this year's Ideal Loon Exhibition,"* which features the classic Python voice-over: "Numbskulls and boobies from all over the country have been arriving to go through their strange paces before a large paying crowd." Among the more absurd exhibits that Idle announces are "Brian Boomers, the Battling British Boy who for three weeks has been suspended above a tin of condemned veal," and "Italian priests in custard, discussing vital matters of the day." Both are accompanied by compelling visuals that illustrate the surreal nature of the exhibition, including a sign on the priests in custard exhibit that states: "Italy, Land of Custard." What is fascinating about this sketch is not only the controversial art that is being parodied—specific performance art pieces, which were becoming increasingly popular in the 1960s, or even the Fluxus movement, which included artists such as Yoko Ono—but how the intentionality of the performance artists they were parodying was not that dissimilar from the work the Pythons themselves were doing in terms of deconstructing the nature of television. What Python was specifically parodying in this sketch (stock footage of Prime Minister Edward Heath opening the exhibition is inserted for an additional political jab) was similar to the concurrent Situationist movement in France.

Taking their cue from Dada, Surrealism, and the Fluxus movement, the Situationist movement in the 1950s and '60s was similar to Python in its critique of media, art, and the everyday. In his book *The Society of the Spectacle*, Guy Debord argued that what he calls the "spectacle," basically

---

*Darl Larsen noted that this was a play on the "Ideal Home Exhibition" that the *Daily Mail* had sponsored since 1908 featuring new appliances and furniture (459).

an entertainment-based atmosphere where the constant bombardment of unconnected information makes real reflective thought almost impossible, serves to perpetuate itself as "the existing order's uninterrupted discourse about itself, its laudatory monologue" (1983, 32). It also eventually subverts humanity itself into a sort of living spectacle, where life is performed instead of lived. As Debord goes on to note, ". . . even in those moments reserved for living, it is still the spectacle that is seen to be seen and reproduced, becoming even more intense. What was represented as genuine life reveals itself as simply more genuinely spectacular life" (153). The Loons at Python's exhibition (whether in custard or hanging from the air) and even the judge in the sketch (who curiously wins first prize) represent a world that is overly mediated, out of linear order, and incapable of making sense. It is pointless to ask what the "art" in the exhibition means; it does not mean anything (conversely, it could mean *everything*, but let's put that one aside for the moment). Meaning and linearity are broken, and so meaning only takes place in an environment where prescribed ideas about what constitutes "real" art are mindlessly spouted, taught, and eventually regurgitated.

PROSE
"No one has read Proust."

In the same way that Gilliam's interstitials and the "Art Critic" sketches underscore the aesthetic knowledge at the Pythons' disposal, it's hard to understate the literary erudition of *MPFC*—but we will anyway. The Pythons were a well-educated lot replete with what is now known as a "classical education," including a deep understanding of canonical literature; think of all those *Classics Illustrated* comics you never bought or those "way old" stories your high school English teacher always droned on about—you know, *Beowulf, The Iliad, Wuthering Heights*—the stuff that used to mark every person in the Western Hemisphere as "moderately intelligent." And, as one might expect, the tropes and ideas within the Western Canon do resurface throughout the works of Monty Python—

hell, *Life of Brian* relies heavily upon an understanding of the New Testament and *Monty Python and the Holy Grail* is at once a retelling and a comic critique of the many medieval romances surrounding King Arthur and his Knights of the Round Table. Yet in *MPFC* direct literary parody is largely absent.

Of course, if you're not in the mood to read or watch, you could always just listen. On the LP (that's long-playing record, a sort of primitive CD or "non-compact" disc for you youngsters) *Matching Tie and Handkerchief* (1973), the Pythons present a brief treatise titled "Novel Writing" for our intellectual consideration:

After a brief welcome introduction from Idle ("And now it's time for 'Novel Writing,' which today comes from the west country from Dorset"), a radio commentator (Palin) excitedly describes the entrance of Thomas Hardy, author of such quintessential English novels as *Tess of the d'Urbervilles* and *Far from the Madding Crowd*, into what is—to judge by the canned sounds of crowd cheers—a large sports arena:

Hello, and welcome to Dorchester, where a very good crowd has turned out to watch local boy Thomas Hardy write his new novel *The Return of the Native*, on this very pleasant July morning. This will be his eleventh novel and the fifth of the very popular Wessex novels, and here he comes! Here comes Hardy, walking out toward his desk. He looks confident, he looks relaxed, very much the man in form, as he acknowledges this very good-natured bank holiday crowd. And the crowd goes quiet now as Hardy settles himself down at the desk, body straight, shoulders relaxed, pen held lightly but firmly in the right hand. He dips the pen . . . in the ink, and he's off! It's the first word, but it's not a word . . . oh, no! It's a doodle. Way up on the top of the left-hand margin, it's a piece of meaningless scribble . . . and he's signed his name underneath it! Oh dear, what a disappointing start. But he's off again—and here he goes—the first word of Thomas Hardy's new novel, at ten thirty-five on this very lovely morning, it's three letters, it's the definite article, and it's . . . "The."

Palin then abruptly throws to a second commentator (Chapman), who provides a dour bit of statistical analysis regarding the "play" on the field:

> Well, this is true to form, no surprises there. He started five of his eleven novels to date with a definite article. We've had two of them with "it," there has been one "but," two "ats," one "on," and a "Delores." Oh, that of course was never published.

Palin's commentator interrupts Chapman's riveting statistical analysis, however, as the action on the pitch begins again: Hardy has crossed out the first word he's written. And so the short sketch proceeds, very much like the broadcast of a football match: one commentator narrating the action, another offering color commentary and statistical analysis. The excitement of the fans echoes that of the narrating commentator, as Hardy adds word upon word to his first sentence until (three hours later) "Hardy has just completed his first sentence, and it's a real cracker!": "A Saturday afternoon in November was approaching the time of twilight, and the vast tract of enclosed wild known as Egdon Heath embrowned itself moment by moment." A "Hardyesque cracker" indeed (lifted accurately from the novel, we might add).

Does Python's audience need to have read *The Return of the Native* to "get" this joke? Does one need to know where/what Egdon Heath is? Or have read any of Thomas Hardy's many works? Or—for that matter—really know who Thomas Hardy is before the sketch begins?

Let's pretend for a moment that you didn't even know who Thomas Hardy was before the beginning of the sketch. By the time the Pythons were done, you would know that he was a famous and reasonably prolific English novelist, that he wrote a series of tales set in Wessex (wherever t'hell that is), and you might even recall the names of two of those novels. See? You weren't even paying that much attention and you still learned something! (And for those of you still interested in more, see the following Factoid Box!)

The serious enthusiasm of both announcers and the rising and falling roars of the crowd show that "Novel Writing" is serious business. Meanwhile, the patent absurdity of the event (a: this sort of thing never

> ## FACTOID BOX: Thomas Hardy
>
> Generally considered one of the great Naturalist writers, Hardy (1840–1928) produced a dizzying array of poetry and prose (for which he was the more famous), much of which was set in Wessex (a fictional section of England akin to Dorchester). According to his own reckoning, his works fall into three categories: Novels of Character and Environment; Romances and Fantasies; and Novels of Ingenuity. Known for employing naturalistic language, especially evident in his characters' speech (which often reproduced various English dialect sets).
>
> **BONUS FACTOID:** Hardy's father was a stonecutter . . . er, stonemason.

happens; b: no one cares this much about novel writing; c: even if you could get a stadium full of Hardy fans, who could see what Hardy was writing, anyway?)* elicits the typical frisson of humor inherent in a juxtaposition typical of the Python mash-up.

Now a literary scholar (or a bleeding-heart Liberal, or, indeed, anyone alienated by the Pythons' "fancy pants education") might ask *why* this is so silly, really. Why do we pay good money to crowd into a stadium and watch one man "hit the ball first time and there it was in the back of the net" and yet we would not pay to watch another man create a work of art that might define a generation? Why don't we, as a culture, laud our authors as we laud our athletes? Are our priorities really that screwed up?

By seating Thomas Hardy (one of Britain's most beloved authors—both critically and popularly) at the center of a football stadium cheered

---

*Of course, given the Jumbotrons of many arenas and stadiums today, the practical aspects of the sketch are less insurmountable than they once were.

on by adoring fans, Python *seems* at first blush to be lionizing the act of literary creation and authorship. Clearly (the skit seems to say), we should venerate authors just as we venerate sports heroes. And yet ... the enthusiasm of the announcers and the crowd ultimately seems misplaced. Hardy is important, certainly, but the act of writing fails as a spectator sport; furthermore, Hardy's writing in this particular moment is especially disappointing. While on the surface "Novel Writing" may offer another attack on the status quo (mindless fans watch mindless sport; intelligent thinkers watch intelligent thinkers), it offers no simple one-for-one corrective. Mental creation cannot—should not—replace physical competition. Neither should *simply* be watched. Nope: not even *Python*.

Ironically, Python worship itself would—at least in America—reach levels of sports-arena adulation. The albums *Live Monty Python at City Center!* (1976) and *Monty Python Live at the Hollywood Bowl* (1982), for example, record two of their American outings before masses of highly enthusiastic fans reciting alongside—and sometimes even correcting—their highly literate heroes onstage. One should recall, of course, that the seventies and eighties were the era of stadium rock and arena comedy—George Carlin, Richard Pryor, Steve Martin, {**a trout**}, and others could pack stadiums as well as their more musical stage brethren (and sisteren). Comedy was king—even if the king wore no pants, perambulated via silly walk, or espoused the overthrow of the king itself.

Is the mass veneration of authors any sillier than the mass veneration of sports figures? Or is Python taking us all to task for hero worship? At first blush—from a rebellious and overeducated perspective—the Pythons seem to be asking why we don't replace the one activity (football) with a more erudite, worthwhile activity (literary philosophy), but in the end the result would be the same. Fans of either type of endeavor are literally relegated to the sidelines in the Python-verse, just as in "real" society fans of either sort are encouraged to be passive observers rather than active participants. Yet ultimately literary creation—even more so than sport—is a solitary endeavor, one that stymies audience participation. Literary appreciation, of course, is another story, but even that can be fraught with a sense of alienation.

WELCOME TO THE MIDDLE OF THE BOOK!
Did you spot the fish?

One of the Pythons' favorite authors—Marcel Proust, the titular focal point of episode 31: "The All-England Summarize Proust Competition"—created at least one literary work that famously mocks the ability of even the most learned fanboy to re-express the thoughts and writings of another human being. Granted, the cards in this sketch are stacked against those comfortable with standard communication, but still.

Set on a typical auditorium stage, hosted by a high-coifed and gold-sequined Jones, and judged by black-and-white cardboard standees of contemporary cricketers, actor Omar Sharif, and violinist Yehudi Menuhin, the game-show atmosphere is accented by the "Proustometer"—a cheap cardboard poster to mark the progress of each contestant. As Mee (Jones) delineates, the rules are simple: ". . . each contestant has a maximum of fifteen seconds to sum up À la Recherche du Temps Perdu (translated as Remembrance of Things Past or In Search of Lost Time). The comic impossibility of the sketch stems from the length of La Recherche: it is a massive seven-volume French epic, one of the longest novels ever composed. Further, the work's main theme—involuntary memory—gives the work a fragmented, uncontrolled, disjointed feel,* making summarization a practically futile endeavor.†

Not that the contestants don't try, of course. The first contestant (Chapman) gets as far as page one of the first book; the second (Palin) freezes onstage and barely recalls the name of the lead character; the third contestant is the Bolton Choir Society, whose lyrical a capella rendition doesn't even get to the first book at all.

As Darl Larsen pithily notes: "The significance of Proust (1871–1922) to the Pythons and their generation of university wits can't be overstated, as he and/or his works are mentioned and mimicked throughout

---

* Much like many episodes of *Flying Circus,* really.
† Makes trying to synopsize one's own doctoral dissertation onto a three-by-five card (a hallowed academic tradition) seem like child's play by comparison.

> **FACTOID BOX:** *À la Recherche du Temps Perdu*
>
> Valentin Louis Georges Eugène Marcel Proust (July 10, 1871–November 18, 1922) French novelist and critic.
>
> His infamously long novel has over two thousand characters, is over three thousand pages long, and is over one and a half million words strong. First translated into English in the 1920s/1930s.
>
> Considered by many to be the definitive novel of the modern age. Considered by others to be the work of a raving loon. Makes a nice gift, if spread out over seven years. Goes well with sponge cake.

FC and even their feature films" (156). In particular, Larsen posits that the Pythons

> clearly draw on [Proust's] "involuntary memory" [trope] throughout *FC*. The "recovery of the past" so important to Proust allows for a more structured reading of the seemingly random and chaotic Flying Circus world, where university reading lists and cherished historical figures and cartoon violence and contemporary, topical faces and foibles come together in a sort of noisome ever-present. (155)

Whether the Pythons chose to memorialize Proust in this sketch because his investigation into the recollected past struck a chord with them or because *La Recherche* was universally recognized as one of those long novels that smart people read (like *War and Peace* and *Ulysses*) or say that they've read (like *War and Peace* and *Ulysses*) remains unanswerable. Ultimately, none of the contestants succeed "in encapsulating the intricacies of Proust's masterwork," so Mee (Jones) decides to "award the first prize this evening to the girl with the biggest tits." This last unexpected turn puts the nail in the coffin of Proustian appreciation onstage . . . for the moment at least.

While, to the best of our knowledge, no one has ever succeeded in satisfactorily summarizing Proust on a game show, there have been "more academic" contests that attempt to synopsize his magnum opus in the fewest words possible. Here are a few favorites, in no particular order:

> Marcel becomes a writer.
> Marcel remembers.
> Multi-hued sentiment passing through flowers and decay.
> Remember the à la mode!
> In looking back one learns to see.
> Mmm . . . cookies.*

There is also a three-minute plot summary available, should one find oneself in a hurry while eating one's biscuit; see Patrick Alexander's *Marcel Proust's Search for Lost Time,* which includes a six-hundred-word summary of the seven volumes. Or watch any of the YouTube videos of Proustians reading Alexander's synopsis. Or read Proust. The Pythons did. Well, maybe not Chapman.

POETRY

"Lend us a couple of bob till Thursday. I'm absolutely skint."

The poet McTeagle—whose entire poetic output amounts to variations on the common theme: "Lend us a quid till the end of the week,"

---

* Some entries translated from the French. Guess which one your American authors snuck in? For a more impressive list, see Mark Calkins, "Summarize Proust" http:// tempsperdu.com/summ.html.

(ep. 16)—reveals the field of poetry (and by extension the arts) as one big scam:

> There seems to be no end to McTeagle's poetic invention. "My new cheque book hasn't arrived," was followed up by the brilliantly allegorical "What's twenty quid to the bloody Midland Bank?" and more recently his prizewinning poem to the Arts Council: "Can you lend me one thousand quid?"

Sidetepping the possible Scots Highlander "skin-flint" stereotyping, the tale of McTeagle draws attention to the structure-less flimflammery of modern poetry, the interchangeable commentary of modern poetry critics ("what McTeagle's pottery . . . er . . . poetry is doing is rejecting all the clichés of modern pottery . . ."), and the fiscal abuse of liberal arts programs. Why on earth should we, the taxpayers, fund the arts? It's just a bunch of gays parading around in tights and homeless artists filming their own poop! Or criticisms to that effect. Compared to the relatively positive light cast upon prose (Hardy and Proust, at least as far as the Pythons represent them), poets come across as duplicitous wordsmiths, at best.

DRAMA
"All anyone wants me to say is, 'To be or not to be . . .'"

Until the manuscript of *Gay Boys in Bondage* is verified by the Folger Institute as truly belonging to the Bard of Avon, this section must remain unfinished.*

---

* Or see Darl Larsen, *Monty Python, Shakespeare, and English Rennaissance Drama* for a comparative analysis of Shakespeare and Monty Python. "Holy Grail, it's entertaining!" raves Rex Reed!

CINEMA

MONTY PYTHON AND THE HOLY GRAIL

THE BEGINNING

**"You've got two empty halves of a coconut
and you're banging them together!"**

Stepping outside the confines (as limitless as they sometimes seemed) of
television for the first time, the Pythons burst, bloodily, onto the big
screen in 1975 with their self-directed effort, *Monty Python and the Holy
Grail*.* Like the episodes of *Monty Python's Flying Circus*, the film is essentially a series of loosely connected sketches, in this case a series of scenes
set in a pseudo-medieval England circa A.D. 932. However, there is also,
as in a few of the later televised episodes (34: "The Cycling Tour" and 44:
"Mr Neutron," for example), a common thread or purpose uniting the
sketches; if we might so be so bold as to cite God (Chapman) as an authority for the moment, the entire purpose of the film is "the quest for the
Holy Grail."

    The film, once it breaks free of the opening credits,† starts slowly, as
Arthur travels "the lengths and breadths of this land seeking Knights" to
join him at Camelot; while sometimes stopping to ineffectively argue
with the local peasantry or to be ridiculed by the French.‡ As the voice-
over notes (to accompanying manuscript pages, à la Disney's *The Sword in
the Stone*), Arthur's compact *comitatus* includes the following (mostly)
illustrious knights:

---

* Jones and Gilliam shared the directorial duties while all the Pythons contributed to
the script and acting. For various views on the sometimes-tense production of the
film (which included Machiavellian power plays, delirium tremens, soggy chain
mail, and perturbed rabbit owners), see Morgan (2005).
† You didn't know llamas were so talented, did you?
‡ Or the Normans, as they were called at the time.

"Ni!"
Sir Bedivere (Jones) and King Arthur (Chapman) encounter the tallest of The Knights Who Say Ni (Palin) in *Monty Python and the Holy Grail.*

> Sir Bedivere (Jones) the Wise
> Sir Lancelot (Cleese) the Brave
> Sir Galahad (Palin) the Pure
> Sir Robin (Idle) the not-quite-so-brave-as-Sir-Lancelot
> And the aptly named Sir Not-Appearing-in-This-Film (Palin's
>   infant son William)

Of these, only the first three are traditionally named Arthurian knights; others with medieval provenance who will join the quest along the way include the short-lived Sir Bors (Gilliam), as well as Sir Gawain and Sir Ector (named only in the roll call of Killer Rabbit victims).

But before the many meet their fates, Arthur's troupe meet a Gilliam-animated God (voiced by Chapman)* who sends them on their sacred

---

* Since Chapman plays both Arthur and the Voice of God, he has the rare privilege of talking to himself here.

task: to seek the Grail and thus serve as an example in these dark (i.e., medieval) times.* Arthur and his knights then set out on their "Quest for the Holy Grail"; along the way, they variously encounter French taunters, construct a Trojan Rabbit, "fight" a three-headed ogre, nearly withstand sexual temptation, answer the call of a helpless . . . maiden in a tall tower, complete seemingly endless fetch quests, glean wizardly wisdom, answer trivia questions, and face fearsome monsters (some "with nasty big pointy teeth," even).[†] All of these scenes are—to greater or lesser extent—based upon medieval literary traditions[‡] and again reveal the literary erudition of the Pythons.

On the whole, the film relies heavily upon comic juxtaposition and gets some good mileage out of setting romantic medieval idealism against contemporary real-world pragmatics. As Palin notes in the film commentary, Arthur often embodies "authority not getting to the common people." In perhaps the most critically popular example, the "Constitutional Peasants" (scene 4, before Arthur has gathered his knights) spout modern Marxist theory that confounds Arthur, who claims he was rightfully granted his Kingship when "the Lady of the Lake, her arm clad in the purest shimmering samite, held aloft Excalibur from the bosom of the water, signifying, by Divine Providence, that I, Arthur, was to carry Excalibur. That is why I am your King!" Upon hearing Arthur's romantic proclamation, the peasant Dennis counters by logically noting that "strange women lying in ponds distributing swords is no basis for a system of government." Furthermore, and despite Arthur's protests, Dennis continues to denigrate the Lady of the Lake and Arthur's claim to Kingship; at a generic and ideological impasse, the romance-fiction

---

*In Chicagoan vernacular, they are "on a mission from God" (*The Blues Brothers*, 1980).

[†] And so *MP&HG* echoes the plot of every D&D campaign and RPG ever produced.

[‡] The odd man out in this list is the Trojan Rabbit, a clear parody of the Trojan horse (a figure from "The Matter of Rome" rather than "The Matter of Britain"), but since the medieval English saw their great heritage extending back to the Romans (in fact, both Wace and Layamon called their literary histories of Britain *The Brut*, after the mythical Trojan hero Brutus), we'll call it a draw.

Arthur is reduced to shouting down the unexpected voice of modern political dogma before galloping (coconutting?) off into the next scene.

As Cleese has said, the *Holy Grail* is full of "angry political crap" (typical of the 1960s) that is exemplified by taking myths and "exposing them to reality." Here the tropes of medieval romance directly clash with the tenets of modern political theory, setting up an incompatibility of dialogue that is played for laughs.

One needn't be deeply versed in either Arthuriana or Marxism to "get" the general humor in this scene: the general high/low dichotomy should suffice. But if you'd never read Marx before seeing this film, congratulations: you now know some of the jargon. Perhaps surprisingly, the same holds true if you'd never paid any attention to Arthurian literature before—there's a nice bit of genre-specific verbiage deployed on both sides of the conversation in this scene. While Dennis may win the densest vocabulary contest (dropping such charged political phrases* as "self-perpetuating autocracy," "working class," "anarcho-syndicalist commune," and "mandate from the masses"), Arthur also informs the audience of some key figures suited to his own milieu ("The Lady of the Lake," "Excalibur," "divine providence," and even "samite"). Neither conversant speaks the other's language, but by the act of speaking they effectively inform the audience (if not each other) of their respective stances.

For those intrigued by the information alluded to in this scene, here's a handy crib sheet:

---

* And, depending on the dinner parties you attend, "politically charged phrases" as well.

FACTOID BOX: Politics and Other
Watery Bedfellows

"ANARCHO-SYNDICALIST COMMUNE": a revolutionary cooperative economic system that rejects the capitalism of the state in favor of a democratic, wageless labor movement. The self-governing body described by Dennis is in many ways more radical than that in Marxism, even.

"DIVINE PROVIDENCE": the Christian God's direct intervention in the mundane world. In medieval romances, for example, God determined the victor of any "trial by combat" (for who could win in battle unless God was on his side?). God also chose Kings, who, in accordance with "The Great Chain of Being," were closer to God than simple peasants. From a purely theological mind-set, Arthur invokes "special providence" here under the broader "divine" heading.

"EXCALIBUR": Arthur's legendary sword; sometimes magical, sometimes indicative of Arthur's divine right to Kingship, sometimes pulled from an anvil/stone, sometimes granted to Arthur by the mystical Lady of the Lake, sometimes held in a magical scabbard that prevented blood loss. While the details vary, Excalibur is *always* identified with King Arthur.

"THE LADY OF THE LAKE": oddly enough, a mystic title, not the name of a single individual. The various ladies of the lake are credited with giving Arthur his sword, advising Arthur (after magically removing Merlin from the picture), and helping to ferry Arthur to Avalon at his final wounding.

"MANDATE FROM THE MASSES": From John Locke to the present, the idea of democratic representation comes from the hoi polloi, not the privileged aristocracy. Hobbes would disagree, but we hear he was "short nasty, and brutish."

"SAMITE": a luxurious, glossy, silken textile, often laced or embroidered with gold or silver thread; highly valued among the nobility in the Middle Ages. Samite's satin liquefaction—shimmering like fish scales—makes it suitable raiment for any aquatic maiden, but it is especially suitable for an upper-class moistened bint.

"SELF-PERPETUATING AUTOCRACY": a government in which one person holds all the power and, by virtue of that power, retains power (or thus enables the next single individual to similarly retain that power).*

"WORKING CLASS": also known as the proletariat; a clearly Marxist term, often identified as the lower class (as opposed to upper or middle class). Karl Marx knew the working class as those who sold their labor for wages without a stake in or ownership of the means of production. However, Marx did not know who won the English Football Cup Final in 1949. See *MPFC*, "Communist Quiz" (ep. 25).

---

* Sir Terry Pratchett's popular *Discworld* series of novels includes the Patrician, a (generally) benevolent autocrat who enters office via a specialized form of democracy: "Ankh-Morpork had dallied with many forms of government and had ended up with that form of democracy known as One Man, One Vote. The Patrician was the Man; he had the Vote" (1987, 136).

"Constitutional Peasants"—while perhaps the most academically cited scene in the entire film—is only one skit of many that rely upon gothic juxtaposition for humor. And yet ... there's far more to *HG* than simply upset expectations and contrary points of view. In many ways, *HG* actually supports, even as it subverts, the medieval literary tradition it parodies, and a great many professors (including the current writers) include a viewing of the film in their courses and still feel justified in cashing their paychecks for that week. In other words, *MP&HG* is another fine example of the learned comedy produced by the Pythons; with some guidance, the film can actually teach you something about a largely defunct medieval genre and the fictionalized English history that is Arthuriana. Without some guidance, it still teaches you something. As one of the Pythons' contemporary comic scholars once wisely noted: if you're not careful you may actually learn something before it's done! Hey, hey, hey.*

But why, of the host of options available to them, did the Pythons choose King Arthur to lampoon? Did the Kennedys and Camelot suddenly target Arthur for parody after one thousand years in the English consciousness? Of course, it's not as if the legend of King Arthur is *not* worth bringing to the public's attention. John Milton *almost* chose Arthur as the subject of his magnum opus, before settling to simply talk

> *Of Man's first disobedience and the fruit*
> *Of that forbidden tree whose mortal taste*
> *Brought death into the world and all our woe . . .* [85]

So perhaps the Cambridge Pythons thought it time to elevate King Arthur to the heights their slightly more famous fellow alumnus had once promised. Or, more likely still, the well-read Pythons noticed something in the literary tradition of the English hero that resonated with them—and again, it is worth noting the genre of the disjointed, practically postmodern, format: the romance.

Although the legends of Arthur survive in various forms—alliterative poetry, lais, lyrics—the romance was the medieval genre of choice for the tales of Arthur and his knights. Medieval romances (aka chivalric romances) were popular and fantastic tales of high adventure told in both verse and prose. These popular tales starred heroic knights who perform extraordinary feats of derring-do, encounter magical creatures, defeat supernatural foes, go on quests, and (occasionally) win over winsome damsels. Incidentally, the name "romance" derives not from the centrality of a "love story" in each tale but because such stories were initially told in one of the medieval vernacular or "Romance" languages

---

* Popular just as the Pythons were hitting their stride, Bill Cosby's *Fat Albert and the Cosby Kids* animated series ran on American Saturday morning television from 1972 to 1985. IMDb politely describes the show as "[t]he educational adventures of a group of Afro-American inner city kids."

[85] Milton (2005, book 1, lines 1–3). Big shout-out to Elise Cavaney! Woo hoo!

> ## FACTOID BOX: Courtly Love Triangle
>
> Also known as *ménage à fin'amors.**
>
> Courtly love was popularized by Andreas Capellanus in his (potentially satirical) twelfth-century "handbook" *De Arte Honeste Amandi* or *De Amore* (known to the English as *The Art of Courtly Love*), which includes thirty-one rules for wooing correctly. Importantly, a man should only love a woman already married (but *not* his own wife), he should afford her all power over him, and they should never consummate their love. Satire? Surely not!
>
> ──────────────
>
> * Okay: we're making that up. But "courtly love" is, really, more accurately known as *fin'amors* and since it's a love triangle we're talking about and a ménage à trois is already (conveniently) French for a threesome, we figured, why not portmanteau?

(languages descended of the Romans, that is, derived from the Latin) but *not* told in the language of the authority—they were not told in Latin but, say, in Old French. NB: Do not confuse the medieval romance with Hellenistic Romance, Harlequin romance, Jane Austen, or anything in the "tween" section of the bookstore! No, we don't care how old/rich/noble the shiny vampire is or how triangular the vampire/werewolf/maiden relationship gets: it still ain't a medieval romance.

Arthurian romances helped comprise what was called "The Matter of Britain": stories about the (often-legendary) Kings of Britain and their knights. There were in fact three "Matters" that mattered to the medieval English: their own "Matter of Britain," "The Matter of Rome," which involved tales about Roman Kings and their mythical histories (including Virgil's *Aeneid*), and "The Matter of France," which focused on stories of Charlemagne (notably, *Le Chanson de Roland,* an epic poem showcasing an endless stream of bloody dismemberments—of pagans, priests, and horses—that put those in *Holy Grail* to shame . . . but more on that below).

All of these nation-building (some might say propagandistic) tales of larger-than-life aristocratic warriors were terribly popular and helped stoke the imperialistic and ethnocentric values of pre-Empire Britain. It's worth recalling that before there was an America and its Cowboy Diplomacy there was King Arthur and his heavily armored, horsebacked, awe-inspiring regime enforcers. For the Pythons, the British Empire had come and gone, the Queen was a political appendix, and authority was the enemy. Yet folks still looked upon the legendary King of all Britons with fondness.

On the plus side, the legends of Arthur and his Knights of the Round Table had endured, popularly, for as long as there had been an England, and so the figures would have been known (if not exactly read) by Python's audience. Arthur was alive in 1960s culture through a variety of media, including the children's versions by Howard Pyle, *Classics Illustrated* comic books, musical theatre (*Camelot*) and, in particular, film: Disney's animated *The Sword in the Stone*, the historical epic *Siege of the Saxons*, and the bildungsroman adventure *Prince Valiant* (based on Hal Foster's popular comic strip), all show the range of Arthurian tales still resonating in film when the Pythons sought their first cinematic thematic.

The longevity of the Arthurian tradition, as well as Arthur's role as an upper-class authority figure (Question: "How d'you know he's King, then?" Answer: "He hasn't got shit all over him."), made Arthur the perfect target for the Pythons' big-screen anti-authoritarian debut. The loosely connected vignettes that comprised the romance genre were—*toujours déjà*—likewise ideally suited to the Pythons performance style.* It was a match made (pardon us, Dr. Milton) in heaven.

The Pythons did not appropriate the whole of Arthuriana, of course—they conspicuously sidestepped (read: ignored) the courtly love triangle often depicted between King Arthur, his queen, Guinevere, and their favorite knight, Sir Lancelot, in favor of a grittier, generally earlier

---

* *Toujours déjà*: "always already"—a tricky philosophical idea in the hands of some, but in this context just a fancy way of saying "ready-made." Sorry to drag y'all down to the footnote for that, but the authors can now say that we cited the arch-deconstructionist Jacques Derrida in the original French (from *De la Grammatologie*, no less!), so—*toujours déjà!*—we've made this book suitable for our tenure review. Thank you for your patience.

> ### FACTOID BOX: Howard Pyle,
> ### American Illustrator and Author (1853-1911)
>
> Famous for writing and illustrating *The Merry Adventures of Robin Hood* and the four-volume collection *King Arthur and His Knights*. Both are loose, and often bowdlerized, adaptations of medieval materials aimed at children (especially young boys).
>
> **RANDOM FACTOID:** Pyle is credited with inventing the Gypsy-inspired attire of swashbuckling pirates that remains in vogue today. Arrgh!

literary tradition—one that focused on martial prowess and nation building rather than love. This is not to say that sex is entirely absent from *HG*—Carol Cleveland again plays a memorable "Glamour Stooge" (or two) to the boys at Castle Anthrax*—but otherwise *HG* focuses on the typically Howard Pyle–esque "boys adventures" that remained popular in the sixties while also directly drawing upon the early medieval tradition (such as the *Bruts* of Wace and Layamon and the *History* of Geoffrey of Monmouth).

THE MIDDLE

"'TIS BUT A SCRATCH!"

Some of the scenes (one might as easily say sketches) of knightly derring-do in *HG* have long and storied histories, with character types and literary tropes that can claim provenance well into the medieval period.

---

*But more on Castle Anthrax later, as the Grail-shaped beacon is (drat!) currently on the fritz.

"The Black Knight always triumphs!"
Cue the buckets of blood in *Monty Python and the Holy Grail*.

While many medieval romances focus on the exploits of individual Knights of the Round Table rather than on those of Arthur, the rightwise King of all England does have a history of smiting mightily himself. Arthur's martial dominance (and patience) is emphatically, and bloodily, demonstrated by the Pythons in one of the hallmark scenes of *HG*, "The Black Knight" (scene 5).

In a typical romance trope (popular in Robin Hood lore as well),* the hero encounters an armed foe blocking a river crossing, the blocker refuses passage unless he is beaten in battle, battle ensues, and the hero continues on his quest. While traveling through the woods en route to (literally) God-knows-where, Arthur and Patsy encounter the Black Knight fiercely engaged in mortal combat with a similarly violent but unnamed knight in green (let's call him Milton). Once the Black Knight has rather viciously defeated his foe (by hurling a sword through Milton's visor slit), Arthur

---

* In a six degrees of Kevin Bacon moment, John Cleese would later play Robin Hood in the partial-Python effort, *Time Bandits* (1981)—written by Palin and Gilliam, directed by Gilliam. "Jolly, jolly good!"

approaches to ask the victor to join him in his court at Camelot. When silence greets his every entreaty, Arthur (saddened) moves to pass the knight:

BK: None shall pass.

A: What?

BK: None shall pass.

A: I have no quarrel with you, good sir knight, but I must cross this bridge.

BK: Then you shall die.

A: I command you, as King of the Britons, to stand aside.

BK: I move . . . for no man.

A: So be it!

At this point, one is apt to ask when reading many medieval romances: why doesn't the hero simply go around the blocker or cross the creek farther along? As the scene is shot in *HG*, the trickle of water that must be crossed makes the practical concerns of the encounter minimal. Similarly, the gravity of the initial encounter between Robin Hood and Little John (in Errol Flynn's boyish romp *The Adventures of Robin Hood*, 1938) is undermined by the easily forded stream into which the hero ultimately falls. In *Robin Hood*, the test of the hero's mettle is all in good fun; in medieval romances, the test is all about honor; in *Holy Grail*, the test is, well, not much of a test at all, really. With no other alternative before him, Arthur engages the Black Knight and handily (get it? "handily!") dispatches his foe . . . or so it seems.

Following a few perfunctory lunges and parries, Arthur cleanly severs the Black Knight's arm from his body, sending streams of blood spigoting from the knight's exposed shoulder. Thinking he has won the fight—and in a world governed by practical physiology the still-standing Black Knight should, by all rights, be swooning from lack of blood—Arthur commands, "Now stand aside, worthy adversary," only to have the Black Knight casually respond, "'Tis but a scratch!"

Faced with a foe in clear denial ("Your arm's off!" "No it isn't!") and finding noble words again proving insufficient, Arthur lops off the Black Knight's other arm. Assuming he has won, Arthur then proclaims, "Victory is mine!" and kneels in thankful prayer,* only to be buffeted again by the Black Knight, who—although now armless and, hence, harmless—refuses to relent, running up to Arthur and kicking him repeatedly. Long story short, Arthur next removes the knight's leg, then the other, until the once-puissant knight sits, armless and legless (yet bolt upright), upon the ground—and still he challenges the "yellow bastard" Arthur to "come back here and take what's coming to you! I'll bite your legs off!" In the end, Arthur and Patsy simply walk away, leaving the "invincible!" Black Knight to declare their martial encounter "a draw."[†]

As over-the-top as the bloodshed appears in the scene, there *is* medieval literary precedence for the material. In fact, the Black Knight might even be considered a typical member of Arthur's medieval rogues' gallery of tireless, nigh-invincible foes. Here are a few for consideration:

The Giant of Mt. St. Michel, an enormous cannibal rapist[‡] whom Arthur stabs in the face, emasculates, and then disembowels—all while the ogre continues, obliviously, to fight against the king (see the anonymous fourteenth-century alliterative *Morte Arthure*).

Mordred, Arthur's illegitimate son (born of his half-sister: ew!), who manages to deal Arthur a potentially fatal blow to the head even after the traitorous bastard has been "smote . . . under the shield, with a foin of his spear, throughout the body, more than a fathom" (see Malory, book 21—c. 1485).[§] Often portrayed as your stereotypical mustache-twirling baddie in modern films.

---

* Or "Tebowing," as it's sometimes known in the U.S.

[†] Shameless plug: The Black Knight is a direct example of why beheading was so popular in medieval tales—unless you cut off your foe's head, he's not really dead (and thus might very well remain a vocal annoyance). See Tracy and Massey (2012) for consideration of various beheading tropes in medieval and Early Modern literature.

[‡] Sadly, the giant does not only rape cannibals. He eats Christian babies, rapes noble Englishwomen, and thereby threatens Arthur's nascent civilization. Really: he's a raging gustatory phallic symbol with whom Arthur deals severely. Oh—and depending on the manuscript one reads, the monster is Italian. Or Spanish. Definitely NOT English!

[§] Interesting factoid: Arthur's spear, like his more famous sword, has a name: Ron. Imagine if Boorman had chosen to name his blood-and-armor epic *Ron* rather than *Excalibur*. Sometimes Hollywood gets it right.

And of course, there remains the most famous of all medieval dismemberments, that of the **Green Knight** in the anonymous fourteenth-century poem *Sir Gawain and the Green Knight*. Seated on his throne at a Pentecostal feast, King Arthur is terribly surprised—and not a little amused—when the Green Knight is beheaded before the gathered nobility of Camelot . . . without serious side (e.g., death) effect.

> *Gawain gripped the Green Knight's axe and gathered it on high [. . .]*
> *He let it down so "lightly" on his naked neck,*
> *That the sharp edge sundered the bones of the man*
> *And sank through the meat cleanly and split him in two*
> *So that the bite of the browned steel bit into the ground.*
> *The fair head, hewn from the neck, hit the earth.*
> *Many there found it with their feet as it rolled forth;*
> *Blood shot from the body, black on the green.*

(Translation Massey)

In short, the Pythons may be playing up the ludicrous side of armed (and unarmed) combat in the Black Knight episode, but they neither created this nigh-impervious character, nor the blood-soaked scenario, out of whole cloth. You may not have realized it when you were snorting with surprise and laughter at the blood spurting out of the Black Knight's many joints, but you were actually learning something about the representation of violence in medieval romances. Not for nothing did Ving Rhames' proclamation to "get medieval on your ass" to a hillbilly rapist in Quentin Tarantino's oddly Arthurian *Pulp Fiction* (1994) catch on with modern audiences.[*]

Speaking of Tarantino, even the "splat-stick"[†] effect employed by the Pythons (used with somewhat more seriousness by Quentin in his *Kill*

---

[*] For analyses of courtly triangles and other medievalia in *Pulp Fiction*, see Terkla and Reed (1997, 39–52) and Jewers (2000, 39–61).

[†] Peter Jackson (of *The Lord of the Rings*—and *Meet the Feebles*—fame) is credited with dubbing such over-the-top comic violence "splat-stick"—see John McCarty's *Splatter Movies: Breaking the Last Taboo of the Screen* (1984).

Bill films)* has medieval provenance. Take, for example: the ultraviolence of the twelfth-century French epic *Le Chanson de Roland* (The Song of Roland), which similarly shocks those who expect a polite "chivalric" romance, only to find repeated passages describing beheadings, bisected pagans, drawing and quartering, various dismemberments, and—in one particularly bloody scene—a horse and its rider who are split asunder from the force of a single blow:

> [Roland] Slices the cap and shears the locks in two,
> Slices also the eyes and the features,
> The hauberk white, whose mail was close of woof,
> Down to the groin cuts all his body through
> To the saddle; with beaten gold 'twas tooled.
> Upon the horse that sword a moment stood,
> Then spliced its spine, no join there any knew,
> Dead in the field among the thick grass them threw.[†]
>
> (Moncrieff 2008, 1326–1334)

In addition to the usual sword- and spear play, the medieval German epic the *Nibelungenlied* (*The Song of the Nibelungs*), includes a rather gory scene in which the hero, Siegfried, is nearly decapitated by his trained tiger. As the blood spurts in an arc across the stage, Siegfried's partner, Roy, looks on in abject horror. Then, while the jaded Vegas audience recoils . . . just a moment . . . I see . . . my apologies: I've just been handed a correction. In the medieval German poem, the hero Siegfried guts a dragon and bathes in its blood, an act that conveys upon the hero near invulnerability. A classically trained audience (or any blossoming folklorist) will note the

---

* In an interview with the *New York Post* (October 2, 2003) Tarantino claims the "*Zatoichi Blind Swordsman* movies and *Shogun Assassin*" as the chief inspirations for the ultraviolence in *Kill Bill*, noting that in those martial arts films "the lopping off of the arm is a staple" and "people have garden hoses for veins and the blood shoots up like the fountain at the Bellagio Hotel!" But for the potential influence of Python on modern splatterfests (both comic and horrific), see "Monty Python" (2009, 15).

† Chapman's King Arthur may have chopped off the Black Knight's arms and legs, but at least he didn't cut his coconuts in two.

similarity between Siegfried's magical bath and that of the Greek hero Achilles, who was dipped in the river Styx as a child and likewise received limited invulnerability. The difference—which many uppity Renaissance and Victorian scholars might view as "typical" of the respective time periods—is that the classical tale depicts a magical "rebirth" while the Germanic *Nibelungenlied* simply recounts yet another medieval bloodbath.

Possibly the most read example of the bloody bunch is the fourteenth-century "Knight's Tale" from Geoffrey Chaucer's *Canterbury Tales*, wherein the two knights, Arcite and Palamon, nobly vie for the hand of fair Emelye by fighting "like wild boars" until they are literally "ankle deep in their own blood" (Chaucer 1987, lines 1656–1660). In short, the Bellagio fountains of blood in *HG*, while Pythonesque, are ultimately trés medieval.

While the encounter with the Black Knight proves to viewers the mettle of King Arthur, just as in the medieval romances, every knight has his turn "onstage" in *HG*. Here are three scenes—featuring Sir Robin, Sir Galahad, and Sir Lancelot—typical of the loosely connected romances comprising "The Matter of Britain."

"THE TALE OF SIR ROBIN"

Sir Robin, accompanied by his favorite minstrels, randomly encounters a typical faerie realm/supernatural monster—a three-headed ogre—but in *HG* neither knight nor monster acts in traditional fashion. The knight proves to be a backpedaling coward, more apt to disavow his identity than prove his reputation, and the monster voices itself as an effete and self-critical chatterbox who, by the time he comes to a quorum with himself regarding how to dispose of the pesky Sir Robin, finds that the knight has "buggered off": "He's scarpered!"

Unlike in the Black Knight scene, here the Pythons are turning away from traditional tropes and instead inverting our modern expectations of a pseudo-medieval tale, much in the same way that beloved English author J. R. R. Tolkien did in *The Hobbit*, the prequel to his neo-medieval fantasy *The Lord of the Rings*. In *The Hobbit*, the hero is not a Hero (as Tolkien orthographically emphasizes) or typical knight but an undertall, overfed, hairy-toed Halfling (and a burglar to boot!) named Bilbo Baggins. Unlike the abject failure of the cowardly Sir Robin in *HG*, in Tolkien's tale the initially reticent Bilbo does, at least indirectly, succeed on his heroic quest (to recover stolen gold from a dragon), thus proving to a generation of children that looks aren't everything and that even small people can, eventually, become heroes.

Yet Bilbo does not become a hero on his first outing.* His initial monstrous encounter involves not a bickering three-headed ogre but three bickering trolls (Bert, Tom, and Bill) who argue with one another about how to kill and eat the dwarves who disturb their evening repose. Like Sir Robin, Bilbo, upon first seeing his giant foes, is so stunned by their enormous and monstrous appearance that he stammers when asked, "What are yer?" offering that he is "Bilbo Baggins, a bur—a hobbit." (Tolkien 1966, 47) Practically ignoring Bilbo as a threat and having captured and bagged his dwarf companions, the trolls argue with one another (and, unbeknownst to them, with the biloquist Gandalf) for so long that their gustatory hopes are dashed as they turn to stone with the sun's rise (as trolls are wont to do, according to medieval lore).

The hesitant, stammering "hero," the three monstrous and self-conflicted enemies, the escape without active victory—these all suggest that *The Hobbit* is an unlikely literary precedent for "The Tale of Sir Robin," but let's not forget that Tolkien was a medievalist, if not an actual medieval. So rather than suggest that the Pythons stole ideas from J. R. R. Tolkien, let's say that the similarity of the scenes suggests that the Pythons aren't the only ones to employ, and even subvert, medieval ideas, especially medieval ideas that everyone already knows (or thinks that they know). What the Pythons significantly add to this Tolkienesque inversion of medieval tropes is the very self-reflexive, indeed synchronous, minstrelsy that echoes Robin's every move (narrative in "real

---

* Discounting Peter Jackson's filmic *Bilbo*, of course.

time," as it were*). When Robin flees his monstrous encounter, the minstrel (Neil Innes) intones, against Robin's insistent protests:

> *Brave Sir Robin ran away.*
> *(No!)*
> *Bravely ran away, away.*
> *(I didn't!)*
> *When danger reared its ugly head*
> *He bravely turned his tail and fled.*
> *(No!)*
> *Brave Sir Robin turned about.*
> *(I didn't!)*
> *And gallantly he chickened out.*
> *Bravely taking to his feet.*
> *(I never did!)*
> *He beat a very brave retreat.*
> *(All lies!)*
> *Bravest of the brave, Sir Robin.*
> *(I never.)*

The insistently repeated "brave" epithet the minstrel attaches to Robin—that's eight "braves" or variants on "brave" (plus one "gallantly") in nine lines—seems cannily reminiscent of the noble epithets attached, perhaps too often, to Chaucer's Knight in the *Canterbury* Prologue (he is *repeatedly* called "worthy," for example). Terry Jones would eventually cite such conspicuously overabundant adjectives as one indication that Geoffrey Chaucer was being ironic (and his narrator naïve) in his portrayal of the Knight.

Jones—the Pythons' in-house medievalist—would go on to publish the compellingly controversial *Chaucer's Knight: The Portrait of a Medieval Mercenary* (1985). That the Pythons were overachievers in terms of knowl-

---

*At least the result for Sir Robin is less existential than for Harold Crick (Will Ferrell) in *Stranger than Fiction* (2006), who finds his life suddenly narrated by the disembodied voice of famous author Karen Eiffel (Emma Thompson).

edge of esoteric subjects was never in doubt. It's hard to dismiss a man as a simple comedian when gems such as this start his "academic" work:

> This historical rather than purely literary approach to the knight's character necessitates a new reading of the Knight's Tale, which emerges, in my view, as a darker, more disturbing piece—a hymn to tyranny dressed up in the rags of a chivalric romance.*

Jones' cultural historicism—a critical lens employed by a great many readers of Chaucer's *Canterbury Tales* (those who seek to understand more about fourteenth-century England via Chaucer's three-dimensional characterizations)—reveals an underlying suspicion of "face value" interpretations. Rather than employ a "purely literary approach," Jones employs a hybrid approach, one that acknowledges the fiction of the knight but assumes that such fiction reflects historical trust. Jones paints a persistent distrust of authority within the medieval period that reflects the Pythons' postwar views as well; not only should readers not trust Geoffrey the narrator (who seems to view the Knight as truly noble), but we should consider that Geoffrey Chaucer was somehow hiding a "hymn to tyranny" beneath the veneer of fiction (akin to the spin doctors who would hide the veil of post-9/11 tyranny under the veil of patriotism and justified revenge). Chaucer thus offers an early predecessor to the Pythons' favorite trope, the "mash-up" (a "real" historical figure placed in a fantasy setting).

In short, "The Tale of Sir Robin" both upholds and subverts medieval tradition by framing the cowardly actions of an "Arthurian"† knight within the panopticon of a historically accurate minstrelsy.

---

* And further, for a very recent publication examining the erudite medievalism of Terry Jones, see Yeager and Takamiya (2012).

† Sir Robin is the only named knight among Arthur's retinue who does not claim a direct literary forebear. That is, while Lancelot, Galahad, Bedivere, and even Bors are all recorded in the medieval tradition, there is no mention of a Robin among Arthur's entourage. Whether this is done to take the cowardly curse off a "real" Arthurian knight (unlikely) or to further connect Idle's knight to his accompanying minstrel via a Robin Hood–esque moniker (likely) remains a matter of speculation. Still, it's worth noting that Robin Hood, who gained fame via medieval ballads, was sometimes accompanied by a minstrel, Alan-a-Dale, in his own tales.

"THE TALE OF SIR GALAHAD"

Sir Galahad's nearly salacious encounter with the ladies of Castle An-thrax ("eight score young blondes and brunettes, all between sixteen and nineteen and a half" who lead a "lonely life ... bathing ... dressing ... undressing ... knitting exciting underwear") parodies two common medieval forms: the temptation and hospitality tropes. Such tropes were common in many medieval saints' lives, such as those recorded in the *Golden Legend*, but the medieval tale most familiar to modern audiences likely remains *Sir Gawain and the Green Knight* (*SGGK*).

In *SGGK*, Sir Gawain—one of Arthur's most trusted knights—defends the honor of Camelot after a reasonably jolly green giant of a knight challenges the court to a medieval version of "Irish One-Stand." To briefly review: the giant will allow any knight a free swing at his neck with his enormous axe, provided that—afterwards—the Green Knight will be allowed a similar blow in return. Gawain accepts the challenge and chops off the Green Knight's head, only to have the knight pick up his severed head, laugh, and then ride off into the mists of Arthurian geography.

The Beheading Game aside, what is most relevant in *SGGK* to Gala-had's/Palin's encounter at Castle Anthrax is the seductive encounter Ga-wain "enjoys" en route to finding the Green Knight. Cheerfully lodged at Lord Bertilak's castle, Gawain is thrice seduced by his host's wife—she even comes to his bed one afternoon clad only in a shift, not unlike the scantily clad maids of Castle Anthrax. Gawain, although torn between his Christian duty to his host (no canoodling your buddy's wife) and his chivalric honor (always do what the lady asks), ultimately escapes this "perilous danger" by offering the Lady Bertilak (and her husband, oddly enough) six kisses—one and two and three.

Gawain also receives a magical girdle, escapes decapitation with but a scratch, loses his honor (maybe), and is then laughed at in Camelot, which seems a silly place to him upon his return. But that's not impor-tant right now. What is important is that the conflict between how a good Christian knight should act (chastely!) and how a good chivalric knight should act (subservient to women) plays out in *Holy Grail* much as in its medieval antecedents. *HG* is simply funnier.

While it's often easy for modernists to look down upon the conflicting sexual mores depicted in medieval literature, we should remember that, for the first half of the Middle Ages, literature—even the seemingly secular—was generally recorded by monks (the only ones who were taught how to write). Some tales—such as those in the Vulgate Cycle (a collection of Old French romances, c. 1225)—tell not only of puissant knights engaged in manly combat but of knights who behave as good Christian soldiers ought, with purity of spirit and flesh. One particular section of the Vulgate Cycle, the *Queste del Saint Graal*, features not only Galahad (the Chaste) achieving the Holy Grail (or *graal*)* but also a very familiar scene involving Sir Bors resisting the temptations offered by a castle full of comely maidens. Noted medievalist and teratologist Jeffrey Jerome Cohen summates Bors' challenge nicely:

> The monastically manufactured *Queste del Saint Graal* serves as an ecclesiastically sanctioned antidote to the looser morality of the secular romance; when Sir Bors comes across a castle where "ladies of high descent and rank" tempt him to sexual indulgence, these ladies are, of course, demons in lascivious disguise. When Bors refuses to sleep with one of the transcorporeal devils . . . his steadfast assertion of control banishes them all shrieking back to hell. (1996, 18–19)

As Bors demonstrates, the avoidance/refusal of sexual temptation was one of the defining characteristics of a truly great Christian knight. As a result, in Thomas Malory's collated opus, *Le Morte d'Arthur*, the virginal Galahad is the only knight who ultimately succeeds on the Grail quest, whereas his more puissant father, Lancelot, fails and then blames his failure on his own distracting carnal desire for Guinevere.

---

* As the Wizard Tim (and Chrétien de Troyes) might say.

Purity of heart trumps might of arms—at least in the later medieval romance.*

Clearly, one can see the conflation of the Vulgate in the Python version—Galahad, not Bors[†] is the intrepid knight who comes upon Castle Anthrax, who . . . nearly . . . avoids the sexual temptation[‡] of the Carol Cleveland "twins" (Zoot and Dingo) and her/their lonely sisterhood. No suggestion is made in the film regarding the hidden demonic nature of the women of Anthrax, and upon losing her desired conquest (thanks to the forceful abduction of Galahad by Sir Lancelot), rather than "shrieking back to hell," all Dingo can muster is a frustrated, "Oh . . . shit!"

The Pythons returned to noodle with the idea of knightly/saintly temptation again after *Holy Grail*, particularly in their audio sketch "The Martyrdom of Saint Victor" (*Monty Python's Contractual Obligation Album,* 1980). In this mock sermon, Palin intones, with appropriately echoic effect, the temptation of Saint Victor,[§] a tale that adds a more modern, er, happy ending to their own "Tale of Sir Galahad":

> "And it came to pass that Saint Victor was taken from this place to another place. Where he was lain upon pillows of silk and made to rest himself amongst sheets of muslin and velvet. And there strokéd was he by maidens of the Orient. For sixteen days and nights strokéd

---

*The legend varies, of course. In Chrétien de Troyes' version (*Perceval, or The Story of the Grail*), the naïve knight Perceval seems destined to achieve the grail . . . if only Chrétien had not died before completing his romance.

[†]Bors (played by Gilliam, who tends to die on-screen a goodly bit) does appear in *HG* but utters only one line: "One rabbit stew, coming right up!" seconds before he is nearly decapitated by the Killer Rabbit in scene 21. Other Gilliam deaths in *HG* include that of the Green Knight (sword through the visor slit), the Old Man or Bridgekeeper (who is hurled into the Gorge of Eternal Peril) and the Animator (himself, who suffers a fatal heart attack). Patsy, Arthur's trusty coconuteer, was last seen outside the Cave of Caerbannog and (as far as we know) escaped the film unscathed.

[‡]Including, but probably not limited to, the spanking and the oral sex.

[§]According to *Martirologia Romano* (Roman martyrology), Saint Victor was a Christianized Roman soldier who refused to swear upon false (Roman) idols; upon his torture, Victor was "comforted" by the young wife of a fellow soldier. She too was then executed.

they him, yea verily and caressed him. His hair, ruffled they. And their fingers rubbethed they in oil of olives, and runneth them across all parts of his body for as much as to soothe him. And the soles of his feet licked they. And the upper parts of his thigh did they anoint with the balm of forbidden trees. And with the teeth of their mouths, nibbleth they the pointed bits at the top of his ears. Yea verily, and did their tongues thereof make themselves acquainted with his most secret places. For fifteen days and nights did Victor withstand these maidens. But on the sixteenth day he cried out, saying: 'This is fantastic! Oh, this is terrific!' And the Lord did hear the cry of Victor. And verily came He down and slew the maidens. And caused their cotton-wool buds* to blow away, and their Kleenex to be laid waste utterly. And Victor, in his anguish, cried out that the Lord was a rotten bastard. And the Lord sent an angel to comfort Victor for the weekend. And entered they together the Jaccuzzi." Here endeth the lesson.

Unlike the monks who penned the corrective *Queste del Saint Graal*, the Pythons were not stringently religious men (even if Gilliam once toyed with the idea of becoming a Presbyterian minister), and neither were their target audience. Remember: *Holy Grail* was released in 1975 to a largely counterculture audience. In the film, the attractive, semi-clad maids of Castle Anthrax do not serve as a monstrous warning (something for good Christian men to avoid) but as a commentary on the "unhealthy" attitude of medieval monastics (and their uptight modern descendants) who feared both sex and women. It's the seventies, people! Free love, man! Galahad's final protest to Lancelot (his father, according to medieval tradition) as he drags him from Dingo's "much too perilous" clutches further affixes a non-normative label upon those who violently impose their normative moral values upon others: "I bet you're gay!" Galahad's final utterance may fall upon politically sensitized ears nowadays. Yet the joke still works if one recalls that in the medieval tradition Lancelot was the most overtly (albeit often closeted) heterosexual among

---

* Q-tips (or cotton swabs) for the Americans, once again.

Arthur's troupe. When not secretly dallying with Guinevere behind her husband's back, the puissant Lancelot was being sexually pursued by every Elaine in the kingdom. It's the emptiest of insults for a son to hurl at a womanizing father, really.

"THE TALE OF SIR LANCELOT"

As noted before, *HG* sidesteps the illicit courtly romance between Lancelot and Guinevere (there is nooooo ... Guinevere in *Holy Grail*), and instead focuses on Lancelot's other traditional attribute: his puissance, or might in battle. In *HG*, "The Tale of Sir Lancelot" is both a traditional "save the Princess" adventure—perhaps the most popular Arthurian trope in modern cinema, alongside the love triangle—and a critique of genre (or idiom, as noble Concord might say). Lancelot—who is often called the "best of Arthur's knights," earns his reputation through his might in combat; and significantly, within the realm of the Arthurian romance, combat was used for far more than war.

The trouble with Lancelot in *HG* is that he is a loaded gun (or sword) with a wonky sight. As Idle says in the commentary for *HG*, Lancelot "is Errol Flynn gone berserk." Instead of engaging in a "noble" mission to save a helpless maiden (as Herbert's note suggests) that would justify the flexing of Lancelot's hyper-violence, he instead enthusiastically slaughters the innocent revelers at a wedding. Even after he realizes his mistake and the King of Swamp Castle has forgiven him his bloody indiscretion (another example of genre clash, as the politically pragmatic King ignores Lancelot's swashbuckling antics out of potential monetary interests: "Mmm ... very nice castle, Camelot. Very good pig country"), Lancelot cannot help but be ... Lancelot: Killing Machine. Exiting Herbert's now-vacant tower, Lancelot again tears through the distraught wedding survivors until restrained by the King. Even after Lancelot's second rampage, all he can say is, "Sorry. Sorry."

Surely such behavior has no precedence in the medieval tales of the Knights of the Round Table, right? I mean, they were violent men, sure,

FACTOID BOX: Trial by Combat

Medieval romances often relied upon a quasi-magical/quasi-legal proof of guilt: Trial by Combat. In Trial by Combat, any accused party (or, if the accused was a female, like Queen Guinevere, her champion) was entitled to a duel with their accuser. The winner of the fight was deemed in the right, since all such contests are ultimately determined by God (who would not, certainly, back a guilty party).

FUN FACT: Lancelot *always* won—even when he was, technically, guilty. In addition to being a most puissant fighter, Lancelot was also quite an equivocator.

but they all held to a noble code of conduct, right? Especially Lancelot. Right?

Nah. Malory's *Morte d'Arthur* more or less establishes Lancelot as an unrestrained beast in the mold of *HG* (albeit one sometimes morally conflicted by his infidelity with Guinevere). At one point, caught in flagrante delicto with the queen, an unarmed Lancelot first buffets an armed knight, strips him of his armor, then fights his way through the pack to escape. Later, when ambushed by a pack of knights led by the traitorous Mordred, Lancelot slaughters a dozen of his fellow knights, including his two innocent, and unarmed, cousins who happen to be present. When he is later accused of the deed by Gawain, all Malory's Lancelot can say (as Cleese's Lancelot is wont to do) is, "Sorry."

Ultimately, the pragmatics of knighthood conflict with the romanticized ideal of knighthood in *HG* and in *Morte d'Arthur*—save the maiden/ protect the innocent, but do so with extreme violence. It is, after all, Lancelot's . . . idiom.

CAMELOT

In 1960, Alan Jay Lerner and Frederick Loewe adapted T. H. White's beloved tetralogy, *The Once and Future King,* into a Broadway musical. Surprisingly (from our jaded millennial perspective, at least), the play was a huge success, garnering excellent box office, four Tony Awards, a best-selling cast album, and, in 1967, a very popular feature film. Let's repeat that: in 1967, one of the most recognized films out of the Hollywood establishment was a musical about King Arthur. How could the Pythons resist?

They didn't, of course, and in one of the most oddly displaced scenes in a film full of displaced scenes, King Arthur and his knights dramatically look out across the vale of England to an impressive distant castle ("It's only a model!"*). Arthur then proclaims, seriously (as ever): "Knights, bid you welcome to your new home! Let us ride! To Camelot!"

What ensues is as close to a direct parody of modern culture as Python engages in during *Holy Grail,* a seriously silly song-and-dance number in the (general) style of Broadway extravaganzas, involving armor-clad knights (and one nearly unclad dungeon prisoner) dancing, singing, playing timpani on (occupied) helmets, kicking chickens, et cetera. In response to this melodic vignette of life in Camelot—including a basso knight who admits to pushing "the pram a lot"†—Arthur (who, along with his companions are *still* a cut scene away from the castle), says, "On second thought, let's not go to Camelot. 'Tis a silly place." And when a bunch of wool-knit/chain-mail kuh-nigguts, accompanied by servants who bang coconuts together in lieu of actual steeds call you "silly," the silliness must be extreme indeed.‡

---

*The only line spoken in the film by Arthur's companion Patsy (Gilliam)—a breaking of the fourth wall made doubly funny since Gilliam was, as usual, responsible for the animation (the castle) the knights are gazing out upon.

† "Pram" (short for "perambulator") is a somewhat archaic British term for baby carriage or stroller. Think of the carriage that bounces down the stairs during the gunfight in *Untouchables* (Kevin Costner reference number two!).

‡ Chapman is obviously echoing his recurring *Flying Circus* character the Colonel, who was apt to interrupt scenes that he deemed "too silly" to continue. Of course, this breaking of the fourth wall by Chapman's character was itself silly and only amplified the metatheatrical silliness of the interrupted sketch at hand, but there was no Colonel to call shenanigans on the Colonel.

FACTOID BOX

Camelot (musical) 1960 Broadway—four Tony Awards

Camelot (film) 1967 Hollywood—three Academy Awards

MUSICAL: Julie Andrews, Richard Burton, Roddy McDowell, Robert Goulet

FILM: Richard Harris, Vanessa Redgrave

FUN FACTOID: Goulet practically made his career offa this thing. No, really.

The repeated invocation of the castle's name in this scene (no less than three . . . no, five! times by Arthur and his knights and five . . . no, three! times by the castellated singing knights) brings direct attention to the name Camelot (it is barely mentioned elsewhere in the film). And, while Camelot remains a nearly constant, and indeed central, location in medieval Arthuriana, for the audience of *Holy Grail* (1975), who likely grew up with the sound track to the identically named *Camelot* playing on their parents' phonograph, the silliness undoubtedly resonated doubly.

THE END [?]

"SO, YOU THINK YOU COULD OUT-CLEVER US FRENCH FOLK WITH YOUR SILLY KNEES-BENT RUNNING ABOUT ADVANCING BEHAVIOR! I WAVE MY PRIVATE PARTS AT YOUR AUNTIES, YOU HEAVING LOT OF SECONDHAND ELECTRIC DONKEY BOTTOM BITERS."

The abrupt, jarring, and anticlimactic "end" to *Monty Python and the Holy Grail* is—from the perspective of two professors who delight in showing this film to our classes, at least—the single most problematic moment in all of Python. And yes: we're including the alien abduction scene from *Life of Brian* AND the explosion of Mr. Creosote from *Meaning of Life* in our very scientific calculation.* Without fail, after we show the film to a class there will be at least one honestly irate student who feels gypped by the ending, who demands an explanation for what just happened, and who will write a term paper that largely expounds upon the theme of WTF? You can hardly blame them.

Although the ultimate juxtaposition of medieval past and modern present is foreshadowed earlier in the film (when the historian is decapitated by the helmeted knight), many viewers get caught up in the quest for the Holy Grail by the end and seem to shunt off the intruding modern scene as an aberration of little consequence. On the one hand, the non-ending is a fine final deflation of the Arthurian legend, a mythos that the anti-authoritarian Pythons have criticized as being overly rosy throughout the film. It is, in this view, subverting its medieval source materials.

On the other hand, the non-ending of Arthur's quest and the non-ending of Arthur himself are entirely in keeping with the medieval tradition. As noted earlier, the Arthurian legend was popularized through a variety of tales, but it was most often associated with the romance. One romance in particular—the late twelfth-century *Perceval ou le Conte du*

---

*This is our theory, and it is ours.

Graal by Chrétien de Troyes—is generally considered the premiere example of a grail narrative. In this slice of Arthuriana, the young, untrained Perceval (of Wales) goes on a quest to become a knight; along the way he is repeatedly asked questions, repeatedly fails to ask the right questions, and ultimately finds love and knighthood. He never—despite the promise of the romance—attains the Graal, however. Chrétien, you see, never finished his narrative.*

So the most famous grail narrative of the Middle Ages ended—like Python's later version—without the attainment of the grail object that served as the focal point of the whole damn adventure. It's disappointing, perhaps, but not without precedent.

Likewise, the non-ending of King Arthur himself (who is, apparently, trundled away in the back of a paddy wagon by the modern gendarmes at the end of the film) can also claim medieval precedent. In fact, one of the most alluring, and enduring, traditions in Arthuriana is the possible non-death of Arthur. In various medieval versions of Arthur's "mort," Arthur faces his final conflict against his bastard son Mordred, who deals him his deathblow even as Arthur deals him his. Malory, for example, provides a lovely (if bloody) end to the two:

> Then the king gat his spear in both his hands, and ran toward Sir Mordred, crying: Traitor, now is thy death-day come. And when Sir Mordred heard Sir Arthur, he ran until him with his sword drawn in his hand. And there King Arthur smote Sir Mordred under the shield, with a foin of his spear, throughout the body, more than a fathom. And when Sir Mordred felt that he had his death wound he thrust himself with the might that he had up to the bur of King Arthur's spear. And right so he smote his father Arthur, with his sword holden in both his hands, on the side of the head, that the sword pierced the helmet and the brain-pan, and therewithal Sir Mordred fell stark dead to the earth; and the noble Arthur fell in a swoon to

---

* Scholars still quibble over why Chrétien never finished Perceval's story, but the bookies lay heavy odds on Chrétien's death as a major factor. Black Beasts may have been involved.

the earth, and there he swooned ofttimes. (Malory 1485, book 21, chapter 4)

After swooning, Arthur commands his vassal Bedivere to cast the sword Excalibur into a nearby lake (which—upon his third attempt—he manages to do). Upon his return to the dying King, Bedivere is ordered to set his liege upon a barge attended by three mysterious Queens, for, in the words of Arthur: "I will into the vale of Avalon to heal me of my grievous wound." The King is never seen again, but perhaps—just perhaps—he will return again, whole, to guide England in a time of need. Or, as the sometimes-unromantic Malory notes:

> YET some men say in many parts of England that King Arthur is not dead, but had by the will of our Lord Jesu into another place; and men say that he shall come again, and he shall win the holy cross. I will not say it shall be so, but rather I will say: here in this world he changed his life. But many men say that there is written upon his tomb this verse:
>
> Hic jacet Arthurus, Rex quondam, Rexque futurus.*

Ultimately, Monty Python's ending for King Arthur is likewise open to interpretation—we each may offer an answer to the "WTF?" moment presented to us at the end. Arthur is denied his grail (lousy French taunters!) and, bereft of Excalibur, he is led away by the police, but whither goes the King? To certain doom? To a just trial?† Or "by the will of Jesu into another place"? Certainly, Arthur's cinematic tale—and his constitutional peasant littered, Killer Rabbit–ridden, coconut-laden quest—is over for now, but is it (or Monty Python) ever really done?

---

*The Latin reads: "Here lies Arthur, the once and future King."
†If the helm don't fit, you must aquit!

"Whatever happened to my part?"
The Lady of the Lake (Sara Ramirez) and her Laker Girls strike a pose in *Spamalot*.

THE CODA

"I'M WITH A BUNCH OF BRITISH KNIGHTS PRANCING 'ROUND IN WOOLLY TIGHTS!"

The musical *Spamalot* (co-created by Eric Idle) opened on Broadway March 17, 2005, and ran for over fifteen thousand shows until its close on January 11, 2009. It was nominated for fourteen Tony Awards, winning three, including Best Musical (that's one shy of *Camelot*, for those keeping score at home). The show is currently (as of 2012) on its third U.S. national tour; it has also played in London, Australia, Las Vegas, Spain, New Zealand, Germany, Hungary, Sweden, France, Belgium, the

Czech Republic, Poland, Canada, Ireland, Italy, the Netherlands, Japan, and South Korea. By most standards of musical theatre, it's been a success.

Spamalot is a Broadway treatment of a film property that actually works because it goes well beyond its source material.* In particular, the show lampoons theatre-specific generic conventions (the Hebraic requirements of a Broadway production, for example, or the "extremely expensive prop forest" that must be utilized as often as possible), pulls in musical and dance numbers from other Python outings (fish slapping makes an extended comeback early on and "Always Look on the Bright Side of Life" from *Life of Brian* closes the show), and even fills a conspicuous absence in *HG* by providing a love interest for Arthur—in fact, it provides a love interest for just about everybody, as befits a standard Broadway musical comedy. The Lady of the Lake (and her Laker Girls) works to rectify the gender imbalance inherent in most Python efforts and we can personally attest that Sara Ramirez was a definite scene stealer as the original Lady of the Lake. Despite, or perhaps because of, these deviations from the Python formula, critical reactions to the play have sometimes been mixed.

Not all the Pythons were exactly thrilled with Idle's proposed musical project. Cleese seemed the most on board and even recorded the voice of God for the show. Palin saw no harm in it so long as the checks cleared. Gilliam considered the project nothing more than "Python-lite" but recognized that it was futile to try to stop something "with a life of its own." Jones was perhaps the most contrary before the show opened ("*Spamalot* is utterly pointless. . . . Regurgitating Python is not high on my list of priorities") but seemed to have changed his mind slightly once he saw it, admitting that "it was terrific good fun . . . It isn't really 'Python.' It is very much Eric . . . the best parts of the musical are the new things," in particu-

---

*Unlike, say, the Broadway production of *Young Frankenstein*, which left at least one audience member silently ticking off points every time the cast—who were largely reciting known dialogue—got a cinematic beat "wrong."

lar "Whatever Happened to My Part," which ridicules musical theatre (and the very performance of *Spamalot*) itself. Chapman offered no comment.

There are obvious reasons to be concerned: the musical takes its title from the lyrics ("We eat ham and jam and SPAM a lot") of the song sung at Camelot Castle in *Holy Grail*—the song that results in Arthur derisively saying, "On second thought, let's not go to Camelot. 'Tis a silly place." In other words, it's a musical partially based off a song that exemplified what was *wrong* with modern Arthuriana. To turn around and "cash in" on the very thing that they once derided would be the ultimately sell-out, no?*

While the majority of critical reviews of the show were positive (it did win three Tony Awards after all), some have noted how the jokes are too often "broadcast" or underscored by explicitly calling attention to the punch line (Anderson 2005). These moments are, sadly, the unironic equivalent of the once-metacritical Glamour-Stooge refrain "but it's my only line" in the original BBC series. As Palin notes, "It's not 'Python' as we would have written it. But then, none of us would get together and write a 'Python' stage show."

Personally, I (Massey here—sorry)[†] found the most troubling part of the show to be the audience of Python poseurs—like the extremely exuberant woman in front of me who kept misquoting Python "scripture" just before the cast cited it. Onstage, the one deviation from the original that seemed misplaced was the self-awareness and comic asides of Tim Curry's Arthur. Unlike the straightlaced Chapman, who serves as a Romance Foil to many of the modernist characters, Curry repeatedly broke character. Nudging and winking, commenting upon the artificiality of the stage, breaking the fourth wall: these are certainly Pythonesque actions, but without the Arthurian straight man acting as a rigid tent pole the medieval parody collapses. Then again, *Spamalot* is less a riff on medieval Arthuriana than it is a riff on modern Broadway. As Jones said, the best parts

---

* Idle has never had any problem with the "sellout" tag sometimes attached to him and has—on many occasions—embraced it (in voice-overs, reissues, and interviews).
[†] Cogan: "I'm still in the room."

were the new bits. While they may not have been fully Python, the satire and parody of known show tunes and showbiz were well conceived and catchy. And like much of Python proper, *Spamalot* is potentially educational: "despite your pretty lights and naughty girls in nasty tights," you "won't succeed on Broadway if you don't have any Jews." That's a lesson of sorts, right?

Ultimately *Spamalot* is not angry or anti-authoritarian or even biting satire; it's a mild nibbling of the show hand that feeds it. But whether it is considered Python, Pythonesque, or Python-lite, *Spamalot* is evidence of the enduring appeal of *Holy Grail*—regardless of whether the two million theatregoers (so far!) have ever seen the original movie or not.

GILLIAM: THE GRAIL

In an interview for the magazine *Film Comment* ("Terry Gilliam's Guilty Pleasures") Gilliam confesses that, growing up,

> I was a great fan of Walt Disney. Everything Disney did, I fell for: the live-action stuff—*20,000 Leagues Under the Sea, Treasure Island*, all the cartoons, *Pinocchio*. As far as other animation, *Mr. Magoo* was good. I never knew who the other great animators were, despite watching their cartoons. Even after I was in Python, I never knew who Chuck Jones was. Or Tex Avery. They represented a shift from Disney, but in all of them there is the creation of these amazing worlds. That's what Disney always did . . . And then going to college, when I discovered more serious films, then my old favorites were an embarrassment to me. Then I spent my whole time trying to get away from Disney. That's why my cartoons were like that: I was going in the opposite direction, away from everything that Disney stood for. And the awful thing is, I love those things. (1991, 70)

Gilliam's love/hate relationship with the Disney aesthetic is evident in one of the interstitials in *Holy Grail* in particular: the "book to film" bleed-in involving a quasi-medieval manuscript, a lady's dainty hand, and a gorilla's hairy mitt. The "book to film" trope occurs in many of Disney's early films, especially those based on literary or folkloric works, such as *Winnie the Pooh* and *Cinderella*, or—as is likely in this context—*Robin Hood* and *The Sword in the Stone*. Disney's animated *Robin Hood* (1973), for example, begins with a shot of a hardbound book, *Robin Hood*, which opens with the text "Long ago, good King Richard of England departed for the holy land on a great crusade." As the pages turn, an illuminated rooster in the margins (Alan-a-Dale) "comes to life" and begins whistling and walking through the text, the credits, and then into the "film proper." While Disney used the image of an open book transitioning into animated film to lend "serious" literary weight to their "light" animated fare, Gilliam upends the practice in *Holy Grail*. There he films a woman's delicate hand (rumored to be that of his wife) turning the pages of a manuscript, only to have her hand snatched away by a gorilla's hand (reportedly his own costumed hand). Later, in the metatheatrically illumined scene 24, the gorilla hand returns to turn the chapter and continue the story. And so, rather than lend literary authenticity to the film's legendary content, Gilliam's directorial choice to subvert a well-known Disney trope ridicules "mainstream" tropes (the film is *not* the book), breaks the fourth wall visually, and calls attention to the very artificiality of both literary and cinematic performance.

The Holy Grail is, throughout, a highly self-referential tale, replete with on-the-spot minstrelsy, self-aware characters, blatantly anachronistic ideologies, and a conclusion that beggars temporal and generic description. Not surprisingly, Gilliam's interstitials likewise reflect the metatheatrical mission of the Pythons. In one instance, Gilliam animates an illustrator limning the manuscript title for "The Tale of Sir Lancelot" only to have his calligraphy ruined by the "bloody weather" leaping about; in another, illuminated monks proceed along a typical medieval manuscript's floral design (decorating "The Tale of Sir Galahad") only to find one monk springboarding up into an illuminated initial, landing upside down and bare assed, to be incongruously fingered by a waiting nun.* Reflective of the medieval illuminator's practice, sometimes these interstitial animations seem more relevant to the tale at hand than others (Galahad's sexual temptation by the "girlies" of Castle Anthrax is at least hinted at by the diddling nun and monk in his tale's initial *G*, for example).

Another Gilliam-intensive bit of metatheatrical awareness occurs before Arthur and his knights learn of the Broadway-themed castle, Camelot. As Arthur proposes that his knights ride forth to Camelot, Gilliam—who is playing Patsy, Arthur's squire/steed—remarks that the distant image of Camelot is "only a model," which, of course, Gilliam the set designer would have constructed. While it is funny enough that a minor character in the story recognizes the artificiality of the setting while the leads do not, the joke is partially predicated upon the audience

---

*Compare this to the happy innocence of the rooster Alan-a-Dale, lounging in his illuminated initial for *Robin Hood*.

recognizing Gilliam as Patsy and upon their knowing that Gilliam is the troupe's animator. It's meta-meta.

But surely the most in-your-face moment of interstitial metatheatricality occurs with the death of the animator in the "Black Beast of Arrrghhh" scene. Here Gilliam appears on camera—as himself!—hunched over a drawing table as the Black Beast chases after the (suddenly animated) Knights of the Round Table, who seem in dire straits until (as the narrator's voice-over intones) "escape for Arthur and his knights seemed hopeless. When suddenly the animator suffered a fatal heart attack." This meta-appearance (meta-meta-meta-appearance?) summates nicely the role of an artist known for his *fumetti* strips before he joined Python.

Part IV

THERE IS NOOOOO ... PART 4

"And of course, there'll be sport"*

Part V

PYTHON ON SPORT

TAG UNDER: rugby, football, cricket, wrestling, sex, dating, war, violence, and pornography.

* At the very opening of episode 21, Idle introduces, via voice-over, the wide variety of programming available on BBC One, which ranges from variety and comedy to drama . . . all of which is actually sport.

"YOUR WIFE, IS SHE A SPORT?"

In the grand tradition of British athleticism, Monty Python proved that brains and brawn do go hand in hand. Or do they? In Python the manly (or Pepperpot-y) pursuit of competition was a recurring part of their television series, various specials, and films. But, like all other topics, various sports are presented by the Pythons as particularly silly, and often particularly British, concerns. Despite the fact that Python tackled great literary figures, philosophers, historical personages, and complex theoretical subjects, the most puzzling aspect of Python to many viewers not native to the British Isles is the way in which Python examines sport.* This may simply be a cultural difference. As Pierre Bourdieu mentions in his article "How Can One Be a Sports Fan?" it is essential to understand sport in the "context of economic and social conditions of the corresponding society" (2000, 429). In many ways, sport is the ultimate "location joke"—to get it, you had to be there.

The disdainful way that the U.S.A. largely refuses to accept soccer (which is called football *everywhere* else . . .) as a serious sport is but one of the many ways that Americans set themselves apart from the cultural

---

* And no, that's not a typo. Although Americans use the plural, in most other counties and in academic writing it is referred to as "sport." Small world eh?

FACTOID BOX: Midfield Play

A key difference between the American view of football and that of the rest of the world is the concept of midfield play. Most American fans of "soccer" enjoy the attempts at goals and are frustrated when no one goes near a goal for more than a few minutes. This was best articulated in a *Simpsons* episode in 1994, where the Simpson family goes to watch an exhibition game between Mexico and Portugal. While observing the midfield action, we hear two very different takes on the game. The American announcer, Kent Brockman, looks bored as he recites: "Halfback passes to the center, back to the wing, back to the center. Center holds it. Holds it. Holds it . . ." Meanwhile his Mexican counterpart almost leaps in the air as he frenetically announces (translated from Spanish): "Halfback passes to center, back to wing, back to center! Center holds it! Holds it! Holds it!!"

pursuits of the rest of the world. Yes, Americans often define themselves through sports (after all, what is more American than baseball and apple pie?), but so does the rest of the world. Yet the fact that a great many Americans choose to define themselves via a distant cousin (several times removed) of cricket, a sport that accompanied British colonialism around the world and is still immensely popular in most of the former "colonies," reveals a national sports mythology radically different from the world at large. They (UK) define themselves via teamwork and cooperation and nil-nil "victories." We (U.S.) define ourselves through monumental ninth-inning home runs, buzzer-beating three-pointers, and Hail Mary touchdowns. The differences, as one can see, are vast.

When watching sports, true fans do not sit passively but instead feel a sense of involvement and participation. In his article "The Sports Star in the Media: The Gendered Construction and Youthful Consumption of Sports Personalities," Gill Lines argues that the audiences of sports can "actively define their own experiences and articulate certain pleasures that they gain from participation in mediated sports events" (2002, 213). A football game is not merely "game" but a grand spectacle that evokes a visceral and emotional response. Fans do not cry at a loss because they have wagered money on the outcome* but because of their emotional involvement: Note how "we" lost or "we" won a game. The level of emotional involvement must seem strange to those not afflicted with sports on the brain. Michael Novak argues that sports are more like "symbolic public dramas than entertainment" (1985, 35), and in many ways sport functions not just as a grand spectacle but also as a form of high drama, where heroes are born, villains defeated, and vicarious involvement is felt, whether we sit in the stadium or in our comfy chair (Yes! The Comfy Chair!) eating snacks and drinking our Watneys Red Barrel. Better than most sports commentators, Python realized that because sporting games are high drama, they can also be deconstructed and turned into comedic fodder. And the more involvement one has in a sport, the more potentially absurd the situation.

FANDOM

". . . at least one ageing football commentator was gladdened last night by the sight of an English footballer breaking free of the limpid tentacles of packed Mediterranean defence."

One particularly telling example of fan involvement from Python is in "Literary Football Discussion" (ep. 11), wherein the Pythons (Idle as "smart" Interviewer, Cleese as "not overbright" Footballer) highlight the sometime discrepancy between those who analyze sport and those who play sports. Idle opens the segment with a highly articulate synopsis/ analysis of last night's match:

---

* Except for the authors. In the words of the poet McTeagle: "Lend us a couple of bob till Thursday."

From the plastic arts we turn to football. Last night in the Stadium of Light, Jarrow, we witnessed the resuscitation of a great footballing tradition, when Jarrow United came of age, in a European sense, with an almost Proustian display of modern existentialist football. Virtually annihilating by midfield moral argument the now surely obsolescent *catennachio** defensive argument of Signor Alberto Fanfrino.[†] Bologna indeed were a side intellectually outargued by a Jarrow team thrusting and bursting with aggressive Kantian positivism and outstanding in this fine Jarrow team was my man of the match, the arch-thinker, free-scheming, scarcely ever to be curbed, midfield cognoscento, Jimmy Buzzard.

Unfortunately, Buzzard turns out to be—to the dismay of Idle's interviewer (Brian)—something of a dullard. Failing to understand much, if anything, of Brian's erudite and philosophically laden analysis, Buzzard answers all of his interviewer's queries regarding his game play with one of three repeated responses: "Good evening, Brian"; "Well, Brian . . . I'm opening a boutique"; and "I hit the ball first time and there it was in the back of the net!"

The main thrust of the sketch seems predicated upon yet another Pythonian subversion of expectation: Idle's Interviewer treats football, and Cleese's Footballer, as the embodiments of intellectual exercise, rather than physical exercise. Football, for the Interviewer, *is* Argument. Football, for the Footballer, is simply football. The result is, yet again, a humorous breakdown in communication.

Andrew Stott notes this sketch in his critical survey of comic theory, *Comedy*, as an example of a "recurring technique" in Monty Python: "the discussion of quotidian topics in an elevated register, exploiting discontinuity between form and content" (2004, 9); in this case, a "sports report that blends philosophy with soccer" results in a "form of incongruity . . . to produce ambiguity and the feeling that normality has been momen-

---

* Also *catennaccio*: lit. "door-bolt"; a defensive style of football.
[†] To the best of the Internet's knowledge, this is a fictional personage—whether intended to denote a philosopher or footballer remains (appropriately) unclear.

tarily decentred for pleasurable ends."* Yet such incongruity—and the feeling that normality has been suspended—need not be cut from whole cloth. That is, the disjoint in this sketch is not a wholly absurd or surreal one. As Larsen notes, there have been real sports reporters who waxed as rhapsodically as the fictional Brian; Larsen even presents a fine trio of "real-world" newsprint analyses of contemporary sporting events wherein the "euphuistic pretentiousness" of the essayists rivals—and even surpasses—the "splendiferous" verbosity of Idle's Interviewer (2008, 152–153). British columnists such as Arthur Hopcraft, Alan Gibson, and Brian Chapman penned some truly florid prose in service of sports reportage in the late sixties and early seventies. A brief excerpt from Brian Chapman's report on a Middlesex/Yorkshire cricket match should suffice to set the standards of sports erudition:

> A match that had for two days dragged its leaden feet rose in the end to heights of drama. Reluctant heroes on both sides buckled on Homeric armour. The lotus-eaters, in Tennysonian idiom, rose from their soporific banks of Amaranth and gave battle.[133]

On American shores, no one epitomized the erudite announcer quite like Howard Cosell (primarily active from 1953 to 1985). A polarizing figure among fans and athletes even in his prime, Cosell was renowned for his lilting, staccato delivery and oddly Shakespearean diction. As he saw (and said) it, every sporting event was a grand event of cosmic importance, every action on the field, in the ring, or around the track a moment of physical poetry. For Cosell, "Sports is human life in microcosm." Setting himself in sometimes-aggressive opposition to the then-current "jockocracy"—especially former athletes promoted to announcing positions regardless of their intellectual or verbal skills—Cosell championed a new intellectualism among American sports broadcasters. Opinionated, learned, and idiosyncratic, Cosell became the model that many

---

*Yep: he calls football "soccer" but spells "decentered" like he's Derrida. Go figure.

[133] Brian Chapman, *Guardian* (quoted in *Private Eye*, 14 August 1970, 4), as quoted in Larsen (2008, 153). It's called "embedding," kids—look it up!

announcers—for a time in the seventies and eighties, at least—followed. Through such learned (some would say "highfalutin" or "needlessly pompous") diction, physical action became grand theatre.

Yet while the Hopcrafts, Gibsons, Chapmans, and Cosells of the world danced the rim of excessive "euphuistic pretentiousness," the final test limit of intellectually verbose sportscasting—epitomized by Idle's Brian—may have finally appeared in the real world in the guise of a stand-up comic turned sportscaster: Dennis Miller. Miller—an *SNL* alumnus who delivered "fake news" with a laconic wit, who often combined strings of comically obscure referents, and who rattled out metaphor-laden rants like nobody's business—served as the color commentator for *Monday Night Football* on ABC in 2000. The results were, as far as user-friendly sportscasting goes, disastrous. His literary, pop-culture, and political allusions often ran three and four deep, and by the time a viewer lined up Miller's point the relevant play had been long blown dead. Witnessing a personal foul, Miller noted, "That hit was later than Godot"; on the retirement of a player after "twenty-eight [knee] operations," he opined, "Trust me, Captain Ahab had a better right knee than this guy." The list—like Miller's stand-up rants—is long and educational.[134]

Ultimately, Miller was replaced in 2002 by retired player and coach John Madden, a man known for his enthusiasm, not his erudition (sample Madden on-mike insight: "If this team doesn't put points on the board I don't see how they can win"). Eight years later, TV Guide Network declared Miller's brief run on *MNF* one of their "25 Biggest TV Blunders." As Miller might say, "That hit was later than Godot."

In short, the Pythons do not always need to invent wild mash-ups in order to upset their audience's expectations (à la the bloody violence of Peckinpah overlaid upon the idyll of a British picnic or the incongruity of the artist Picasso participating in a bicycling race). In the case of sports commentary, their focal point (the overintellectualizing of sport) is a

---

[134] For an entertaining and informative parsing of his many in-booth bon mots, see "The Annotated Dennis Miller Archive" at ESPN online. http://espn.go.com/abcsports/mnf/s/annotatedmiller/archive.html.

sometimes-common practice in the "real" (non-Python) world, one that we as consumers generally accept . . . up to a point. The Pythons simply explore the point up to which we accept such intellectualizing and the point at which we cry foul.

Our often-fanatical investment in sport is rarely without intellectual content—sports fandom is populated by analysts and fans who memorize long lists of statistics, have deep understanding of the rules (and exceptions) of the game, and who voice passionate theories regarding the play on the field. And there are likewise sundry athletes who share their fans' intellectual passion, who are the "brains on the pitch." But there are also—and these cases form the popular stereotype capitalized upon by Cleese in the "Literary Football" sketch—those athletes who embody the "physical" in our culturally perceived "body/ intellect" dichotomy: those who play without thought, those who simply "hit the ball first time."

The separation of the body from the intellect is not, of course, an exclusively sports-related ideology. It is instead a long-held—indeed Classical— philosophical conceit, embraced by many Western theologians, that posits a split between human intellect (spirit) and human corporeality (the flesh). For some, this dichotomy reflects the divide between god and man, between immortal and mortal, between human mores and animal urges. On the positive side, a belief in such a dichotomy gives humans a happy excuse for our failings; as many an armchair theologian has said after breaking a New Year's resolution: "The spirit is willing, but the flesh is weak." On the negative side, such belief can give rise to practices like scourging, corporeal mortification, and the cilice.* Yet however one personally leans, the intellectual/physical divide expressed in "Literary Football Discussion" is not a divide found only in sport but a part of Western culture in general. Nevertheless it informs a fairly stereotypical understanding of sports figures on both sides of the Big Pond.

For what is quite likely the most erudite on-screen examination of the split between intellect and physicality in sports, we might fruitfully

---

*Unless you're into such things, or you're Dan Brown, in which case: win-win!

turn to the Kevin Costner/Tim Robbins/Susan Sarandon film, *Bull Durham* (1988). Named the "Greatest Sports Movie of All Time" by *Sports Illustrated* in 2003,* *Bull Durham* presents the clash of athlete brains versus athlete brawns (both on the field and off), within the milieu of American baseball. On the one hand (or lobe), we have the intellectual (and incidentally philosophically and poetically well-read) catcher "Crash" Davis, who is the brains on the field; on the other, we have the naïve pitcher Ebby Calvin "Nuke" LaLoosh (a comic-book-reading bumpkin, appropriately nicknamed Meat). Between the two lies (ahem!) Annie Savoy, their common love interest. By the end of the film, the intellectual catcher quietly amasses a minor-league record of his own (and wins the girl), while the physically talented pitcher captures headlines and attention, ultimately making it to "the Big Show"—the American major leagues. As a tag line from the movie neatly summates: "It's all about sex and sport. What else is there?"

In *Bull Durham,* as in the "Literary Football Discussion," the importance of adroit interview skills is examined, and while the results are the same (athletes who offer seemingly unintelligent responses), the achievement of such responses varies greatly. While Jimmy Buzzard manages to naturally convey almost no intelligent commentary upon the game in his interview with Brian, in *Bull Durham* LaLoosh must actually be taught by the older and wiser Crash to talk to reporters *only* in non-committal platitudes, in empty sports clichés. Among the clichés to be studied and memorized by LaLoosh are:

"We gotta play them one game at a time."
"I'm just happy to be here. Hope I can help the ball club."

---

* *Bull Durham* beat out other sports classics, including *Rocky, Raging Bull*, and *Hoop Dreams*. And in a later turn of events that Terry Jones might appreciate, the Baseball Hall of Fame canceled fifteenth-anniversary celebration of the film because then Hall president (and former Ronald Reagan assistant press secretary) Dale Petroskey took umbrage at the "very public criticism of President [George W.] Bush" voiced by Sarandon and Robbins during the Iraq conflict. See SI.com, "A Load of *Bull*," 09 April 2003, http://sportsillustrated.cnn.com/baseball/news/2003/04/09/hall_bull-durham_ap/.

"I just want to give it my best shot, and the good Lord willing,
   things will work out."

To the intellectual athlete, clichés "are your friends" presumably because they enable you to avoid controversy (as LaLoosh says, "they're
boring"), while to the intellectually challenged athlete, clichés "are your
friends" because they substitute for actual thought (or lack thereof). In
either case—according to the wisdom of *Bull Durham*—the result is that
all athletes intentionally do not *sound* intellectual. Hence the common
stereotype that all athletes are not, in fact, intellectual.

Such clichés are indeed a major part of the industrial sports complex
and—as Crash notes—terribly useful. They fulfill a player's need and a
fan's expectations. It's only when a professional athlete or coach goes
"off script"—that is, deviates from the acceptable list of empty phrases
and clichés—that they make unfortunate and distracting headlines. On
the one hand, if a coach says, "We lost because of [name a player]," it can
lead to locker-room infighting; if a player says, "I'm not getting paid
enough to play any better," it can distract from the team's performance
and decrease fan loyalty. On the other hand, when a coach says, "We play
as a team and we lost as a team," the fan base may not respect his intelligence, but no one is distracted by his comments; when a player says, "I just
hope I can help the ball club," even if the player is amidst a protracted contract renegotiation, no one is distracted by her comments. By playing it
verbally safe, athletes can concentrate—to whatever their innate ability—on the game before them. In short, sports clichés, including the
"dumb athlete" stereotype, create a communally agreed-upon false reality.

Yet for the non-athletes heavily invested in sport, such safe clichés
can be frustrating. In the "Literary Football Discussion" sketch, the divide between intellect and physicality is even starker than in *Bull
Durham*:* Idle's interviewer is all intellect, engaging in excessively prosy
and obtuse language (note the nods to long-winded writers Marcel

---

* The current writers respectfully refuse to comment on an intellectual comparison
between footballers and baseball players. We reached our quota of wedgies in high
school, thank you very much.

Proust and Immanuel Kant in his panegyric) to describe a sport that is succinctly distilled by Cleese's player as hitting the ball into the net.* One character is so excessively cerebral that his words amount to nothing; the other is so excessively vapid that his responses add nothing to the conversation. The divide between the two is so wide that communication simply fails and—as is the case with many *Flying Circus* sketches— the interview is abruptly ended via a quick cut to the next sketch. One imagines many a coach and player looking on in envy from the sidelines.

PHILOSOPHY ON THE FIELD
"Well there may be no score, but there's certainly no lack of excitement here."

In terms of football, the "Philosophers Football Match" is as boring as watching paint dry (although most likely a real philosopher would derive some enjoyment from watching paint dry). The game's usual smorgasbord of overt athleticism, as enacted in the second of the two German Python "episodes" (*Monty Python's Fliegender Zirkus*)†, is completely devoid of even the midfield action that European football fans so delight in watching. The philosophers stroll up and down the pitch, they idly gesticulate into the air, they think deep thoughts, and finally, at the very end of the game, they actually score a goal. Essentially, this is a distillation (almost forty years early!) of how Simpson-era Americans perceive the game of football. Most Americans look at sport as something that not only is constantly exciting (baseball and golf being obvious exceptions) but usually involves feats of individual heroism and breathtaking feats of athleticism on a regular basis. To the British, and to most of the rest of

---

* Or, as the coach of the Durham Bulls notes regarding baseball: "This is a very simple game. You throw the ball, you catch the ball, you hit the ball. Sometimes you win, sometimes you lose, sometimes it rains." Think about that for a while.
† The sketch was performed as well in *Live at the Hollywood Bowl*.

the world, sport is more intellectual, involving team efforts and almost intuitive knowledge of where the ball will be in the near future. The "Philosophers Football Match" epitomizes the *idea* of football, because while it does have its one moment of individual achievement, it also involves long stretches amidfield, where the "ball" is worked back and forth.

In a game where Greek philosophers play against German philosophers, it is tempting to think of how football works as philosophy, about how deeply refined the game is, and how football "explains the world." But, in the most important ways, it explains nothing. The philosophers are not playing football well (or at all), because "for eighty-nine minutes the players wander around too lost in thought to actually kick the ball." Until, that is, Archimedes has his "Eureka!" moment. To Terry Jones, football is not philosophical at all. To him, the parody works because of the lack of action; football, as it turns out, is a game of continuous action and almost instinctual, rather than intellectual, effort. "The clash of opposites is the whole point," according to Jones. "You can't think about football too much, you just have to do it" (Baggini 2010). This apparent truth is essentially lost on the philosophers up until the very end of the game. It is unclear as to whether this is a better parody of sport or philosophy.

WRASSLING WITH GOD
"Is God really real, or is there some doubt?"

Python also attached philosophical and theological questions to other sports as well as to football. In the world of Python, matters of belief are not the fodder for extended intellectual debates but instead matters of brute force. The sketch "The Epilogue: A Question of Belief" (ep. 2) begins, as many intellectual debate shows do (or did, sigh. Remember the good old days?), with an introduction of the scholars and a brief presentation of their credentials. Idle, as the interviewer, starts by saying:

Good evening, and welcome once again to the Epilogue. On the programme this evening we have Monsignor Edward Gay, visiting Pastoral Emissary of the Somerset Theological College and author of a number of books about belief, the most recent of which is the best seller *My God*. And opposite him we have Dr. Tom Jack: humanist, broadcaster, lecturer and author of the book *Hello Sailor*.

This is a fairly standard introduction to a program where serious topics are presented and debated. However, as Idle's announcer continues, "Tonight, instead of discussing the existence or non-existence of God, they have decided to fight for it. The existence, or non-existence, to be determined by two falls, two submissions, or a knockout."

At this point, Jack and Gay move into a literal wrestling ring, where real wrestlers then indulge in actual (as opposed to WWE) wrestling moves, albeit for higher stakes than the usual gold lamé belt. The commentator breathlessly relates that

Dr. Jack's got a flying mare there. A flying mare there, and this is going to be a full body slam. A full body slam, and he's laying it in there, and he's standing back. Well ... there we are leaving the Epilogue for the moment; we'll be bringing you the result of this discussion later on in the program.

Ultimately, the Lord ends up reaffirming his existence via "two falls to a submission." The juxtaposition of literal wrestling instead of intellectual wrestling reaffirms Python's ability to take an idea to its ridiculous and natural extreme. Why argue when you can wrestle? In the end, which one is more convincing, might or right? Famous scholars literally roll up their sleeves and, in actual instead of intellectual conflict, illustrate the distance we instinctively apply to the physical and the mental.

The German episodes of *MPFC* were a chance for Python to experiment outside the parameters of the BBC's almost constant complaints about minor details.* The disputes over on-air language—what could and could not be said—were exasperating for the Pythons, whose best efforts at breaking new ground could be reined in by the BBC. Sometimes this was because the censors got the hidden meaning buried in a joke, most often because they didn't.

In the "Colin 'Bomber' Harris" sketch, Chapman plays a wrestler who, due to the archaic rules of wrestling, finds that his next challenger is . . . himself! While normal people would ask what kind of bureaucratic foul-up had led to this (mis)match, Harris—who is, after all, a Python creation—accepts his lot in life. Much like the terminally frustrated Vladimir and Estragon in Beckett's *Waiting for Godot*, Harris realizes that he cannot escape his fate. He must fight himself, much as we all engage in internal struggle. However, Harris is also engaged in external struggle, and his battle against himself is quite violent. At one point he attempts to cheat by biting his own leg, but the referee sees this and issues him a warning. After several more strenuous acrobatic moves, Harris manages to knock himself out. The referee counts him out, declares him the winner, and announces that he will now be going on to face yet another challenger in the finals: Colin "Bomber" Harris.

It is tempting to read this sketch as not just an existential parable of man's never-ending inner struggle or psychomachia, especially with Chapman as the protagonist. While Chapman was struggling with alcoholism at the time the sketch was filmed, there is no clear indication that this is meant to represent Chapman's own struggles. Rather, it may well be that as a rugby player and mountain climber he was simply the most limber of the Pythons. He later went on to perform the sketch in the *Live at the Hollywood Bowl* concert film, and the act was also a staple of his college campus tours towards the end of his life.† As in all Python representations of sport, the existential struggle is always profoundly silly.

---

* Another reason this sketch was in the German series is that it is largely mimed, with an announcer's voice-over. A much easier presentation than trying another sketch in broken German.

† One of the writers did get a chance to see it on that tour. It was a grand occasion, but Cogan still lost money putting twenty bucks on Colin "Bomber" Harris!

LOVE?

". . . this gentleman is interested in the 'India Overland'—and nothing else."

Love is, of course, a sport and Python reveals ways in which love, like cricket and football, is just as silly as any other kind of organized game. In the "Nudge Nudge" sketch (ep. 3) for instance, one of the things Norman (Idle) asks the squire is if Jones' wife is a "sport"; Jones responds that indeed, she does like sports and, "She's very fond of cricket as a matter of fact."* Just as cricket and football have rules and standards that, when devoid of context, make no real sense, so do relationships.

In "The Visitors" sketch (ep. 9), Victor (Chapman) has invited Iris (Carol Cleveland) over for a quiet romantic evening at his home, one that he seems to have planned out for quite some time, when they are interrupted by an unexpected guest. As Python demonstrates elsewhere, social mores are more important than dating rituals. Even though Idle's character Arthur (who looks to be the same character from "Nudge Nudge," only with an air of arrogance that only the nouveau riche possess) had not been invited, but he has nonetheless shown up, due to the fact that down at the pub—three years ago!—Victor had causally remarked that "we must have a drink together sometime." There is some logic in this case of Arthur dropping by. Victor's original invitation was incredibly ambiguous and "sometime" could indicate that any evening was therefore acceptable. However, in most cases, invitations of this sort are not meant to be ambivalent but are social indicators of companionship lubricated by alcohol. The invitation was simply polite and would very likely have not been made under other circumstances, but in this case Arthur has taken the suggestion literally and therefore has shown up, wrecking the quiet evening alone.

Of course, in a world where any bad situation can go downhill with absurd speed, Arthur has not come alone. Arthur has "taken the liberty" of inviting several wildly objectionable friends over who will fur-

---

*Say no more!

"Say, is it my imagination or is it getting crowded in here?"
The Marx Brothers (and sundry) engage in vaudeville slapstick upon the ocean in
A Night at the Opera.

ther disrupt the equilibrium of the situation. First to arrive are the
brutish Brian Equator (Cleese), who grabs at Carol Cleveland's cleavage,*
and his wife (Pepperpot Jones) who, while laughing uproariously "wets"
herself. They have in turn invited Mr. Freight (Gilliam), as a costumed and
extravagant "great poof," followed by what looks like the return of Ken
Shabby (Palin, here called Mr. Cook), complete with a very un-house-
trained goat. When Victor quite naturally tries to show them the door,
Equator responds by shooting him dead and they go into a rousing
chorus of "Ding Dong Merrily on High."

This is not just a typical Python sketch where excess breeds more
excess and silliness begets more silliness. While there are precedents for

---

* Say that ten times fast. Go ahead, we'll wait.

this type of additive absurdity—the increasingly crammed ocean liner stateroom scene in the Marx Brothers' film *A Night at the Opera* is a clear ancestor of the sketch—Python is reaching for something subtler here. Instead of simply demonstrating comic absurdity, they are also looking at the rules and conventions of socialization and dating. By exploiting British class-based ideas of politeness, Python demonstrates that socially constructed rules are just that: rules designed to keep the fabric of shared interactions intact. Of course, Chapman need have not answered the door or he could have forcefully asked Arthur to leave the moment he came in, but this would have both stopped the sketch cold and also demonstrated that rules can be broken. It's simply not done: one must live (or die) by convention.

Likewise in another sketch about love that also demonstrates Python's critiques of film and television, Bevis (Jones) and Dora (Cleveland) play lovers about to consummate their passion ("Newsreader Arrested," ep. 5). As was customary in Hollywood films for many decades, scenes involving overt sexuality could not be explicitly shown. Instead Hollywood invented the concept of the "ellipsis" where, instead of showing explicit sex, the camera panned to blowing curtains, or waves crashing upon a rocky shore, or, perhaps more daringly, a train going into a tunnel or a smokestack blowing smoke. Python ups the ante by showing a montage of sexually connotative images including (as the script puts it)

> *collapsing factory chimney in reverse motion; pan up tall soaring poplars in the wind; waves crashing; fish in shallow water; fountains; exploding fireworks; volcano erupting with lava; rocket taking off; express train going into a tunnel; dam bursting; battleship broadside; lion leaping through flaming hoop; Richard Nixon smiling; milking a cow; planes refuelling in mid-air; Women's Institute applauding*

and then, with passions presumably sated, "*tossing the caber; plane falling in flames; tree crashing to the ground; the lead shot tower collapsing.*" We then return to the bed, where we see that a frustrated Cleveland is pouting about being ignored, while Jones has literally been showing film clips—the *assumed* ellipsis—the entire time. The "explicit" juxtaposition of sexual activity, along with the images that had previously been substituted for sex, is a demonstration of not only how we give symbolic meaning to unrelated phallic and yonic imagery but also the ways in which the conventions of film and television have become so codified that we understand the visual shorthand without being prompted. Naturally though, in the world of Python, we are asked to read such images literally. Yes: even images of Tricky Dick Nixon.

THE MEANING OF LIFE AGAIN
(Sex, Sport, and Death in a Nutshell)
"Why are we here? What's life all about?"

In the grand panorama that is *The Meaning of Life* (1983), sport is sandwiched between sex and war, between what some would call love and violence, or what the more classically minded poets would have anthropomorphized as Venus and Mars.

Considering some of the more risqué themes and performances the Pythons and their British contemporaries (like the bawdy Benny Hill) had previously explored, the direct discussion of sex in *Meaning of Life* begins in the least titillating setting possible: the classroom of a rather posh-looking English boarding school. Sadly, bam-chicka-wa-wa music doesn't suddenly well up as the tight-bloused substitute teacher, Miss Behaven, enters the classroom sucking a cherry lollypop and looking demurely over her reading glasses; clad in a short, plaid skirt and knee-high stockings, she drops her books, giggles, and bends invitingly over the desk . . . her pert thighs . . . tumescent . . . er . . . uhm. Well.

No. Rather, the paunchy Headmaster, Humphrey Williams (Cleese), enters and, in a rather distracted fashion, asks the disengaged students, "Did we cover foreplay? Did I or did I not I do vaginal juices?" While the students in the class (and many are played by the then-thirty-year-old Pythons in schoolboy outfits) are clearly disinterested in the lector's questions, his blunt inquiry regarding sexual taboo terms certainly gets the film viewers' attention. And once the Pythons have your attention, it's just possible you might learn something. Imagine that: learning something in a classroom setting. Will wonders never cease?

And oh! The things that are taught at this school! As the Headmaster continues to drone, in traditional lecture format, he brusquely summates his raison d'être for their daily review: "Foreplay is necessary to cause the vagina to lubricate, which will allow the penis to penetrate more easily." Is this all one should know about foreplay? Surely not! (But—fellahs, take note—it's a start.)

As the boys' oral (ahem) exam continues, they offer myriad "ways to get [the vaginal juices] flowing." Among the many techniques proffered: rubbing the clitoris (not recommended right off the bat, BTW); kissing; sucking the nipple; stroking the thighs; biting the neck; nibbling the ear; kneading the buttocks; and so on and so forth. Wisely, albeit conde-scendingly, the Headmaster concludes the Q-and-A portion of the lec-ture by noting that "there are all these possibilities before we stampede towards the clitoris." For pubescent viewers (and others, alas) in 1983, this was an education in itself,* let alone what follows. . . .

After the chalkboard ingeniously transforms into a four-poster bed, the Headmaster and his wife† disrobe and deliver an unexpectedly prac-tical demonstration of "penetration and coitus, that is to say, inter-course" for the benefit of the class (foreplay being now taken as a given). As the script prompts suggest, the Headmaster's sexual mounting of "his good lady wife" in the front of the room is about as interesting as a lecture on "binomial theorem" to the assembled boys, who engage in the usual bored classroom antics, including passing notes. As Jones notes in the DVD commentary, "You can put anything into a classroom context and it would be boring. It's just the way it's taught." However, by placing a highly atypical mock classroom upon the screen as they do

---

* Granted, all sorts of parental and decency groups did their best to keep the movie, and this knowledge, from the eyes and ears of impressionable teens. Upon release, the film was banned in Ireland and given an 18 rating in England and an R rating in the USA. Very likely these ratings caused an uptick in attendance, but never mind.

† The Headmaster's wife, Mrs. Williams, is played with admirable indifference by Patricia Quinn, who is perhaps better known for her portrayal of the more volatile "Magenta—a domestic" in *The Rocky Horror Picture Show* (1975).

here, the Pythons transform classroom education into something else entirely; as a result, their viewers invariably learn something . . . about foreplay, coitus, the British school system, and the consequences of passing notes in class.

Speaking of notes—he says knowingly, by way of transition—one of the boys, Biggs (Jones), is caught with a passed note and the Headmaster, still "more-or-less erect" and in mid-mount, declares: "I think you'd better be selected to play for the Boys team in the rugby match against the Masters this afternoon!" The film then transitions directly from sex to sport, in what many a schoolboy may recall is an almost absolute inversion of the traditional order of events.

The rugby match—or ruggers—is a horror show, ominously heralded by the opening flourish of Johann Sebastian Bach's Toccata and Fugue in D minor.

The Boys team (all played by truly young boys, not the Pythons in schoolboy attire, as in the classroom scene immediately previous) is literally

FACTOID BOX: Bach's Toccata and Fugue in D Minor

Johann Sebastian Bach (1685–1750) was one of the most highly regarded composers of the Baroque era and composed over one thousand different pieces in the course of his prolific lifetime. Bach's Toccata and Fugue in D minor is perhaps one his best-known compositions, likely because of its use in horror films and most notably in Walt Disney's *Fantasia*. The piece contains a free opening (a toccata) and a reoccurring subject (a fugue). Aaron Copland, writing of Bach's fugues, noted that each theme "mirrors a different world of feeling" (1988, 14). If this is true, then abject creepiness may well be the theme of Toccata and Fugue in D Minor and explains why it was a staple of the early horror genre, appearing in films such as *Dr. Jekyll and Mr. Hyde* (1931), *The Black Cat* (1934), and *The Raven* (1935), as well as *Fantasia* (1940).

outmanned by the Masters squad, who are all played by beefy men in their twenties; no Pythons are on the field. By removing themselves from the casting on the field, the Pythons largely remove the expectation of comedy from the pitch—the violence upon the children in the scene is so over-the-top that it might be considered cartoonish but never funny ha-ha.

Compare, for example, "Derby Council vs. All Blacks Rugby Match" (*FC*, ep. 23), in which the humor of the match derives not from the abuse of children but from the dominant professional New Zealand rugby squad (the All Blacks) ludicrously competing against not only a small-town team but a small town's mayor, mayoress, and clerks (still enrobed, no less). That the All Blacks lose to the Derby Council (and other non-rugby "teams") underscores the humor. *Flying Circus* does not present these victories as underdog tales: it is just a silly premise. Importantly for the comparison at hand, violence is not the focal point of the "All Blacks" sketch, whereas violence is the entirety of the Boys vs. Masters match in *Meaning of Life*.

Ultimately, rugby is not portrayed in *Meaning of Life* as a real sport (see Factoid Box) but as a violent, cruel, and unfair rite of passage suffered by children, mastered by those in the flower of youth, and gleefully celebrated by the mature and elderly. For the boys, it is punishment, not play.

FACTOID BOX: Rugby

Originally a version of football played at English public schools throughout the nineteenth century, early rugby set no limit to the number of players per side, which often yielded anarchic play and unfortunate injury. Current rugby, by comparison, abides by much more stringent rules (although these can vary by league and country) but is still considered by many a rather violent and anarchic sport. Oi oi oi!

RANDOM FACTOID: Rugby union football holds with fifteen players per team, while rugby league football holds with thirteen.

Had the then-thirty-year-old Jones been beaten while wearing knickers, easy slapstick humor might have resulted. Instead, the ensuing "ballet of ruggers"—which focuses on the repeated bludgeoning of children and the entirely unsportsmanlike behavior of the adults present, including the Headmaster tripping a runaway boy and the antic celebration of the elders after the boys' trouncing on the field—shocks but does not amuse; indeed, the violence on the pitch sets up the gravity of the following scene, set in the trenches of World War One.

Needless to say, the field after the rugby match is riddled with the wounded Boys team, which leads—via a direct fade from Biggs as a boy holding his head in horror to Biggs as a "Tommy"* amidst the trenches of the First World War, holding his head in horror.

Many have compared sport to war before: indeed, for the ancient Greeks the Olympics were essentially an "off-season" way of occupying military forces between engagements. Philosopher Thomas Hobbes saw "war" as a natural state of humanity and sport as a sort of mini-war, an outlet necessary for our social survival.† Less optimistically, American President Theodore Roosevelt is quoted as advising: "In life, as in a football game, the principle to follow is: hit the line hard."‡ Far less optimistically, the great dystopian author George Orwell once reputedly wrote: "Serious sport [. . .] is war minus the shooting."

More significantly, perhaps, for the Pythons and their audience, were two modern sports philosophers: the extremely popular Dutch football coach Rinus "The General" Michels (creator of the "total football" system of play) and the American stand-up comedian George Carlin.

Michels famously opined before the Netherlands' 1974 World Cup Final against West Germany: "Voetbal is oorlog!" ("Football is war!") Although, actually, what he said was: "Topvoetbal is zoiets als oorlog. Wie netjes blijft, is verloren" ("Professional football is something like war. Whoever behaves too properly is lost"). Nevertheless, the catchphrase everyone attributed to him in the seventies was "Football is

---

* A British colloquialism equivalent to the American "doughboy" of the same war.
† See Aicinea 2010, 15–25.
‡ *Bartlett's Familiar Quotations*, 17th ed., 615:3

war." Incidentally, Netherlands lost the match—"The Mother of All Defeats"—to Germany, 2–1. For a group of comedians steeped in English and European football lore, Michels' observation may have resonated as they contemplated the role of rugby in *The Meaning of Life.**

Simultaneously, albeit on a very different front, American comedian George Carlin once compared—in rather impressive detail—(American) football and baseball to war and peace.† A born cultural anthropologist, Carlin noted: "Baseball and football are the two most popular spectator sports in this country [USA]. And as such, it seems they ought to be able to tell us something about ourselves and our values." In particular, Carlin observed that

> ... the objectives of the two games are completely different: In football the object is for the quarterback, also known as the field general, to be on target with his aerial assault, riddling the defense by hitting his receivers with deadly accuracy in spite of the blitz, even if he has to use the shotgun. With short bullet passes and long bombs, he marches his troops into enemy territory, balancing this aerial assault with a sustained ground attack that punches holes in the forward wall of the enemy's defensive line.
>
> In baseball, the object is to go home! And to be safe!—I hope I'll be safe at home!

Like American football for Carlin and European football for Michels, British rugby resonates for the Pythons as a stand-in for real war; however, the Pythons add the unexpected observation that scholastic rugby has no decorum while (for stereotypical Brits, at least) war has far too much. And speaking of war ...

---

* Sepp Herberger, the famous German football player, was also reported to have said, "The ball is round, the game lasts ninety minutes, anything else is pure theory."
† The first recorded version of the "Baseball and Football" skit is on Carlin's album *An Evening with Wally Londo* (1975). The more elaborate routine cited here is from his book *Brain Droppings* (1997, 51–52). Carlin performed yet another version of this routine as part of the opening monologue for the very first episode of *Saturday Night Live* (October 11, 1975) as well. The Pythons were likely aware of it, and Carlin, in any case.

FACTOID BOX: CORPSING

Idle "enjoys" a particularly prolonged death scene, and as Jones points out in the commentary, "Idle is corpsing throughout." Corpsing (also known as "breaking") is a type of "dying" onstage—when one starts to laugh uncontrollably, even if one's character is supposed to be serious or, in this case, dead. For Americans of a certain age, Harvey Korman (on the old *Carol Burnett* show) could be relied on to "corpse" at least once an episode, thanks largely to the antics of Tim Conway. Horatio Sanz managed to corpse quite a bit on *SNL* during his tenure there. Idle opts to hide his laughter (with limited success) in a terrible rictus grin, thus corpsing comically.

As Biggs is about to embark on a heroic/suicidal raid against an enemy gunpost, those serving under Biggs try—while still entrenched and under heavy German fire—to present their captain with some tokens of their appreciation: "a handsome ormulu clock" encased in fragile glass, a short grandfather clock, a wristwatch, a card, a cheque, a cake, and so forth. As their heartfelt but ill-timed presentation goes on, so does the death and carnage, as soldier after soldier dies on-screen.

The decorous behavior under duress, the bonding of soldiery, the self-sacrificial hero: all are tropes that parody every British "stiff upper lip" war film ever shot; think Alec Guinness in *The Bridge on the River Kwai* (1957)* or Michael Caine in *Zulu* (1964), the latter of which is subsequently

---

* Interesting factoid: the Pythons' much-revered Goons spoofed the film in their radio show "An African Incident" (1957) and again on the LP *Bridge on the River Wye* (1962). Source: thegoonshow.net. The Pythons themselves riff on the film in their "Scott of the Sahara" sketch (ep. 23), renaming it alongside other not-so-exotic films including *Lawrence of Glamorgan, Bridge over the River Kent, The Mad Woman of Biggleswade,* and *Krakatoa, East of Leamington.* For the non-Brits, all the place-names are indigenous to England (replacing the more exotic Arabia, Kwai, Chaillot, and Java, respectively). The titles parodied all belonged to films of the fifties and sixties.

directly parodied by the Pythons in scene 29, wherein[*] one officer (Cleese) continues shaving, unperturbed, as hand-to-hand combat ensues around him and another (Idle) sits nonplussed in bed despite having somehow lost an entire leg during the night. As these scenes suggest, war may be hell, but that's no reason not to be civilized about it.

Ultimately, war, as presented in *Meaning of Life*, is more civilized than rugby, which is at least more interesting than sex. Sport thus holds a particular place in this version of the Python-verse, wedged tightly between sex and violence. It's possibly the most accurate description of sport in human history.

CRICKET: A FINAL NOTE

"But for all the mumbo jumbo and superstition, the batsmen of the Kalahari are formidable fighters."

A problem with analyzing the sports in Monty Python, for a pair of Americans at least, is precisely how very *British* their sketches on sports are. Because there was no need to appeal to an American audience during the production of the original series, they stuck to sports that would be familiar to Europeans and hence looked at sport more in terms of the rituals and media coverage involved, as opposed to American notions (see Ken Burns for this argument) about any specific sport "being a national pastime." According to Michael Palin, John Cleese once joked about Americans and sports, noting that Americans are unable to appreciate "cricket, or any sport not directly based on greed" (Palin 2006, 552). Cleese's rants on Herman Vaske's *The Art of Football from A to Z* are likewise educational, if humbling.

The difference between American sports and British sport is that British sport—like the empire—can seem to go on forever. American sports are to some extent about individual achievement, about stars and

---

[*]As the shooting script prompts: "RORKE'S DRIFT DAY LOCATION; CUT TO the thick of battle. A Zulu attack on British Army encampment circa 1890. (We could even buy it from *Zulu* maybe.)"

superstars and agents working back rooms for maximum exposure and money.* In American sports, the audience is presumably waiting with bated breath for a superstar to hit a home run or score a goal or touchdown, to perform an act of individual talent and expertise. British sports are more communal; again, British football is about the midfield action. Americans want high-scoring games and glory and the British like a 1–0 game; this is much like philosophy, which is why the Greeks are able to come up with the idea of kicking the ball into the back of the net. Cricket is much, much, much longer than football. Matches literally go on for days at a time. There is no sudden rush of adrenaline in cricket. The match has to be watched carefully. The action is dynamic but subtle. Err. Okay . . . fine. We have a confession to make: despite the two of us having watched every Monty Python episode over and over again for decades . . . we still have no real idea how cricket works. We believe that there is no easy explanation or Proustian summary possible. Cricket is cricket is cricket.

---

*For a fine fictionalized version of this truth, see *Moneyball*.

GILLIAM: THE ACTOR

Believe it or not, one of Terry Gilliam's strengths is as an actor. And for those of you who were children of the eighties, we are not referring to his cameo in *Spies like Us* (although there was a pretty cool Bob Hope cameo in the same bad film). Instead we think that Gilliam should be lauded for the small but pivotal roles he played on-screen and -stage in the Python-verse.

Although he would never become a "lead" actor like Chapman or Cleese, Gilliam—although at first reluctant to appear on camera at all (and normally too busy working on the animations to leave his lonely garret)—grew to be a fine character actor. Even though he was not always listed as performer or writer (especially in the first season of *Flying Circus*), some of his acting roles have become major contributions to the Python canon. If the Python habit of cross-dressing and overt caricature was intended to point out the grotesque extremes of humanity, Gilliam *started* at grotesque and worked his way up from there.

His naturally rubbery and eminently pliable face also led to increasingly escalating humor in characters such as Cardinal Fang (who nods menacingly) in the "Spanish Inquisition" sketch (ep. 15) and the bean-encrusted, couch-bound Kevin Garibaldi, described in the script as "too fat and flatulent to get up," in the "Most Awful Family in Britain" sketch (ep. 45). While Gilliam's only lines in this last sketch are desperate primal screams for "more beans," his caricature would become an increasingly familiar sight in both Britain and America in the following decades; the ubiquitous, morbidly obese, family member still rings true today. On the big screen, his roles in *Holy Grail* alone, as the cackling Bridgekeeper, filthy steed/page Patsy, and dead Animator, are marvels of character acting. He may have had relatively few lines, but his twisted, often-muck-encrusted form not only effectively portrayed the time period of *Holy Grail*; it also reflected his ability to *inhabit* the roles he took, no matter how much suffering (or beans) was involved.

In addition to his physical traits, Gilliam was also brilliant at conveying that most common of American workplace traits: smarm. In the "Twentieth Century Vole"/"Splunge" sketch (ep. 6), his one-line, playing against Graham Chapman's exceedingly dim film producer Larry Saltzberg, practically oozes smarm and obsequiousness. His writer character manages to outdo all of the others in his over-the-top praise for Saltzberg's nonsensical movie idea, stating, "Sir, I don't know how to say this, but I got to be perfectly frank. I really and truly believe this story of yours is the greatest story in motion-picture history." He is then sent from the room (as Saltzberg cannot stand a "yes-man").

Gilliam managed a similar style in several smaller appearances, including one notable metamoment where he announces that "this is my only line" (a telegraph joke often reserved for Glamour Stooges, of which he was certainly *not* a member).* His most naturally comfortable role may have been as one of the "guests from America" (Mr. Howard Katzenberg, from Philadelphia) in the death scene in *The Meaning of Life*, who insists upon looking at Death's arrival as a "potentially positive learning experience" before being told to shut up by Death itself.

And speaking of death . . . no one dies like—or as often as—Gilliam. Gilliam dies thrice in *Holy Grail* (as the Bridgekeeper, Bors, and himself), is disemboweled and poisoned in *Meaning of Life*, and is crucified in *Life of Brian*. And not once does he corpse. That's talent.

---

* A Pepperpot, surely, and whatever m'lady Joeline is intended to portray, yes, but never a Glamour Stooge.

"And now for something completely different . . ."

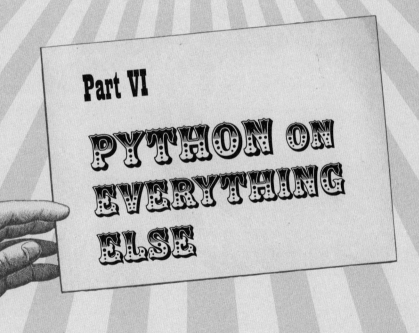

Part VI

PYTHON ON EVERYTHING ELSE

TAG UNDER: Spotting trees, foreigners, women, the meaning of life, death, transvestites, Sam Peckinpah, religion, televisuality, effective camouflage (you won't find it, it's hidden far too well), film, the French, mimes (aka the French), SPAM and, of course, fish-slapping.

This chapter analyzes the surrealistic and often-haphazard side of Python, their debt to Dada and other art movements, and the historical likelihood of Knights Who Say Ni! (highly likely). You might suppose that this section is essentially the rubbish bin wherein we put things that do not quite fit neatly into common schema, but look at it this way: have you seen Part V? It's nice pristine land, unsullied, beautiful, you could build a council estate there, or some kind of geodesic dome had you the mind. Do you really want to dirty that chapter with mime? So let's just say that Python is so chock-full of—shall we use an academic term here, okay?—well, *stuff* that it had to go somewhere, and here it is at last! Please feel free to browse this part in any order, whether it be alphabetical, numerical (good luck with that choice!), or chronological.

SPOTTING TREES
"The Larch. The Larch."

As with a great many British men of a certain age, the members of Python were certainly familiar with "spotting." Many British citizens, going far beyond the usual eccentricities of American bird spotters (definition: Americans who have far too much time on their hands and who have had their gun licenses revoked), actually take their obsession even further, as is seen in the grand old British traditions of trainspotting and planespotting. There are some obvious connections to both. After Python, Michael Palin starred in a variety of television specials about travel (including a reimagination of *Around the World in 80 Days,* where Palin attempted to re-enact the book's journey using Phileas Fogg's original—albeit fictional—locomotive methods) and also did two different "Great Railway Journeys" specials, including "Confessions of a Trainspotter" in 1980 and "Derry to Kerry" in 1994. Bird spotting can also be spotten in the "Book Store" skit available on *Monty Python's Contractual Obligation Album,* where one of the many non-existent books the customer is looking for is *Olsen's Standard Book of British Birds,* a key tome for any astute British birder. However, as this is Python, we learn soon that the (illiterate) customer wants the expurgated version, or the one without the gannet as it "wets its nest."

A similar Python obsessive was Mr. Spotworth (Idle), the camel spotter from episode 7. As a reporter (Cleese) interviews him, Mr. Spotworth reveals himself to be a particularly inept camel spotter. He has been waiting in the same location for three—no, five—years, and has seen "Nearly, ooh, nearly one." Before that, he had been a Yeti spotter. When asked to describe that experience, he relates that it was ". . . extremely interesting, very, very—quite . . . it was dull; dull, dull, dull, oh God, it was dull. Sitting in the Waterloo waiting room. Course once you've seen one Yeti you've seen them all." When pressed further by the reporter (who was clued in by the "Waterloo Station" mention, as well as Idle's assertion that camels have a number "on the side of the engine above the piston box") to admit that he is merely a trainspotter (a fairly typical British eccentric), he replies, "Oh, you're no fun anymore," the start of a catchphrase gag that continues throughout the episode. Such British eccentrics are, if Python can be believed, quite typical of the species. As Christopher Hitchens observed about England, "the entire place has something batty, squiffy, potty and loopy about it" (2008). Indeed, Hitchens' article in *Vanity Fair* contains a particularly good portrait of Gavin Pretor-Petty, founder of the British Cloud Appreciation Society—living proof positive of Python's astute portraiture.

Underscoring the "Camel Spotting" skit is an obsession with obsessions and pathology. Many of the Cleese/Chapman sketches are obsessed with wordplay or endless variations on a theme such as in the "Cheese Shop" sketch, where, in particular, Cleese names over forty-three different kinds of cheese (Cleese's original family name actually was Cheese, until his father wisely changed it), all in a rather futile gesture towards obtaining fromage from a shop that is completely bereft of dairy products. However, the sketch is not just about the futility that bureaucracy inevitably foments or linguistic futility in general, but also about the way in which people become obsessed with a concept, desire, or object. In this case, the cheese is a metaphor for control and Cleese is not merely an expert on cheeses but also a completist.

Eric Idle was also a keen critic of national obsessions and his knack for wordplay is evident in sketches such as "Me Doctor" (ep. 13), and Palin also got into the act with his "Déjà Vu" sketch (ep. 14). But perhaps Python's most maddening example of wordplay is the famous composer Johann Gambolputty de von Ausfern-schplenden-schlitter-crasscrenbon-fried-digger-dingle-dangle-dongle-dungle-burstein-von-knacker-thrasher-apple-banger-horowitz-ticolensic-grander-knotty-spelltinkle-grandlich-grumblemeyer-spelterwasser-kurstlich-himbleeisen-bahnwagen-gutenabend-bitte-ein-nürnburger-bratwustle-gerspurten-mitz-weimache-luber-hundsfut-gumberaber-shönedanker-kalbsfleisch-mittler-aucher von Hautkopft of Ulm. The name is repeated a full five times by characters in the "It's the Arts" sketch, as well as one shared recitation by a Viking, a knight in armor, and various animated characters including a pig, the *Mona Lisa*, and others later in the episode. Illogical excess (see also the Factoid Box on Surrealism) is a key to understanding the uniquely British eccentricity that the Pythons parodied oh so well, because it was a defining trait in their own lives.

SPAM
"Bloody Vikings!"

SPAM is a canned lunch meat created by the Hormel Corporation in 1937, the name coming from an amalgamation of the words "spiced" and "ham." After World War II, it caught on as a staple in places across the world where fresh meat was scarce, particularly in the Pacific Rim; it remains a particular favorite in Hawaii today, where over 6.7 cans are consumed (per capita) very year. Hawaiians seem to follow the lead of the Python Vikings in simply not having enough SPAM, and to this day "Spam is still daily fare in Hawaii, a must-have on any self-respecting breakfast menu, including at McDonald's, and a staple of community cookbooks" ("Spam That Isn't" 2003). So, there does seem some truth to Python's assertion that there are communities or cultures that favor SPAM over other kinds of meat products. It is unclear how many modern Vikings eat SPAM; an article on a typical Norwegian contemporary meal makes no mention of SPAM, whether with eggs, sausage, or even more SPAM (Saglimbene 2011).

SPAM is vacuum sealed in a can, where it is cooked for three hours and guaranteed fresh for years to come, leading many to believe that this would make the perfect food in case of an apocalyptic emergency, although as Patrick Di Justo notes, Hormel concedes that the "flavor may change after three or more years on the shelf" (2012, 40). SPAM also includes modified potato starch (as a preservative), sodium nitrate (to stave off botulism and add that oh-so-lovely pink color), sugar for flavor, and, in the new bacon version, "the cured belly of a swine carcass" (Di Justo 2012, 40). If this is beginning to sound a bit like Python's riff on the Whizzo Chocolate Company (ep. 6) and their many suspect confections—such as "ram's bladder cup," "cockroach cluster," and "anthrax ripple"—it is probably best not to examine too closely the ingredients of any food source.

Hormel's new SPAM with Bacon (introduced to quivering tastebuds in 2004) nears Pythonesque levels of absurdity itself. As the Hormel Web site hubristically claims:

Perfection, by definition, cannot be improved upon. This SPAM® variety is the exception. We married the timeless taste of SPAM® Classic with the irresistible flavor of bacon. It's swine on swine, and that's a scrumptious thing. Try it once and breakfast will never be the same.

Neither, we suspect, will our GI tracts. The baconic SPAM label calls itself "pork with ham," which sounds a bit redundant, really, since "ham is the hind leg of a pig that's been preserved, colored and flavored through a process known as curing" (Di Justo 2012, 40) and "pork" is generally considered any meat from a domesticated pig. "Swine on swine" action indeed.

In the SPAM sketch in episode 25, Mr. and Mrs. Bun (Idle and Chapman) enter a café incongruously filled with Vikings and try to order breakfast. To the amusement of Mr. Bun and the horror of Mrs. Bun ("I don't like SPAM!") all of the meals on the menu contain SPAM, some more than others.* The sketch reflects the relative popularity of SPAM in England at the time and is also a particularly silly Python sketch that reveals nothing more than the futility of trying to order outside the parameters of any menu. One just does not do such things. Even when Mr. Bun offers to eat Mrs. Bun's SPAM (and then announces that he will be ordering ". . . SPAM, SPAM, SPAM, SPAM, SPAM . . . baked beans, SPAM, SPAM, and SPAM!") there is still no solution, nor, as usual, any linear conclusion to the sketch. Instead, the Hungarian with the bad phrase book (Cleese) returns, only to be once again hustled off by the police before, in a typical Python comment on the impermanence of televisual events, the scene moves to a historian (Palin) talking about a great Viking victory. However, the recitation of history soon directs us back to the café, as the historian continues that "once in Bomely they assembled in the Green Midget café and SPAM selecting a SPAM particular SPAM item from the SPAM menu would SPAM, SPAM, SPAM, SPAM, SPAM" before the Vikings once again take up the "SPAM" chant and Mr. and Mrs. Bun float off into the air. As usual, the linear nature of the sketch is disrupted as we move back and forth across mediums, away from the obviously staged environment of the sketch, to the presumably historical

---

*The menu includes "egg and bacon; egg, sausage, and bacon; egg and SPAM; egg, bacon, and SPAM; egg, bacon, sausage, and SPAM; SPAM, bacon, sausage, and SPAM; SPAM, egg, SPAM, SPAM, bacon, and SPAM; SPAM, SPAM, SPAM, egg, and SPAM; SPAM, SPAM, SPAM, SPAM, SPAM, SPAM, baked beans, SPAM, SPAM, SPAM, and SPAM; or lobster thermidor *aux crevettes,* with a Mornay sauce garnished with truffle pâté, brandy, and a fried egg on top and SPAM."

"I'm having SPAM, SPAM, SPAM, SPAM, SPAM ... baked beans, SPAM, SPAM, and SPAM."
Chapman and Idle order breakfast from Jones among the Vikings in *Monty Python's Flying Circus.*

veracity of the historian, back again to the original sketch, where even the usual semi-linearity of a Python sketch is ended abruptly, by a fade to black and the credits.

While SPAM has been around since the 1930s (perhaps even that can in the back of your cupboard, eh? Alongside that Twinkie you're saving for the zombie apocalypse?), for many years it lost brand share due to movements away from canned and processed meats in many parts of the world. But while Python may have skewered SPAM in the seventies, the hit musical *Spamalot* afforded the Hormel company some welcome (it seems) free publicity, bringing the canned food back to the public's increasingly self-ironic eye. Hormel even agreed to make a special "SPAM Golden Honey Grail wicked-awesome *Spamalot*" variant of SPAM (with an additional ingredient of "honey granules") to be sold as a souvenir at the musical.* And in 2012, as part of SPAM's 75th Anniversary Celebration,† Hormel introduced its first ever "spokes-character": Sir Can-a-lot, a mascot clearly capitalizing upon their association with the Broadway show's Arthurian thematic. In short, Python's long-running relationship with SPAM serves as a reminder of their wide—and rather varied—influence on the world.

ETHNOCENTRISM (i.e., Lousy Foreigners!)
"Romani ite domum!"

The cast of Monty Python were (and still are) of largely Anglo descent, and given their mother tongues (two kinds of English!) and affiliation with the BBC, they played to a largely Anglo set of audiences (Brits, 'mericans, and Germans). And while they were well aware that by the 1970s the sun had long since set on the British Empire, they nevertheless seemed to delight in portraying non-Anglos with a certain amount of critical contempt . . . possibly even as much contempt as they held for Anglos themselves. Here are a few examples of Python's far-flung xenophobia/philia.

LATIN / THE ROMANS (The Original Evil Empire)
"Also, we're demanding a ten-foot mahogany statue of the Emperor Julius Caesar with his cock hangin' out."

The Life of Brian, while to some heretical or blasphemous, certainly makes you think. And at times, it makes you learn—even if you, like the "native" Jews at the center of the film's struggle, hate the bloody foreigners who

---

* At least one of the writers of this work still has his can. The stamp on the bottom says: "Best by Jan 2008."
† Really? Processed meat product remembers its anniversary? My wife is gonna be pissed!—Jeff

"Romani ite domum!"
A Roman Centurian (Cleese) schools Brian (Chapman) on his Latin grammar in
The Life of Brian.

have occupied Nazareth. Two great cases in point: technology and language.

The film's great conflict is between the authoritarian Romans and the various rebel forces—the Judean People's Front, the People's Front of Judea, the Judean Popular People's Front, and the Popular Front—all of whom struggle against Roman oppression ... and against one another. PFJ spokesperson Reg notes, "The only people we hate more than the Romans are the fucking Judean People's Front." Of course, while their unfocused anger against "the entire apparatus of the Roman imperialist state" is not without merit, even the PFJ reluctantly admits that the Romans weren't without certain positive contributions to society. And so begins a short lesson in "What Have the Romans Ever Given Us" that reads like a crib sheet from an Ancient Civ I course: aqueducts; sanitation; roads; irrigation; medicine; education; public baths; public order; and wine ... ohhh yeah ... the wine.

> ### FACTOID BOX: Aqueducts
> ### (Sanitation, Irrigation, Baths)
>
> The Romans indeed brought "civilization" (or at least "the city") to many of the folks they conquered. Perhaps the Romans' greatest engineering contribution to western civilization was the aqueduct—a means of bringing in (relatively) clean water and shunting out (comparatively) dirty water. While the aqueduct wasn't exactly the flush toilet, it was a huge boon to irrigation, bathing, and general hygiene—especially as city populations bloomed in the first century A.D.
>
> **RANDOM FACTOID:** The Romans had a god/dess for everything, including Cloacina, a goddess whose dark domain was the Cloaca Maxima (the Great Sewer). How one worshiped Cloacina remains, alas, a privy mystery.

While a few of the preceeding Roman contributions can be easily explained by a Factoid Box, one deserves extended explication here: education.

Brian, attempting to get laid . . . errr . . . to impress a girl, seeks to join the PFJ and so is tasked with "a little job": to deface the Roman palace with that timeless marker of social protest, graffiti. That night, we see Brian furtively painting something in red on the walls, only to have a Roman Centurion (played as a combination copper/schoolmaster by Cleese) tap him on the shoulder and say, "What's this then? 'ROMANES EUNT DOMUS?' 'People called Romanes, they go the house'?"

In response to the Centurion's literal translation of his mangled Latin, Brian timidly suggests, "It, it says: 'Romans go home.'" What follows is—rather than a quick march to the hoosegow—a lesson in Latin

FACTOID BOX: Latin

Although it is considered a "dead language" (having no native speakers), Latin remained the primary liturgical language of the Roman Catholic Church until the 1960s and remains the official language of the Vatican in Rome. Since a knowledge of Latin (Ordinary level) was required of all entrants into Oxford and Cambridge until the 1960s, it's a given that the English Pythons eventually knew their Latin well—probably about as well as Shakespeare, who famously (according to Ben Jonson at least) had "small Latin and less Greek."

grammar that, at least in the case of one of your current authors, inspired a short-lived attempt at becoming a Classical scholar. For everyone else in the audience unschooled in the mother of all Romance languages, the scene at least introduces us to cases, numbers, and voices of the heavily inflected Latin language.

After a long and somewhat abusive "lesson," the two arrive at the proper Latinate form of "Romans go home!": "Romani ite domum."

Eventually, Brian is ordered by the Centurion to "write it out a hundred times" (a pedagogical strategy employed by countless schoolmarms over the centuries) and then told "and if it's not done by sunrise, I'll cut your balls off" (a slightly less popular pedagogical strategy nowadays).* Two sentries watch over Brian, who toils all night, until dawn comes and his handiwork is revealed: a towering, massive work of anti-Roman graffiti covering the entire palace. The posted sentry gives Brian one final warning: "Right. Now don't do it again," then departs, but as Brian steps back to admire his night's work a fresh set of guards arrive, visibly

---

* At least among pretenure faculty.

irate at what he's writ; he scarpers, a new set of authority figures on his tail. That'll learn him.

THE FRENCH

"You don't frighten us, English pig-dogs! Go and boil your bottom, sons of a silly person."

The British have always had a love/hate (okay: hate/hate) relationship with the French. This might have something to do with the constant and rather predictable invasions they have launched upon each other for a thousand or so years, but it also has a lot to do with the fact that each nation thinks that the other is filled with loopy eccentrics. They are probably both right. From the French knights who "already have" a Holy Grail of their own in *MP&HG*, to the pseudo-Frenchmen explaining "the commercial possibilities of ovine aviation" in *MPFC*, to the recidivist Montgolfier brothers and Cardinal Richelieu, the French are a reoccurring presence throughout most of Python's work. They even have some key phrases and names, such as "Zatapathique," "perhaps Python's catchall name for any Frenchman," as seen in episodes 2, 14, 22, and 23 (Larsen 2008, 148).* The show is rife with not just French characters but also French writers, philosophers, and historical impersonations—such as Marcel Marceau (ep. 13) and Mr. and Mrs. Jean-Paul Sartre (ep. 27), who live in the same apartment building as Jean Genet. Napoléon, perhaps the most imitated and parodied French figure in the history of comedy, appears in two sketches in episode 13, the "Psychiatry" sketch and the "Silly" sketch. In episode 44, Palin—as the leader of the multi-lingual "Post Box ceremony"—first reads an English dedication of the new box (emphasizing the word "box" every time) and then proceeds to read the surprisingly "fairly accurate"

---

* As in "Brian Zatapathique" in the "Eurovision Song Contest" sketch, the same name as the presenter on sheep aircraft in episode 2 (Larsen 2008, 296). In the French silent film sketch, "Jean Kenneth Longueur's movie *Le Fromage Grand*," "Brian Distel" appears, along with "Briannette Zatapathique."

> ### FACTOID BOX: The Montgolfier Brothers
>
> The Montgolfier brothers (Joseph-Michel Montgolfier and Jacques-Étienne Montgolfier) were French inventors who, on June, 5, 1783, sent up the first balloon capable of carrying human beings, much to the astonishment of Paris. Benjamin Franklin, who was watching, responded to a member of the crowd who questioned the use of the balloon, "Of what use is a newborn baby?" Ultimately, "the balloon flew for twenty-five minutes at an altitude of 100 meters across an astounded Paris" . . . nearly twice as long and half as high as Franklin's infant. (Horne 170–180)

French translation, as well as "the German version that is to follow" (Larsen 2008, 515). In the "Walking Tree of Dahomey" sketch (ep. 45) they call a tree *Arborus Bamber Gascoignus* based on the real-life quizmaster of *University Challenge* Bamber Gascoigne (Larsen 2008, 519). The list goes on, but as Carol Cleveland (as the "girl" in the French film) would have said, "J'ai dit 'oh.'"

It isn't just historical Frenchies who appear in Python. In episode 14, in the "Ministry of Silly Walks" sketch, it is made clear that Palin's applicant will only get a Research Fellowship if he works up a silly walk to rival one that the French are currently developing, "the Anglo-French silly walk," or, as Palin puts it, "La Marche Futile"—a nicely employed francophone phrase denoting the vain uselessness of the French in general.

In the short sketch immediately following the "Ministry of Silly Walks," we see two Frenchmen (Cleese and Palin again) dressed in berets and striped shirts, introducing the Anglo-French silly walk by saying, "Et maintenant avec les pieds à droite, et les pieds au gauche, et maintenant l'Anglais-Française Marche Futile, et voilà!" The man they are addressing, revealed to be dressed on one side as an English businessman and on the other in the stereotypical French outfit, then walks away sped up in a rather silly fashion. In a stark visual bisection, the Pythons seem to argue that the British and French are both equally silly, in walk and thus in behavior.

In a broader sense, even the Fish-Slapping Dance (not difficult to read Palin as French with his small fish and Cleese as British with his larger one) can be taken as another visual metaphor for the British and French class systems, wherein the British response is larger, less effete, and final proof of British dominance (into the Channel with ye!). Or it may simply be the finest moment of pure Pythonic slapstick ever captured on film.

In episode 23, the Pythons present a French subtitled film *Le Fromage Grand* (*The Big Cheese*). A commentator on the film (Idle) remarks on how the obscure foreign film represents the "breakdown in communication in our modern society." Larsen suggests that this utterance "defines *Flying Circus*": ". . . there are very few examples of a successful communication or transaction. In most cases, the message is misunderstood, delivered improperly or received incorrectly" (2008, 301). More specifically, however, Idle's comment may also show the influence of Sartre and the Existentialists on the Pythons and their interpretation of the vacuous nature of contemporary French film. The Pythons did seem to have an avid interest in French film, and in episode 24, the "Mr. Neville Shunte" sketch, they say of Claude Chabrol, "Chabrol stops at nothing," talking about the inventive director's daring approach to filmmaking (Larsen 2008, 311). Not only does this demonstrate Python's astute regard for the contemporary underground, but also, having watched Chabrol's films, we confirm that the statement is quite true.

A particularly French-influenced sketch in episode 27 focuses on two Pepperpots—Mrs. Premise and Mrs. Conclusion (Cleese and Chapman)—who seek to ask the famous French philosopher Sartre a complicated question about one of his seminal works (*Rues à Liberté*). Later in the same episode, when the Pepperpots finally find Sartre his singular response to their allegorical question is a simple "oui," delivered off camera. This suggests the curtness of the French to the English or perhaps provides (as philosophers of all denominations are wont to do) an existential reply to an existential question.*

---

*What is the Meaning of Life? Forty-two (at least according to Python colleague, Douglas Adams).

An example of the typical enmity between the British and French and the continuing wars of succession that marked those countries during the Hundred Years' War can be found in the years leading up to the reign of Louis XI (not explicitly mentioned by Python but conceptually present naytheless). By the time Louis died in 1483, France possessed "a material plenty never achieved in the West" and as a result, "the populous and prospering kingdom of France gave the law to chivalry and learning of all Europe"; "The King of France," wrote the English historian Matthew Paris, "is the king of earthly kings'" (Kendall 1971, 36). The British Kings of the time could not claim such glory, but their antipathy was not based on mere jealousy of French power and prestige. Since the time of the Norman Conquest in 1066 and well over a hundred years before that, France and England had been locked in a bitter ever-escalating war for the throne (the Hundred Years' War, 1337–1453). A typical sequence goes a little like this: In 1346, Edward III of England, his army staffed with archers who could use the far more accurate English longbow, fought an unprepared French army that was shattered "like glass under a hammer" (Kendall 1971, 37). A decade later Edward's son Edward IV crushed Philip's heir, John, carrying him back to London. Subsequently "English armies, unopposed, raided the length and breadth of France, tearing bloody weals of fire and pillage" (Kendall 1971, 36). This was followed by the Peasants' Revolt, the Black Death, and the ineffectual reigns of two subsequent rulers, including Charles V, who gradually drove the English out, until *his* son Charles VI was killed by John of Burgundy, leading to yet *another* invasion of France, led by Edward III (Kendall 1971, 38). You get the picture. It wasn't until Louis XI could stabilize the country that the constant squabbles stopped (up until the English invasion of 1475, followed by the Treaty of Picquigny, followed by, well, yadda, yadda). The English and French fought over thirty-three times over centuries. Surprisingly, as so much of this conflict shaped modern perceptions of English–French relations, Monty Python did not caricaturize any important French officials until they tackled one of the most important French historical figures of the seventeenth century, Cardinal Richelieu, steward of France under Louis XIII (see Part II: History). That the cardinal in question proved to be a "professional Cardinal Richelieu impersonator" only makes the strange British obsession with the French even sillier.

AMERICANS

"That's why nine out of ten small countries choose American defence . . . or Crelm Toothpaste with the miracle ingredient Fraudulin!"

And let's not forget *Americans!** While the satirical portrayal of Americans (and yes, one-sixth of Python was an American . . . until 2006[†]) is remarkably absent in most early Python work, they get around to lambasting them eventually. Americans portrayed in *Flying Circus* are either little more than walk-by characters with flattened accents or direct parodies of Hollywood (hence American) film types, and in the films following *FC* (the medieval *Holy Grail* and the late Classical *Life of Brian*) there is simply no time for them, chronologically speaking. Whether ironically or purposely, the Pythons first turn to target Americans and American stereotypes (vacuous tourism, empty-headed anti-intellectualism) in *Meaning of Life* (1983), *after* their American popularity had become well and truly established—as evidenced, for example, by the fanatical American response to *Live at the Hollywood Bowl* (1982).[‡]

Even in *Meaning of Life,* Americans are simply gauche, showing up to the party late, arriving in "Part IV: Middle Age," just after the surreal "Middle of the Film" sequence. Palin and Idle, as a middle-aged American couple (the Hendys), after happily settling into their lackluster hotel room are greeted

---

*While the U.S. of A is technically Anglo, we're fairly sure the Pythons (and the British) would like to check our birth records on that.

[†]Terry Gilliam, born in Minnesota and raised in L.A. moved to London in the late sixties, took dual British citizenship in 1968, then renounced his American citizenship in 2006—whether in protest of then-president George W. Bush or for tax reasons remains unclear.

[‡]By the late seventies the shows had aired on PBS and ABC (the latter in mangled form), and *Holy Grail* and *Life of Brian* had made headlines; ultimately, the zealous attendees of *Live at the Hollywood Bowl* (1982) gave ample proof of their U.S. popularity.

"It's real Hawaiian food served in an authentic medieval English dungeon atmosphere."

The American Python, Terry Gilliam, as M'Lady Joeline, the cross-dressing hostess of the *very* American "theme hotel" in *The Meaning of Life*.

downstairs by M'Lady Joeline, a cross-dressing Gilliam in a flounced Bo Peep costume who—unsurprisingly—does a fine job projecting a falsetto Minnesotan accent. He/she directs them to dinner in the Dungeon Room, where they will find "real Hawaiian food served in an authentic medieval English dungeon atmosphere." And, true to M'Lady's promise, the setting is replete with bare stone walls, ensconced torches, torture devices, hanging corpses, and a real half-naked prisoner being branded by a hot iron . . . as well as roaming grass-skirted luau performers.

As the vapid Hendys, Palin and Idle do a reasonable job flattening their pronunciation to approximate "general midwestern American" accents, while their waitstaff, Cleese and Carol Cleveland,* adopt somewhat more aggressively urban American patois.† Just as the U.S.A. is a land without history/identity (compared to the U.K.), no one in the scene is really from anywhere; when asked, the Hendys say they come from "room 259" and when she is asked the waitress responds that she comes from "out of those doors over there." The diverse mix of American accents in the sketch suggests that all the U.S. is as one: dialect is a part of the blanding-out parody, no doubt. The idea that Americans can—or care to—approximate European style is belied by the waitstaffs' attire: Cleese is stuffed into a red tartan day jacket and Cleveland is poured into a strip-show approximation of a British Beefeater costume (think of a typical "Sexy Nurse" or "Sexy Lawyer" Halloween costume). "Authentic"—the skit seems to say—means something very different to Americans, a people without history or culture and therefore without taste.

As for taste, the menu choices at the Dungeon Room, should one choose to have food with one's meal, are but two: square-shaped green things or squiggly shaped brown things. By comparison, the SPAM-laden menu at the Viking Café (FC, ep. 25) seems positively decadent.

Ultimately, the scene plays up the stereotypical lack of culture and

---

* Cleveland's bits, alas, appear only in the director's cut.
† Cleveland's emphasis on the dialect markers "caw-fee" and "catch-ip" seem to suggest an attempt at a New Yawk–ese or Brooklyn accent, while Cleese's accent sounds more Chicagoan than aught else.

intelligence among Americans, who are uncritical (or at least unfazed) by the illogic of "authentic medieval Hawaiian cuisine," who have nothing much to say beyond "the Steelers–Bears game Saturday" or "really great World Series," who never bother to think about the meaning of life, and who are, at least by middle age, sexually passionless and literally tasteless.

PYTHON ON WOMEN
"But it's my only line."

There is not much, one might think, that one can (or should) learn about women by watching the sausage-fest that is Monty Python. At first glance (and sometimes that is quite the glance), women seem to be employed as merely salacious props in Python, come across as inherently unfunny, or are not really women at all. Heck: at second glance, that still seems to be the case. But after careful consideration, we have concluded that in the Python-verse there are up to three types of women: Pepperpots, Glamour Stooges, and Girls with Big Tits. Not coincidentally, this triptych of femininity reflects, in rather distorted terms, the traditional folkloric division of the "fairer sex" into three distinct categories: the maid, the mother, and the crone. In popular romances, for example, women were either premarriageable but sexualized (maidens to be rescued, raped, or revered); marriageable equals suitably sexualized (wives and mothers); or postmenopausal and desexualized (granny types to be consulted for sage advice). Since the Pythons tend to turn traditional categories on their heads, we will discuss these categories in reverse order: Pepperpots, Glamour Stooges, and Girls with Big Tits.

Women (Part One): Pepperpots

Most frequently, female roles in Monty Python sketches were performed by the men in drag; this is not only somewhat funny in itself (the boys make, on the whole, fairly ugly women), but such theatrical (and meta-

"This used to be a nice neighborhood before the old ladies started moving in."
A particularly dangerous incarnation of the typical Python Pepperpot inhabits the "Hell's Grannies" sketch from *Monty Python's Flying Circus*.

thatrical) cross-dressing has enjoyed a long tradition in English theatre—Shakespeare was quite fond of the practice, for example. So was the American performer Bugs Bunny, for that matter. When so be-dragged, the Pythons called themselves Pepperpots.

The Pepperpots—generally caricatures of "middle-aged lower-middle-class women"* (such as Mrs. Scum and Mrs. Premise and Mrs. Conclusion)—are all part of the grand British theatrical and music hall tradition of men dressing as women. This may also lead us back to British boarding school, but let's save that for another day. For all of their grotesque nature, the Pepperpots are generally meant to be perceived as (grossly exaggerated) women, not as men—nudge nudge—dressed as women. It was rare in Python for a character in drag to actually be revealed as a transvestite. A

---

* First appearing—and so described—in episode 1.

notable female impersonator, at least, is Gloria (Cleese), the girlfriend of Dinsdale Piranha (ep. 14), who announces to the interviewer, "He was a gentleman, Dinsdale, and what's more he knew how to treat a female impersonator." The bitchy high-court judges who disrobe to reveal themselves in flamboyant women's undergarments (ep. 21) are another example of non-Pepperpotted Pythons in women's clothing. Brian's mother (Jones) in *Life of Brian* introduces us to another odd bit of double cross-dressing. Jones (male) plays Mandy Cohen (female), who dons a fake beard (thus male) to participate in the "male-only" stoning of a sinner. Shakespeare would be proud. But for the most part, at least in *FC*, when a sketch required a female character the Pythons employed real women actresses (typically Carol Cleveland, Connie Booth, or even Eric's mother) or donned Pepperpot costumes themselves. The effects of each show a careful comic distinction.

When the Pythons chose to play Pepperpots, the sketch required not realistic women but exaggerated versions of women, so outrageous and obviously imitative that they could not have been portrayed by "anatomically correct" actresses. It may be useful to think of the Pepperpots as analogous to the Gumbies. If the Gumbies are exaggerations of hypermasculinity, manhood taken to such a ridiculous extreme that the Gumby brain has atrophied and all that is left is impulse and will, then the Pepperpots are the idea of femininity taken to a point where all that is left is a twisted caricature of aged, matronly British stubbornness and carefully cultivated household ignorance. In short, the Pepperpots are not simply gratuitous "funny ugly men in drag" (although that resonates as well); they are informing parts of the overall design of any sketch. As Graham Chapman wrote:

> What we quite liked was the juxtaposition of something that is exemplified in those mad female creatures we played called Pepperpots—I hesitate to call them women. Normally, they would be the last sort of people that you would expect to talk about philosophers and yet they were always quite comfortable talking about John Paul Sartre. That's where a lot of our humor comes from, I

think—the way that intellectual things were treated in a trivial way. (Chapman and Yoakum 1997, 47)

In their own weird way, then, the Pepperpots are the unlikely disseminators of Pythonic Wisdom: comic crones.

There are more examples of cross-dressers intended as camp figures rather than as satirical savants. The outrageously campy and feminine characters of Ginger (Biggles' old companion), and Mr. Freight from the sketch "The Visitors," are hyper-exaggerated and more sexually ambiguous than any Pepperpot; they are more "camp" than anything else. As Susan Sontag wrote in her essay on camp:

> The whole point of Camp is to dethrone the serious. Camp is playful, anti-serious. More precisely, Camp involves a new, more complex relation to "the serious." One can be serious about the frivolous, frivolous about the serious. (2001, 288)

Python characters were never transvestites per se; they were frivolous comments on how we take our sexuality far too seriously.

Women (Part Two): Glamour Stooges

And then there are the often-voluptuous, sometimes-vocal real women of Python: those who belong to the category "Glamour Stooge," as Carol Cleveland proudly called herself. Cleveland may have initially been part of "the BBC's attempt to broaden the show's demographic potentialities" (Larsen 2008, 4), but she soon earned her keep legitimately—if not as a writer, then certainly as an actor.

Carol Cleveland, the unofficial "seventh Python," aka "Glamour Stooge," aka "Carol Cleavage," is described in her first stage prompts (ep. 2) as *"a beautiful blond buxom wench, in the full bloom of her young womanhood (Carol Cleveland)."* Clearly, the Pythons knew what they wanted: an actress who had already cut her teeth in television (including *The Saint* and *The Avengers*) and who had experience in comedy (working with the Two

> ## FACTOID BOX: Carol Cleveland
>
> **Appearances:** *Flying Circus* (34 episodes); *Not the Messiah: He's a Very Naughty Boy* (Mexican/Sheep Lady); *Meaning of Life* (Beefeater Waitress/Wife of Guest #1/Leaf Mother/Leaf Daughter/Heaven Receptionist); *Life of Brian* (Mrs. Gregory/Shoe Follower); *Holy Grail* (Zoot/Dingo).
>
> **Measurements:** 37-25-37 . . . Hello, nurse!

Ronnies, Peter Sellers, Morecambe and Wise, and Spike Milligan). The beauty, blond, and buxom parts were clearly just a bonus.

In her first appearance in *Flying Circus*,* Cleveland plays Deirdre, the "ravishing wife" to Arthur Pewtey (Palin), who harbors suspicions about his wife's fidelity and thus reluctantly seeks the advice of a Marriage Counselor (Idle). Unfortunately for Pewtey, as he explains his suspicions they are simultaneously realized in front of the audience, who watch as Deirdre and the Counselor flirt shamelessly and then retire behind a changing screen; various articles of her clothing are then tossed over the top.

The sketch works, in part, because there is a palpable sexual allure in Deirdre. Idle's Counselor is instantly mesmerized, and there is no doubt on the audience's part that Pewtey's fears are well justified. No male Python in drag would have the same effect.

Cleveland's natural sexuality also played well in live performances, where it could be emphasized in ways that the BBC would have frowned upon. Her role as the provocative Secretary in the "Bounder of Adventure/Mr. Smoke-Too-Much/The Travel Agent" sketch is heightened a tad when performed onstage at the Hollywood Bowl, for example.

---

*As noted earlier: the first episode that aired was the second shot, and vice versa: Cleveland thus holds the distinction of acting in the first *FC* episode ever filmed.

"What is the name of your ravishing wife? . . . Something to do with moonlight; it goes with her eyes. . . ."
A Marriage Counselor (Idle) seduces "a beautiful blond buxom wench in the full bloom of her young womanhood" (Cleveland) in front of her husband (Palin) in *Monty Python's Flying Circus*.

In *Flying Circus* (ep. 31), she greets the tourist (Idle) by "*sexily*" asking, "Do you want to go upstairs?" before quickly and "*brightly*" following up with a counteroffer: "Or have you come to arrange a holiday?" When the Tourist opts for the latter, she dismisses her first offer, but the humor in his "I can't believe what I just heard" has been established and culled.

Cut free from the censors at the BBC, however, the skit can take a slightly different tack. In the version of the sketch recorded for *Live at the Hollywood Bowl*, Cleveland asks, "Uhm, have you come to arrange a holiday or would you like a blow job?" When the Tourist (Idle again) is taken aback by her second offer, she again dismisses it but punctuates his confusion when she escorts him to her boss, Bounder (Palin), by saying, "Mr. Bounder, this gentleman is interested in the 'India Overland'—*and nothing else*." Playing the jokes larger onstage (by both word choice and the dramatic intonation

"I wish I'd been a girlie, just like my dear poppa!"
Palin and a Glamour Stooge perform "The Lumberjack Song."

of "and nothing else"), Cleveland drives home the humor in a manner generally eschewed by the Pythons previously. Still funny. Funny *and* hot—and perhaps bluntly directed at an American audience.*

Again, few would argue that the sketch would not have played rather differently had, say, a Pepperpotted Terry Jones played the seductress instead of a vivacious Glamour Stooge. Take, for example, the "Organ Donor" sketch from *Meaning of Life*. It is a gruesome bit of humor in which a creepy paramedic/organ harvester (Cleese) hits on the almost-widowed Mrs. Brown (Jones, playing a disheveled Pepperpot in grimy house frock) as Cleese's partner (Chapman) disembowels the "Rastafarian Jew Organ Donor" Mr. Brown (Gilliam, dying onstage as usual) on

---

*The Pythons' choice for their opening sketch at the Hollywood Bowl performances— "Sit on My Face" (sung by a Pythonesque barbershop quartet, bereft of trousers)— set the tenor for their American shows in general.

their kitchen table. The seduction in this petite Grand Guignol here evokes morbid fatalism and death, not life. Their courtship is creepy, not titillating, their appearance unattractive, not titillating, as befits the mood of the scene overall: an ugly stereotyped Pepperpot is thus required. Cleveland would have simply introduced mixed messages to this scene.

Of course, *Meaning of Life* also presents a scene in which a real Glamour Stooge (Patricia Quinn*) is practically necessary. During a very "hands on" sex-ed lecture, the Headmaster (Cleese) mounts his good wife (Quinn) in front of a class of bored schoolboys. The two are half-naked (Quinn is topless on-screen; Cleese bottomless) in bed, the man atop the woman. Again—humor could certainly be mined from the scene if Quinn were replaced by a Pepperpot, but the point of the scene—of their very public coitus—is not to be funny but to be boring. As silly as it may be to "accept" the Pythons as teen boys in the scene, it would have been counterproductive (too silly) to force the audience to accept a Pepperpot being mounted by Cleese.

Quinn is not simply a set of tits in the scene; like Cleveland, she is a Glamour Stooge. Her detached delivery of absolutely mundane dialogue with the equally disengaged Cleese brings the sketch to climax, as it were. The couple's blasé coitus underscores their captive audience's distraction—a common set of attitudes that are in stark contrast to the film audience's attention, no doubt. (I can't believe I'm seeing this!)

Women (Part Three): Girls with Big Tits

The authors—in a cowardly attempt at broaching a potentially dodgy topic—would like to now turn the topic of "Girls with Big Tits" over to esteemed thespian (and part-time Sir Robin) David Hyde Pierce. Over to you, David:

---

*As noted earlier, Quinn is undoubtedly better known for her portrayal of "Magenta—a domestic" in *The Rocky Horror Picture Show* (1975). "I'm lucky, he's lucky, you're lucky, we're all lucky, ha ha ha!"

I was sixteen, and I had come home from practicing the organ . . .
[at church] . . . and I got home, it had to be about eleven o'clock at
night, I think . . . [I] was flipping channels and hit the PBS station.
And I still remember, it was "The Dull Life of a Chartered Public
Accountant," and I remember I turned it on at the point where he
walked into the tobacconist, and the woman behind the counter
was completely topless. And I was sixteen and I thought this was
the best thing I've ever seen in my life. Or two of the best things
I've ever seen in my life. (*Monty Python Conquers America*)

Thank you, David! That about sums it up nicely.

When the role in question relied, for its effect, on the shock value of a
naked woman (or women), the Pythons generally stepped aside and let
natural-born females fill their high-heeled shoes. Sometimes, of course,
those women filled little else. Such are the "Girls with Big Tits" in the
Python-verse, the often silent eye candy who tempt chaste and wayward
knights, who pursue male chauvinist pigs to their precipitous deaths,
who dance on Vegas stages with fake plastic boobies, and who win Summarize Proust contests by virtue of their mammary glands alone. They
are the "Page Three Girls" of the Python set, if you will.* Yet rarely are
they simply to be ogled (as is oft the case with similarly cast models in
Benny Hill). Believe it or not, in most of the Python oeuvre nudity seems
to serve a purpose beyond titillation.

The maids of Castle Anthrax are fronted by the supposed twins Zoot
and Dingo (both Cleveland), who stooges it up. After selling herself (and
her diaphanously clad "Girls with Big Tits" maids) as demure and helpless sex objects, Dingo punctuates the scene with a contrastively earthy,
"Shit!" when her desires are thwarted. In *The Meaning of Life* the slow-
motion chase of topless girls sets a stark contrast to the death of Chapman's male chauvinist—sex is sold here as a form of poetic justice, not
simply a titillation. The Vegas showgirls—each wearing identical falsies—

---

* As Larsen notes, "Beginning in 1969, bikini-clad (and then topless) models began to
appear in Rupert Murdoch's tabloid newspaper *The Sun*, called 'Page Three Girls'—
they helped the paper's circulation jump significantly in the early 1970s" (2008, 525).

further underscores not only the falsity of American overproduced stage-craft but also the falsehood of our visions of the afterlife. Naked and jiggly they may be, but women in the Python-verse are never simply naked.

THE MEANING OF LIFE: MUSIC

In the interest of gender equality, let's talk about dicks for a bit, shall we? In the "Penis Song (Not the Noël Coward Song)" sketch from *Meaning of Life,* Idle plays a vampy lounge pianist who (as the title assures us, is certainly *not* a parody of Noël Coward) presents his dinner audience with a dirty little ditty about his penis that he, ahem, "tossed off this morning":

> *Isn't it awfully nice to have a penis?*
> *Isn't it frightfully good to have a dong?*
> *It's swell to have a stiffy, It's divine to own a dick*
> *From the tiniest little tadger to the world's biggest prick*
> *So three cheers for your willy or John Thomas*
> *Hooray for your one-eyed trouser snake*
> *Your piece of pork, your wife's best friend, your Percy or your cock*
> *You can wrap it up in ribbons, you can slip it in your sock*
> *But don't take it out in public or they will stick you in the dock*
> *And you won't . . . come . . . back!*

Part of the joy of the very short bit comes from the delight the entertainer seems to get by enumerating taboo terms, that it all seems frightfully naughty but simultaneously quite quaint. None of "Not Noël Coward's" terms for the penis is particularly taboo, but for the non-Brits in the audience a few might have come as a surprise, at least in 1983.

Python offers a much more depressing enumeration of sexual terms in their "Medical Love Song" (sung by Chapman, the troupe's *de facto* field medic). A truncated version of "Medical Love Song" first appeared on *Monty Python's Contractual Obligation Album* (1980); the full version appeared on *Monty Python Sings* (1989). The deep and somewhat disturbing list of STDs and their symptoms culled below draws from the full version:

FACTOID BOX: Noël Coward

Sir Noël Pierce Coward (b. December 16, 1899; d. March 26, 1973)

Known as much for his flamboyant style and wit as his truly impressive lyrical and theatrical production. A "congenital bachelor" in the tradition of Oscar Wilde, Coward gained some notoriety for his short satire on the English pacifist movement, "Don't Let's Be Beastly to the Germans" (1943); while a favorite of Winston Churchill, the song was banned by the BBC in deference to its war-weary listeners' sensibilities.

RANDOM FACTOID: Known for wearing dressing gowns in public, smoking cigarettes out of a long holder, and affecting a clipped, staccato verbal delivery. Not to be confused with Hugh Hefner!

Anal Snail Tracks
Anterior Uveitis
Ballanital Chancroids
Diplococcal Cephalitis
Dobie's Itch
Epididimitis
Gonoccocal Urethritis
Gonorrhea
Herpes
Inflammation of the Foreskin
Interstitial Keratitis
Meningo Mylititis
Moenilial Infection
Penile Warts
Scrotal Postules
Scrumpox

Streptococcal Ballinitis
Syphilitic: Choroiditis
                Kisses
                Sores
Trichovaginitis

Ultimately, "Medical Love Song" parodies all love songs by focusing on the sometimes-unpleasant physical ramifications of love (as John Wilmot, the Second Earl of Rochester, infamously did in the seventeenth century*). Despite its unpleasant subject matter, the song remains—in every sense of the word—"catchy."

In another bout of listmania, "The Decomposing Composers" (from *Monty Python's Contractual Obligation Album*), Palin offers a morbid but not aggressively taboo recounting of famous classical composers and their deaths. For your further visual study ("There may very well be an exam this quarter! I mean it!"), here are the first thirteen lamented composers:

Ludvig van Beethoven
Wolfgang Amadeus Mozart
Johannes Brahms
Franz Liszt
Edward William Elgar
Franz Schubert
Frédéric Chopin
Frederich Händel
Franz Haydn
Sergei Rachmaninov
Guiseppe Verdi
Wilhelm Wagner
Achille-Claude Debussy

---

* For examples of disease-laden Restoration British bawdy, see Rochester's "The Imperfect Enjoyment," "Régime de Vivre," and "The Disabled Debauchee" (among many, many others).

The chords of Pachelbel's Canon,* and the lyric lament, end with a spoken-word recounting not only of the full names of choice composers but their death dates as well (they have ceased to be; they are ex-composers):

Achille Claude-Debussy—Died, 1918.
Christoph Willebald Gluck—Died, 1787.
Carl Maria von Weber—Not at all well, 1825. Died, 1826.
Giacomo Meyerbeer—Still alive, 1863. Not still alive, 1864.
Modeste Mussorgsky—1880, going to parties. No fun anymore, 1881.
Johan Nepomuk Hummel—Chatting away nineteen to the dozen with his mates down the pub every evening, 1836. 1837: nothing

But composers were not the only dead lyrically praised by Python. Appearing in the Python's stage shows and recorded (with minor variation) on the *Matching Tie and Handkerchief* and *Monty Python Sings* albums, "The Philosophers Song" sings the praises of no fewer than fourteen deep thinkers who—according to the faculty of the Philosophy Department of the University of Woolamaloo (all Bruces)—are also all deep drinkers. They are, in reasonable order:

Immanuel Kant; Martin Heidegger; David Hume; Arthur Schopenhauer; Georg Wilhelm Friedrich Hegel; Ludwig Wittgenstein; Karl Wilhelm Friedrich Schlegel and/or August Wilhelm Schlegel[†]; Friedrich Nietzsche; Socrates; John Stuart Mill; Plato; Aristotle; Thomas Hobbes; René Descartes; Socrates (again: he is "particularly missed").

"Decomposing Composers" and "The Philosophers Song" have found their ways into school curricula, and for good reason: the catchy tunes make effective mnemonics. Granted, there is often some "unlearning"

---

*For a modern take on the ubiquity of Pachelbel's Canon, see Rob Paravonian's "Pachelbel's Rant" at http://robprocks.com/.
[†]The Schlegel brothers, Karl and August, are identified variously in performances.

to be done in the classroom after the songs are played ("No, the most important thing to remember about Socrates is not that he 'was permanently pissed'"), but since many of the DWEMs listed in these songs possess "weird" names by modern students' standards* any help is appreciated.

Lyrical synonymy needn't be racy, taboo, or disturbing to be memorable. Musical satirist Tom Lehrer (a favorite of Palin's) is considered by many the contemporary master of the genre and produced the most copied/parodied/riffed list song in modern memory: "The Elements" (1959). Just as Python should be used to supplement teaching in a liberal arts classroom, Lehrer (who was a mathematician as well as musician) should, by all rights, be required in science classes. "The Elements" (aka "The Element Song") is a tour de force of enumeration, as Lehrer names all 102 currently identified elements to the tune of "I Am the Very Model of a Modern Major-General" from Gilbert and Sullivan's hit comic opera *The Pirates of Penzance* (1879). We won't list all the elements here, but we will say that Lehrer's catchy lyrics hooked not only his generation but every generation since; Daniel Radcliffe of Harry Potter fame, for example, geekily performed the difficult patter on *The Graham Norton Show* in 2010. Smart kid.

THE MEANING OF LIFE: MNEMONICS

Like Tom Lehrer and They Might be Giants, the Pythons produced catchy, musically mnemonic devices that permeate the brain and lodge within. And even when their lists are not attached to memorable tunes,

---

* See the *SNL* sketch "Camp Ujaama" for a parody of modern naming practices. As counselors Daman Wayans and Ellen Cleghorne call roll, the names include: "Abracadabra, Agoraphobia, Algebra, Binaca, Briquette, Bulimia, Chinchilla, Chlamydia, Conundrum, Cornea, Krakatoa, Duracell, Eczema, Fellatio, Frigidaire, Genitalia, Gynolotramin, Harpsichord, Hologram, Hyperbole, K-tel, KamaKamaKamaKamaKamaChameleon, Latrine, Lexicon, Listerine, Lubriderm, Melanoma, Minoxidil, Mylanta, Noxzema, Nutrasweet, Onomatopoeia, Placebo, Pneumonia, Purina, Quesadilla, Ratatouille, Robitussin, Rubikscube, Silhouette, Spatula, Spina Bifida, Testicle, Trifecta, Urethra, and Uvula" (1995: season 20, ep. 17).

the repetitive impact of lists and pseudo-synonymy often resonates with their audience long after the context of a sketch has faded from memory.

Take, for a short example, *The Life of Brian*. As his messiah-tinged bildungsroman progresses, Brian Cohen more and more heartily embraces his identity as a Jew, at one point denying his mother's suggestions to the contrary: "I'm not a Roman, Mum. I'm a kike, a yid, a hebe, a hooknose. I'm kosher, Mum, I'm a Red Sea pedestrian and proud of it!" Brian starts by asserting what he is not (a Roman); that part is simple. More complicated is asserting what he is. Brian is a Jew, yes, but as the force of the repetition asserts, Brian is not simply a Jew: he is all that the term "Jew" connotes, including both the positive and the negative social values. From taboo "kike" to the Exodus-inspired "Red Sea pedestrian," Brian embraces his linguistically delineated identity as a Jew. In other words, Brian's other words proclaim his own self-awareness: identity as framed by language.

While such linguistic wrestling in *Life of Brian* teaches us (and perhaps Brian) something about Brian's character, particular lists in Python are often employed as correctives against other perceived failures of language. That is, the "Thesaurus" sketch is an attempt at clarification. Inarguably the most popular, most memorized, and most recited synonymy in Python history is that in episode 8 of *Flying Circus*: the "Dead Parrot" sketch.*

Palin and Cleese (in roles they would essentially reprise for the "Cheese Shop" sketch in ep. 33) play evasive Shopkeeper and disgruntled customer, respectively; the customer, Mr. Praline, wishes "to register a complaint about this parrot what I purchased not half an hour ago from this very boutique"—a parrot that is, in his estimation, dead. Despite appearances to the contrary, the Shopkeeper repeatedly denies the complaint, and the two men then engage in a protracted "yes it is/no it isn't" schoolyard argument that is elevated to the level of linguistic genius by virtue of the myriad ways Praline can say "dead." Synonyms laced within

---

* "The Cheese Shop" may be a close second in popularity, but far fewer are the fans who have memorized the exhaustive list of cheeses enumerated by Mr. Mousebender.

the conversation include: "resting," "stone dead," "stunned," "deceased," "tired and shagged out," "pining for the fjords," "flat on its back," "bleeding demised," "and passed on," all of which leave the Shopkeeper unconvinced. In exasperation, Praline offers a dizzying volley of deadly assertions:

> This parrot is no more. It has ceased to be. It's expired and gone to meet its maker. This is a late parrot. It's a stiff. Bereft of life, it rests in peace. If you hadn't nailed it to the perch, it would be pushing up the daisies. It's rung down the curtain and joined the choir in-visible. This is an ex-parrot.*

Ultimately overwhelmed by the heaps of deathly verbiage spewed by Praline, the Shopkeeper seemingly relents and sends the unhappy cus-tomer across England to "my brother's pet shop in Bolton," where he may receive a replacement parrot. He doesn't, of course, and after a bit of run-around the Colonel (Chapman) deems the sketch "too silly" to continue; but by then the comic impact—the never-ending litany of euphemisms for "dead"—has been made anyway. An intellectual impact has also been made, as the euphemistic range (simple synonyms and trite clichés, comic neologisms, blunt utterances, and poetic pronouncements) of expressions urges the viewer to reconsider his or her own usage. Why say "dead" when such panoply of verbiage exists?

Partially in response to the perceived penchant of Cleese and Chap-man to write thesaurus-based sketches—like the "Dead Parrot" sketch, which Jones noted "is basically straight out of the thesaurus" and Idle called "pure Roget!" (Morgan 2005, 111)—Jones and Palin would eventu-ally write "What the Stars Foretell" (ep. 37).† In this synonym-laden bit,

---

* Cleese embellished the list of deadly euphemisms in the staged performances.
† Because the Pythons tended to break into pairs for much of their writing (Cleese and Chapman; Palin and Jones; Idle and Gilliam flying solo) there was, at least ini-tially, a sense of style particular to each duo: Cleese and Chapman tended to write wordplay sketches, while Jones and Palin's sketches tended to be more visual. Yet as the troupe now agrees, the longer the show ran, the more there was a crossover of styles, and "after a while, you couldn't tell who wrote a sketch at a certain point" (Gilliam in Morgan 2005, 110–11).

Mrs. O (Pepperpot Idle) asks Mrs. Trepidatious (Pepperpot Chapman), "What do the stars say?" After some minor confusion regarding the intended meaning of the word "stars"—Trepidatious starts recounting the warty opinions of Petula Clark and David Frost—and an overly pedantic, and ultimately fourth-wall-busting set of synonym lists follow. If you were paying attention while watching the skit, here's how the Pythons casually expanded your vocabulary.

> "the stars" = the zodiacal signs, the horoscopic fates, the astrological portents, the omens, the genethliac prognostications, the mantalogical harbingers, the vaticinal utterances, the fratidical premonitory uttering of the mantalogical omens

Not content to redefine what she meant by the noun "stars," Mrs O continues to clarify her question, "what the bleeding stars in the paper predict," by elucidating upon her intended meaning of "predict":

> "predict" = forecast, prophesy, foretell, prognosticate, forebode, bode, augur, spell, foretoken, presage, portend, foreshow, foreshadow, forerun, herald, point to, betoken, indicate!

Further underscoring the pedantic nature of Mrs O's excessive clarification, a voice-over interrupts her rant (between "prognosticate" and "forebode") as "a big sheet is lowered with the words on" to tell the audience: "And this is where you at home can join in." And so the in-studio audience does—and perhaps those at home as well—thus voluntarily engaging in an oral recitation exercise that would be more likely in a language lab or ESL classroom than a comedy sketch. A great many teachers would love to hear that kind of audience vocabulary, lemmee tell you.*

"Vocabulary"* = word bank, word hoard, lexicon, cant, internal dictionary, glossary, glossarium, word-stock, denotative signs and signifiers, phraseology, patois, argot, unique set of viable utterances, concordance, individuated thesaurus.

THE MEANING OF LIFE (Really: No italics!)
"Why are we here? What's life all about?"

There are several possible answers to that question:

ONE

In the movie *The Meaning of Life*, Maria the Cleaning Lady (Jones), after recounting her search for the Meaning of Life in many of the halls of knowledge, concludes (in rhetorical verse):

> *I feel that Life's a game*
> *You sometimes win or lose,*
> *And though I may be down right now*
> *At least I don't work for Jews . . .*

And at that, the Maître D' (Cleese) pours a bucket of vomit over her head. So perhaps there is less worldly wisdom in Maria's philosophy than expected. Never mind—here's another idea:

TWO

Gascon: One day, when I was little, my mother took me on her knee and said: "The world is a beautiful place, Gascon, my son. You must go into it, and love everyone, and not hate people. Try to make everyone happy, and bring peace and contentment wherever you go." So . . . I became a waiter. . . . *There is a rather long pause, while he looks a bit self-deprecating and nods shyly at the camera.* Well . . . it's not much of a philosophy, I know . . . but . . . well . . . fuck you . . . I can live my own life the way I want, can't I? Fuck off! Don't come following me!

And so the French waiter tottles off, leaving us to ponder whether his *Candide*-inspired final non-philosophy amounts to a philosophy or not. We leave it to you to decide. But here's a final option:

FIVE . . . ERR . . . THREE

Lady Presenter (Palin): Well, that's the End of the Film, now here's the Meaning of Life . . . Well, it's nothing special. Try and be nice to people, avoid eating fat, read a good book every now and then, get some walking in and try and live together in peace and harmony with people of all creeds and nations.

Of course, her de facto reading of the "results" *as handed to her* is seriously undercut by her subsequent personal rant that what people (for her, defined as cinemagoers) really want is

. . . some sort of [penis-inspired] controversy which it seems is the only way these days to get the jaded video-sated public off their fucking arses and back in the sodding cinema. Family entertainment bollocks! What they want is filth, people doing things to each other with chain saws during Tupperware parties, babysitters being stabbed with knitting needles by gay presidential candidates, vigilante groups strangling chickens, armed bands of theatre critics exterminating mutant goats. Where's the fun in pictures?

Is Python's final offering that "fun" is the meaning of cinema and thus life? Or could this be Python taking yet another stab at one of the developing genres of cinema they grew up with, cinema verité? As *MPFC* and *Meaning of Life* showed, Python cannot keep to only one genre per sketch and may have decided to remind viewers of how they broke new ground in the 1960s and 1970s, by performing postmodern experiments in cinema long before it worked its way into the mainstream. However, this could also be another attempt on Python's part to hint that the existentialist viewpoint they have more or less espoused throughout their career is no joke. They want you to laugh because there is no meaning, and the reference to the "controversies of cinema" is a sly referent to their many critics, including those who were simply appalled by a man eating until his body literally exploded. So, "feck off!"

THEOLOGY/ORGANIZED RELIGION

"Sarah, today's diocesan lovely, is enough to make any chap go down on his knees."

Python has long been obsessed with the topic of religion. After all, most of them had grown up in private schools, attending chapel and, despite their various belief systems, more or less "enjoyed" the same institutionalized experience of religion as the others. Gilliam, however, had once been so firm in his beliefs that he had considered (briefly) becoming a Presbyterian missionary before college. By the time of Python, while it is difficult to say whether any members held any firm religious beliefs at all, they were certainly united in one belief: the organization and authority invested in religion by any people (and in England by the state) led to inherently silly behavior.

Yet they were not (probably) blasphemous. In *Life of Brian*, the Pythons are not attacking Jesus Christ or any of his teachings, a point missed by the critics of the time; they are attacking mindless obedience to *any* kind of system. It would be easy to see the film as an attack on the institution of organized religion, but it is far more than that: it is an attack on all sources of authority. Python actually took their time to reread the Gospels and found them laudable and in many ways a poor target for satire. Their aim seemed less to make fun of the idea of religion than to ask why people put their blind faith in any kind of authority. According to Eric Idle, ". . . it was an attack on churches and pontificators and self-righteous assholes who claim to speak for God, of whom there are still too many on the planet" (Morgan 2005, 226).

Life of Brian epitomizes this worldview. The film, which again was emphatically *not* about Jesus (they took great pains to mention that he was a historical contemporary of Brian's and that Brian was clearly not a parody of Jesus),* nonetheless caused predictable controversy. What people did not realize was the way in which Python was trying to *avoid* antagonizing the faithful (although considering the delicacy of the subject

---

* As his mother put it, "He's not the Messiah; he's a very naughty boy!"

matter, this may have been a bit disingenuous or naïve on the part of the Pythons). What Python was trying to parody was the mindless way in which people followed, and often perverted for their beliefs, the beauty of belief systems themselves, many of which were not only very moral but also helpful in their most basic forms. As Michael Palin wrote in his diary at the time, Brian was about "power—its use and abuse by an establishment" (2006, 594). The trouble was that across the world almost every religion was an establishment to a certain extent, however decentralized some may have been.

Python was not merely parodying religion; as usual, their canvas was painted broader than simply covering one topic. From the competing prophets, each with their own followings, to the Roman occupiers (who sometimes resemble stern schoolmasters rather than occupiers), to the schisms in the different revolutionary groups (John Cleese was later to say that they were a direct parody of the differing schisms on the British left in that time period), all are equally ridiculous and all equally silly. One of the points of the film is that organizations, especially those with any real sense of responsibility, become inherently silly when they try to consolidate power.

Talking about *Life of Brian*, Palin illuminated the continuity deep down below all of Python's various humorous enterprises. What Python comedy was all about

> was really resisting people telling you how to behave and how not
> to behave. It was the freedom of the individual, a very 60s thing,
> the independence which was part of the way Python had been
> formed, the way Python had gone on, and the way Python had
> sort of arrogantly assumed that whatever we did was right and
> whatever other people did was wrong. (Pythons 2003, 306)

This arrogance caused them no end of controversy with *Life of Brian* and probably did cost them much of their momentum as filmmakers and doubtlessly some of their hard-earned popularity. For Palin, *LOB* was not just about religion but about the abuse of power. In his mind, the film paralleled the Roman occupation of Judea in the way

FACTOID BOX: Sicarii

In *Life of Brian* the different squabbling anti-Roman factions were probably based on the Sicarrii. The

> term applied, in the decades immediately preceding the destruction of Jerusalem, to the Jewish Zealots who attempted to expel the Romans and their partisans from the country, even resorting to murder to attain their object. Under their cloaks they concealed "sicae," or small daggers, whence they received their name; and at popular assembles, especially during the pilgrimage to the Temple mount, they stabbed their enemies, or, in other words, those who were friendly to the Romans, lamenting ostentatiously after the deed and thus evading detection. ("Sicarii" 2012)

The different Jewish freedom fighters, as well as (mostly cut from the film) Eric Idle's Otto, leader of the Judean People's Front, were likely based on this. Although, as many of the Pythons have noted elsewhere, they also based the different factions on the inability of the British left to coalesce against the British right wing.

that Great Britain expanded its empire through conquest. As Palin said, ". . . so you've got the whole British imperialism which was something we were all brought up on" (Morgan 2005, 226); meanwhile, "People in power don't like comedy because it's essentially subversive" (Morgan 2005, 237). Perhaps the real objections to *Life of Brian* were not to its perceived and imaginary attacks on Jesus but instead to how Python challenged the way in which some humans use religion to consolidate power.

Terry Gilliam pointed out that in "*Life of Brian*, in a strange way we were being very cautious about not being blasphemous, by being totally blasphemous but about another guy. My mother, an avid church-goer, saw it but she didn't have a problem because it wasn't about Jesus" (Pythons 2003, 279). But still critics tried to tar the Pythons with the charge of blasphemy, mostly delivered by people who could not bother to even send a representative to see the film, or request a script in order to see if there were actually blasphemous references or theological disputes. John Cleese summed up the Pythons' point of view on religion and *LOB* by pointing out:

> Quite genuinely I don't know how you could try to be funny about Jesus' life, there would be no point in it. What is absurd is not the teachings of the founders of religion, it's what followers subsequently make of it. And I was always astonished what people didn't get. (Pythons 2003, 280)

And Cleese was right: many in the audience did not get this point. Perhaps because Python had erred in tackling what would have been a difficult subject no matter how they had approached it, but perhaps also because by not seeing something they were protesting people did not get to see the nuanced way that Python approached *LOB*. As Cleese remarked on *Life of Brian,* "We were making some very good jokes about some very important things" (Pythons 2003, 307). Python was forced to defend themselves, and in doing so they became both more articulate and more defensive.

As Michael Palin recalled, during a televised debate with Malcolm Muggeridge and the Bishop of Southwark, despite the fact that the bishop had been jocular in the green room, they were attacked on air by both the bishop and a late-arriving Muggeridge, who had apparently not gotten to see all of the film before the debate. Things got testy and Muggeridge became dismissive of the Pythons' point of view, leading to a famous exchange: "When he [Muggeridge] said that Christianity had been responsible for more good in the world than any other force in history, John said, 'What about the Spanish Inquisition?'" (Pythons 2003, 301). Needless to say, the bishop and Muggeridge were not amused.

Strangely enough, with three (major)* films to their credit, the only reappearing character in all three Python films is God. God appears as the (animated) heavenly Father giving direction and purpose in *Holy Grail*, as Jesus in *LOB*, who is seen giving the Sermon on the Mount to a large and largely uncomprehending crowd, and in *Meaning of Life* (where every day is "Christmas in Heaven"). On the whole, the Christian godhead comes across in a rather positive light in the Python-verse.

Human religious figures, however, showed up on Python with less positive regularity, including the dirty vicar (Jones) of episode 39, who could not control himself despite his best efforts (the sketch was also supposed to have won the Mountbatten Trophy, "Show business's highest Accolade"), the dead bishops who mysteriously turned up on the porch of a couple in the "Salvation Fuzz" sketch (ep. 29), and the rough-and-tumble bishop (Jones) continuously late to stop assassination attempts on church officials, despite his best efforts (ep. 17), in the genre parody "The Bishop."

As already noted, one of the more elaborate religious setups was on a talk show titled *The Epilogue: A Question of Belief*. In this sketch from episode 2, a host introduces "Monsignor Edward Gay, visiting Pastoral Emissary of the Somerset Theological College and author of a number of books about belief, the most recent of which is *My God*." His opponent is "Dr. Tom Jack: humanist, broadcaster, lecturer, and author of the book *Hello Sailor*." They are there not to argue about the existence of God but to finally fight over his existence once and for all (God wins by two falls to a submission). Python did have an interest in those who zealously believed in a deity. While making *Life of Brian*, they added and later cut a sequence where Eric Idle appeared as Otto, essentially a religious zealot portrayed along the lines of a Hollywood Nazi. These characters, along with the other revolutionary movements in the film, were based largely on left-wing divisions in the British party system but also on real-life rebels against the Romans (although presumably few of them were forced to write "Romani eti domum" over and over again on a wall until sunrise).

---

*Not counting *And Now for Something Completely Different* or *Live at the Hollywood Bowl*.

BIRTH CONTROL
"Every sperm is sacred."

We said every sperm is sacred: weren't you listening?!

DEATH
"The salmon mousse!"

Python not only showcased an undertaker-themed episode in *FC* (ep. 11), but a major plot point in *The Meaning of Life* involved the personification of Death, who is determined to take away a dinner party, albeit with a rather flimsy excuse as to how they had actually died ("Hey! I didn't eat the mousse!"). However, during the original series one sketch involving death went too far for the BBC. When in the "Undertaker" sketch (ep. 26) the undertaker (Chapman) suggests eating Cleese's recently departed mother (not raw, of course, but cooked) the audience is depicted as growing visibly annoyed and disgusted by the material (although as a matter of fact they were not; this was a condition imposed by the BBC). When the undertaker ends the sketch by mentioning that "if you feel a bit guilty after it later, we can dig up her grave and you can throw up in it" this leads to a staged riot that shuts the show down.

The sketch was *obviously* not advocating interfamilial cannibalism but it was mocking the heavily coded customs of grief that we have standardized in the funeral industry. As Palin later said, sketches like the "Undertaker" sketch were inspired by "a desire to shock an audience by talking about something that was *not* talked about" (Morgan 2005, 57). Like all other lofty topics, Python could not even take funeral rituals seriously.

FILM AND TELEVISION: THE BBC

The British Broadcasting Corporation was founded in 1927 to consolidate and standardize British broadcast radio and was supposed to start broadcasting television in 1936 but, due to wartime shortages, broadcast nothing much visual until the end of the war. The BBC maintains its economic independence from advertising and survives to this day thanks to a license fee paid by anyone who maintains a radio or television receiver in the U.K. Although often presumed to be part of the government, the BBC is independent but operates under a royal charter. Early on strict measures were put in place to guarantee independence in terms of news and programming. Even today, no advertising is permitted and the BBC proper is separated from the BBC commercial services that publish books and sundry. (The commercial services do make a nice little bit of change, thanks for asking!)

The BBC is controlled by a board of governors appointed by the Queen for five-year terms. The BBC operates (in theory) much like American television, in the nebulous concept of the public interest; the airwaves are controlled by corporations that broadcast under license in the public interest (as opposed to the people broadcasting on their own) because of need for coherence and stability. In Britain, J. Reith was the first director-general (appointed in 1927), and was indispensable in forming the BBC's mission. Reith believed that "the medium had great capacity for information and enlightenment" and, thanks to a committee he formed, the recommendation was put forth that "the nation's broadcasting be operated by an independent public corporation" (Brown 1992, 69).

Over time, the BBC has become extraordinarily influential thanks to its television monopoly and thus has informed the vast majority of many in Britain until it was challenged by the creation of for-profit ITV in 1955. The BBC also helped to create a perception of a standardized British language. The diction and familiar phrasing of BBC announcers led to a standard pronunciation and diction sometimes referred to as "BBC English," where one BBC announcer was usually speaking in the same "oval tones" as another (Brown 1992, 69).

From the start, the Pythons could not resist making the BBC one of their targets. In episode 3, the opening title to BBC's *Money Programme* appears and the sketch ends with the BBC globe logo. In episode 4, there is an appearance by Richard Baker, a senior BBC news reader. Not only were news readers considered to be far too "serious" to appear in a light entertainment program, but the use of the "BBC globe in a sketch was unheard of before," as was "BBC style continuity announcers" (Topping 1999, 27).

Because the Pythons were largely left alone (at first) they could gradually tweak their use of the "official" BBC symbology and poke fun at the inherently serious and almost sacred nature of the institution. By episode 13, the BBC "is the medium that's now the fodder for *Monty Python*" (Topping 1999, 43). This led to some of the best comedy of the twentieth century but it also led to the BBC eventually noticing. Early on, no one at the BBC quite knew what to make of the bold and innovative humor the Pythons were creating. They didn't get it (like many others at the time) because Python was not merely "sending up the boss" but actually boldly challenging the conventions of televisuality. One of the problems of creating mind-boggling new innovations in comedy is that that the old guard has no real understanding of what exactly you are doing. As previously mentioned, Python was a reaction to the staid customs and traditions of British culture and one of the establishments that they were addressing was the BBC itself.

Almost from the start, Python had to contend with a capricious and arbitrary system of programming their original episodes. Not only were they stuck in an undesirable time slot on Sunday nights, but they also had to contend with frequently being interrupted or preempted. Part of their rising anger at the BBC stemmed from periods in 1970, when BBC actions included putting them in "opt out" slots so no viewers in Scotland, Ireland, the midland, or the south could watch, leading Palin to joke that "there is to be a break after three episodes where Python will be replaced by 'Horse of Year Show'" (Palin 2006, 35). Despite the lack of attention by the BBC and the lack of any obvious goal towards achieving an audience, Python continued to stretch the boundaries of what was acceptable on television at that time. To Palin, early "Python seemed to fit into this niche of daring, irreverence, therefore only accessible to those of a certain sort of intellectual status" (Morgan 2005, 72). After the first few episodes "the program became more fragmented, more surreal, more violent" (Morgan 2005, 69).

The question remains exactly *why* the BBC ignored them early on.

Perhaps because of the relatively unneeded piece of television real estate or simply because they counted on the presumably bankable Cleese (and, to a lesser extent, the other Pythons) to produce something that would break some ground, just not too much, and not all at once. As Palin noted:

> I think there was always a conscious desire to do something which was ahead of, or tested, the audience's taste, or tested the limits of what we could say or what we cannot say. For us it was more putting together odd and surreal images in a certain way which would not *offend* but really jolt, surprise and amaze! (Morgan 2005, 56)

But offend they did, often spectacularly. It was hard to ignore. Python became progressively less concerned with linear sketches and began exploring sketches that not only involved surrealistic juxtapositions of humor but also were designed to test the boundaries of the BBC. Again, perhaps the most notorious sketch, in "Royal Episode 13" involved John Cleese being given options by an undertaker of how to best dispose of his recently deceased mother. After a few tentative pokes at the topic, eventually it becomes clear that the undertaker is actually recommending that Cleese cannibalize his mother's corpse. The episode is interrupted by BBC-ordered chaos, and as the Pythons are shut down by supposed members of the audience they are forced to apologize for their rude behavior (once again using the BBC logo with a voice-over as the forum for their apology). By rudely approaching the topic of cannibalism, the Pythons threw the gauntlet down, daring the BBC to either censor the show on a regular basis or let the Pythons' comedic imagination proceed in whatever direction they felt (im)proper. For the most part the BBC let the Pythons experiment. As Terry Jones noted, "The BBC took pride in not only *not* looking at the scripts, they didn't look at the shows before they went out" (Pythons 2003, 164).

As Terry Gilliam noted about the first Python audience at the live tapings, "There was just the sound of hundreds of jaws dropping, it seemed to me" (Pythons 2003, 166). As Marci Landy wrote, "The Flying Circus appealed more to university educated, increasingly younger audiences and to the culturally disaffected" (2006, 29). Yet initially the audiences were unreceptive and the Pythons had to bring in their friends and relatives to sit in the live audience before they developed enough of a cult following to fill the tapings with enthusiastic fans.

One of the ways in which the Pythons continued to progress was in the technical aspects of television. While most British performers were content to let others direct and plan their shows, Python early on demanded as much creative control as possible. As Eric Idle noticed, individual writers had their own technical requirements. To Idle, "Mike and Terry always starting with long pans across the countryside, or a typical John and Graham confrontational opening" (Morgan 2005, 111). The Pythons decided the best way to tackle television was to understand how it worked. Because of this, the codes of television became ripe for their brand of comedy. As Marci Landy wrote, "the Pythons form of comedy tackled sexuality, law, medicine, politics, psychiatry, literary classics, comic books, language, cinema, and above all, television" (2006, 5). Terry Gilliam in particular loved the immediacy that television provided for the Pythons, saying, "That's what you get out of television that you don't get out of films—millions of people are experiencing the same thing at the same time" (Pythons 2003, 166).

TELEVISUALITY AND FILM

Monty Python subverted the codes of television so thoroughly that almost every episode contains a reference to some aspect of the medium itself. Actors ask if they have any more lines. Extras do not talk because then the BBC would have to pay them. Nature show hosts chase each other for the sole microphone in competing documentaries, et cetera. Other sketches play with the literal format of television (the standard BBC practice of taping the show with videotape for soundstages and film for the outdoors) as in the "Society for Putting Things on Top of Other Things" sketch (more about this in a moment). Even the switching between animated segments and live action was unpredictable: one could

be a link to the other and the next a non sequitur.* Such anarchy marked
Python as boldly aware of the power of the medium. The films were also
constructed in a similar manner, with Brian being "rescued" by a space-
ship," and *Holy Grail* briefly becoming a documentary as the historian,
who is trying to put this into context, is suddenly thrown (literally) into
the violent world of chivalry. With the death of the historian, we see that
Python is not afraid to combine the two worlds together, to suggest that
the viewer is symbolically fooled by watching a straight narrative, and
that we should not hold them fast to the traditional rules of film or televisual culture. Even *Holy Grail*, despite two mighty armies about to clash
over the fate of the Grail, does not end in a traditional battle for dominance but with police coming to break up the fight ("That's a dangerous
weapon, that is!" one officer exclaims as he disarms a knight); we are
suddenly in a documentary. Or perhaps we are just watching television
in much the same way that coverage of the Vietnam War and the struggle for civil rights in the United States (and Northern Ireland) intruded
into living rooms at the same time.

Python subverts the visual codes and rules we are accustomed to
when watching television; it makes sure that we realize that we have
been following a "grammar" of watching television (and film) all of our
lives. We expect that in certain genres, genre codes—the rules that tell
us exactly what we are watching and give us clues as to how to
respond—are maintained. For example, we *know* that people do not
burst into song in a drama or comedy unless it is obviously labeled as a
musical as well (except in Bollywood, where all bets are off and in the
midst of a car chase or violent duel a song or wet sari scene could break
out . . . but we digress). Python both comments on television genres
and deconstructs them. A sketch can be stopped if it is being "too silly."
A Gilliam animation can take us to another sketch not just as a link,
but also as simply a pause in the action.† Not as a throwaway gag, but
as a way of asking the viewer, "Why haven't you noticed all of those

---

* The "Crazy Ivan" maneuver of sketch comedy.
† Given Gilliam's experience in comics, it is perhaps unsurprising that his interstitials often act as the "gutters" between comic panels.

silly rules in the first place?" Just as Python deconstructed the traditional role of the BBC, it also asked viewers to question the nature of television itself.

For many years the BBC had worked with the assumption that shooting on film was useful for outdoor shots, but that videotape was more effective (and cheaper) for indoor shots. In the sketch "The Society for Putting Things on Top of Other Things," (ep. 18) after the meeting has broken up, Chapman, the group's leader, is confused and then gradually horrified that every time he leaves the building he is no longer on videotape but is instead on film. Try as he might to escape the confines of the building, he is trapped by the BBC's internal televisual logic.

Naturally, the way out is based on the audience's familiarity with the conventions of the genre and the comforting familiarity with the British class system (although no one stops to ask why it would be dangerous or even alarming to be on film as opposed to videotape in the first place!). The society members quickly organize a plan to tunnel under the building and therefore escape below the film. With this the scene quickly morphs into a full-on parody of a British or American World War Two prisoner-of-war film, complete with men assigned to digging and others given various tasks to lull the Nazis into a false sense of security. When two Nazi officers appear, both dressed according to the conventions of the genre, they wonder, "Where's the traditional cheeky and lovable Cockney sergeant?" who then immediately appears to reassure them that all is right with the world.

By the time the series was over, Python had so deconstructed the medium of television that there was almost nothing left to deconstruct, except for their own deconstructions: "the elements of illogicality and playfulness to be found in most comedy are in Python stretched to the limit" (Neale 2008, 77). After it was all over, what could be done with the completely leveled and fallow fields of the television medium, except to rebuild it again with many of the same traditions intact? One option was to be John Cleese's brilliant *Fawlty Towers*, which worked so well within the conventions that Python had worked so hard to destroy. As Cleese put it, "Python was . . . playing games with convention which no one had ever done before, and it was very startling the first time you do it. But once people get used to a convention being broken, it's not startling at all, and then there's nothing left" (Morgan 2005, 314). Python had essentially undermined the televisual landscape so that the only recourse for other programs was to return to more traditional methods of comedy (albeit, sometime more self-aware and sometimes more ironic in nature) and try to forget that Python had ever existed in the first place.

"SAM PECKINPAH'S *SALAD DAYS*"

While it is customary for current cartoon situation comedies such as *South Park* and *Family Guy* (not to mention countless parodic YouTube videos) to engage in mash-ups—the juxtaposition of different media texts with each other (such as *Family Guy* producing winking remakes of the first three *Star Wars* movies) or the combining of two or more disparate genres together to create a new comedic whole, Monty Python largely introduced this process to television. While Python had been engaging in mash-ups since the start of the series, the epitome of the genre is evidenced in *Salad Days* (ep. 33). The title *Salad Days*, a phrase that originates in William Shakespeare's *Antony and Cleopatra* and refers to the days of youth and vigor but also naïveté, serves as a theme for several of the sketches on the show and also works in terms of a specific sketch, one that juxtaposes not only acclaimed and controversial American filmmaker Sam Peckinpah's increasingly violent filmic career but also a whimsical 1950s-era musical about a magic piano that causes all who listen to its music to dance manically and find joy despite themselves.

In the episode, "Sam Peckinpah's *Salad Days*" is the closing sketch, immediately following the now-famous "Cheese Shop" sketch (which introduced viewers to the cheese shop that does not, in fact, stock any cheese). After killing off the cheese shop proprietor, John Cleese dons an oversized Stetson hat and rides off into the sunset, revealing the end of a cowboy (and cheese-related) western imaginatively titled *Rogue Cheddar*, apparently written by early twentieth-century British author Hugh

Walpole. From there the scene shifts to Eric Idle in a talk-show format. Idle, playing a particularly unctuous film critic (based on British film critic Philip Jenkinson), begins by talking about previous cheese-based westerns including *The Cheese Who Shot Liberty Valance*. Then (as various captions urge him to "get on with it" and "stop sniffling") Idle offers a brief overview of the career of Sam Peckinpah as a purveyor of "utterly truthful and sexually arousing" violence, before proceeding to show a clip from Peckinpah's version of *Salad Days*. The clip begins with a group of straw-hat-wearing upper-class British men and women surrounding a piano. When Lionel (Palin) proposes a game of tennis, Graham Chapman's character gently lobs a tennis ball at him that unexpectedly causes an enormous spurt of blood to erupt from his forehead. His tennis racket is tossed aside, only to eviscerate the woman at the party; Idle's arm is then quickly torn off and Cleese's hands are cut off in the piano. The next

"Some pretty strong meat there, from [sniff] Sam Peckinpah."
Pike Bishop (William Holden) and his machine gun unleash hell in *The Wild Bunch*.

"There will be some door slamming in the streets of Kensington tonight!"
Upper-class Twits wrestle with brassieres in *Monty Python's Flying Circus.*

minutes consist of extremely gory shots of most of the other players dying via incredibly bloody dismemberments in slow motion. Idle's critic returns to comment, "Pretty strong meat there, from [sniff] Sam Peckinpah!" He is then gunned down in slow motion by unseen attackers as the credits roll. The entire episode ultimately ends with an apology (supposedly from the BBC) about the over-the-top violence in the sketch.

The pastoral upper-class picnic Python references is based on a British musical, *Salad Days* (1954), with music by Julian Slade and lyrics and book by Slade and Dorothy Reynolds. The musical is ostensibly about two young recent college graduates in love, but it also serves as a nostalgic look at the last vestiges of the British upper class (a group much parodied by Python, particularly in the Upper-Class Twit of the Year contest in ep. 12). The musical is quintessentially British—featuring dancing college dons and easily identifiable Cambridge college undergraduates and graduates in an adventure with a magic piano and a UFO* thrown in as well. Python's members knew this particular vision of undergraduate idyll well, as the troupe was well stocked with members who had attended some of the best colleges in Britain. The British audience for Python had also likely either seen or heard of the musical and known of the ubiquitous Jenkinson, and at that point most would also have known of the controversial new films of American director Sam Peckinpah. Peckinpah, a notorious director, had become well known for introducing a new breed of more cynical westerns, such as *Major Dundee* (mentioned by Idle), to cinemagoers, and Python's audience would certainly have heard of his infamous *The Wild Bunch* (1969), starring William Holden, Ernest Borgnine, and Robert Ryan. Peckinpah's *The Wild Bunch* was a boldly violent deconstruction of the mythic Old West. *The Wild Bunch* is the story of an aging band of robbers who decide to pull one last heist before retiring to Mexico. However, their plans go awry and after a (literal) Mexican standoff the remaining members of the gang are killed in dramatic slow motion, but not before they manage to kill several hundred Mexican soldiers in the battle. If John Ford's *The Searchers* had opened up the debate regarding the myth of the iconic cowboy and the western genre itself, then Peckinpah's *The Wild Bunch* was the nail that shut its coffin.

Peckinpah's controversial over-the-top bloodshed and use of slow motion to emphasize excessive violence demonstrated not just a new late sixties/early seventies cynicism but also a new ultraviolent cinema that made each death as cruel and shocking as older westerns had thoroughly romanticized the shoot-out. While Peckinpah's vision was particularly American, there are precedents in English cinema as well, such as Lindsay Anderson's surrealistically violent ending to *if....* and the ultraviolence of Stanley Kubrick's disturbing *A Clockwork Orange*. But set in contrast with the innocence of *Salad Days*, Peckinpah serves as a tool for Python to deconstruct not just British culture, but also the notion of what was acceptable on television and in cinema.

"Sam Peckinpah's *Salad Days*," a virtual mélange of two radically dif-

---

* No, we're not making that up.

FACTOID BOX: Hugh Walpole

The transition between the "Cheese Shop" sketch and "Sam Peckinpah's *Salad Days*" is also accompanied by Idle's reference to Hugh Walpole's "Rogue Cheddar"; Walpole was best known as a prolific British novelist, perhaps best known for his book *The Inquisitor* (1935), and as far as most biographers agree, he seldom, if ever, wrote cowboy novels involving cheese.

---

ferent film genres, the newfangled ultraviolence of Peckinpah and the jolly nostalgia-drenched British class-based idea of a holiday, is a typical Python mash-up of radically different sensibilities, styles, and genres. Misplacing the visual techniques of Peckinpah's cynical and blood-splattered American Old West within a setting typical of idealized British class sensibilities is more than just an example of how Python invented the televised mash-up (they were well aware of the Dadaist, Fluxus, and Situationist movements, as well as the history of literary criticism); "*Salad Days*" also demonstrates the cultural knowledge necessary for an audience to truly "get" the myriad levels of humor inherent in a Python sketch.

FISH SLAPPING

One of the most beloved, shortest, and funniest of all of Monty Python's sketches was the Grimsby "Fish-Slapping Dance" sketch, which appeared in episode 28. The sketch involves Palin, dressed in a pith helmet and expedition-type outfit, dancing up to a similarly clad John Cleese. Twice Palin slaps him with a small fish before dancing back to place. After Palin is done, Cleese takes out a much larger fish and slaps him, and he then falls over ten feet into a canal. According to Palin, the sketch was a joy to film and after he was done "you experience this pleasant feeling that, just by jumping into the river, you have justified your existence for the day, and can relax into a state of quiet euphoria" (Palin 2006, 57). It was supposed to be "a very silly traditional dance," one complicated by the fact that the river/canal had been at high tide before filming but had returned to its lowest water level. Palin particularly loved the Fish-Slapping-Dance and mentioned that

> of all the Python stuff, that is something that I would show people to determine whether they had any detectable sense of humor at all. That's something you could show to someone devoid of humor and they might just begin to smile. And if they didn't, there would be no hope for them. (Johnson 1999, 135)

To Palin, this was the genius of Monty Python in all its fundamentally silly glory. As Palin also noted, there is "something so elementally silly about it, it works so satisfactorily" (Pythons 2003, 304). If years of university education, training with some of the finest comedians of that time period, and continuous deconstruction of the medium lead us to one final image of Monty Python's final circus, let it be two men in pith helmets, joyfully slapping each other with fish until one falls into the canal. If this makes no sense to you, then you have probably been watching a different television show than we did or have wandered into the wrong book.*

---

* In case you *have* wandered into the wrong book, sitting to the immediate left of this book is *Everything I Ever Needed to Know About Filling in Blanks* and to our right is *Everything I Ever Needed to Know About Ziggurats*. Both books also feature much on Python but relatively little on the Fish-Slapping Dance.

GILLIAM: THE DIRECTOR

In the years since the dissolution of Monty Python, Gilliam has gone from being the "silent Python" to perhaps the most prolific and vocal Python of them all.* As a director, he continues to push the boundaries of cinema (particularly working, as he often has, within "the Hollywood system") and he continues to challenge his audiences intellectually and conceptually, just as he did back in his Python days. His directorial work, both comedic and dramatic, is not simply designed as entertainment for the masses. As his many—and often very public—ideological disagreements with various production companies (including Universal, with whom he struggled to make *Brazil*) attest, he and mainstream Hollywood seem to be perpetually enacting an Americanized version of the Python/BBC conflict. As Gilliam has reportedly complained:

> The [Hollywood] studio's mentality is that Americans are stupid. They try to lower the standard as much as they can to reach what they think is this great dumb audience. And I have always resisted that and wanted to believe in the audience's intelligence. But if you keep feeding people baby food for long enough they begin to like it. (iMDB)

Yet while Gilliam did spend an extraordinary amount of time going through books on classical art and literally cutting and pasting his own animation together, he was also responsible for the hand-drawn artwork that provides much of the visual appeal of Python. In the Python films, he established the visual tropes that would help define his later directorial style. In particular, his design work on *Life of Brian*, with its faked perspectives of grand scale and imposing architecture, became hallmarks of the later Gilliam film style, and the fish-eye lens employed for the surreal "The Middle of the Film" in *Meaning of Life* has seemingly

---

* Although, admittedly, that's a pretty damn subjective claim, given the far-flung talents and opinions of all the surviving Pythons.

"—"

Typically atypical Gilliam cut-and-paste interstitial animation (*Monty Python's Flying Circus*). Gilliam's unique illustrations continue to influence subversive animated comedies from *South Park* to *Frisky Dingo* and *Archer*.

been employed (for various effects) in nearly every Gilliam film since. And according to the director himself, "The 14mm lens is now known as The Gilliam" (Stubbs 2004).

From *Jabberwocky* to *Brazil*, to all of his many completed (and uncompleted) projects, Gilliam's unique "more for less" style,* which bombards the viewer with fantastical and often-disturbing imagery, is unique in the way it gets under the skin. Like the auteurs Kubrick and Hitchcock, Gilliam's visual design is apparent from the first frame and stands out as one of the defining features of his films. In terms of other directors with a similar visual sense of style, only the (early) work of Tim Burton can really be compared with Gilliam. Interestingly, both had backgrounds as artists and cartoonists and worked their way into film almost by accident.

Unlike the "mainstream" purveyors of entertainment who are stereo-

---

*Eventually "more for less" became "more for much, much, more": witness the visual overload in *Fear and Loathing in Las Vegas*, for example.

typically concerned with putting paying arses in the pews, Gilliam strives to agitate, rather than please: "I do want to say things in [my] films. I want audiences to come out with shards stuck in them. I don't care if people love my films or walk out, as long as they have a strong response" (Stubbs 2004).

And the responses to his post-Python films (from the disturbingly trippy *Brazil*, to the disturbingly postapocalyptic *Twelve Monkeys*, to the disturbingly trippy *Fear and Loathing*) have definitely been "strong"—most folks either love Gilliam's works or hate them; pretty strong meat there [sniff], from Gilliam, indeed!*

---

* Ultimately, if you'd like to know what Gilliam has been up to lately, you can check his Twitter account (@terrygilliamweb) or, if timeliness is not paramount, peruse Phil Stubbs' finely obsessive site, *Dreams: The Terry Gilliam Fanzine* (http://www.smart .co.uk/dreams/home.htm), which includes a Gilliam filmography, detailed information on Gilliam's current and future projects, "reviews" of Gilliam-related news from 2006 to 2011, and various in-depth features and interviews through 2005.

"It's . . . ?"

Part VII

THE AFTERWORD

TAG UNDER: errata, wafer thin, and bugger off.

t's? No it isn't! Here we discuss the lasting legacy of Python, or how you too have learned everything you ever needed to know about anything, without ever leaving your living room! Except possibly to go to the bathroom . . . or to get a snack. Well, either way, you can learn everything about everything *mostly* in your living room. Unless of course there are other rooms that are more conducive to learning. Well, pick *a* room and let's get on with it, shall we?

What did we learn from Python? Well, for one thing, we learned about life from Python.* I know we've been saying that for the last bleeding three hundred pages or so, but we really did. Python taught us a lot about comedy, about the world, about history, about authority and (as we move into middle age) exactly how wonderfully absurd everything is and how absurdly wonderful everything is. There is no one correct way to analyze Python, only multiple ways to enjoy it. Again, as Palin said, ". . . once one tries to sort of analyze *why* we're funny, I think it's—I think it's *impossible* to answer for a start and I think once we unpick ourselves and give guidelines, in a sense it takes away from the audience their choice of how they react to Python" (Morgan 2005, 115). Python did not want to dictate a specific style of critical thought, just a natural and, they hoped, mirthful range of responses. After all, not many comedies from the late sixties and early seventies garner such praise as: "Its slippery logic and post-modern

---

* Although the meaning of life? Still not so sure about that.

"Now Mrs. Teal, if you're looking in tonight, this is for fifteen pounds, and is to stop us from revealing the name of your *lover in Bolton!*"
A sleazy television presenter (Palin) offers compelling reasons to tune in to *Blackmail!* from *Monty Python's Flying Circus.*

self-awareness pioneered a style that has never successfully been imitated. Its joyful and singular appreciation of both lowbrow antic vaudeville and a high minded theater of the absurd is a model of the form" (MacGregor 1998). There are more people alive today who didn't get Python than those who did. Hell, some of Python's most ardent critics were members of Python, including John Cleese, who has opined, at times, that

> everyone thinks you can't wait to drive up to Huddersfield to lec-
> ture the local Monty Python appreciation society about some-
> thing you did so long ago you've actually forgotten it . . . If I made
> people laugh back then, great, but is anybody really going to be
> better off going on about the damn comedy show than reading
> "War and Peace" again? (Schmidt 1994)

Despite the pessimism shown by Cleese towards Python, every now and then we would argue that there is real joy to be had in obsessing over Python. Just as a rereading of *War and Peace* will make you a better person (magically!), learning all the words to the "Nudge Nudge" sketch will make you a funnier person. Both admirable qualities, we assure you.

It is also true that among the most reverent fans of Monty Python are academics. There have been books on Python, scholarly papers, disserta-tions, Darl Larsen's mammoth guide (*Monty Python's Flying Circus: An Ut-terly Complete, Thoroughly Unillustrated, Absolutely Unauthorized Guide to Possibly All the References from Arthur "Two-Sheds" Jackson to Zambesi*) and his comparative analysis of Python and Shakespeare, collections exploring Python and philosophy, and even a recent (2011) conference in Poland. According to Professor Randy Malamud (who attended said conference), "Academics venerate Monty Python because we find the troupe's subver-sive critical analysis and its vast portfolio of cultural and intellectual ref-erences congruent with our world" (2011). Malamud remembers that when he first started watching Monty Python "there were still large gaps—many things I didn't get" and that "Monty Python's appeal induces a fanatical (which is perhaps synonymous here with 'scholarly') attempt to understand not just its puns and allusions, but more broadly, its cul-tural context" (2011). We believe that any fan of Python, or anyone who has read this book all the way through to the afterword (having carefully avoided the tiger we released on the last page of Part 4—now that was a bit of a jolly good adventure, wouldn't you agree, Algy?), would have to agree that as they watched Python throughout their lives they were constantly learning not just new allusions to historical events or philosophical concepts but also how to engage with a text and how to wrestle (with or without Plato) with esoteric concepts in an effort to "get" the hidden humor that relied upon an accumulation of human knowledge. Python didn't just entertain their fans: they rewarded them.

So, the question at the end of this book is not only what you learned from Python (of course if you had the *Executive Edition* of the book, this wouldn't be a problem. Discerning buyers of the *Executive Edition* have already had all of their questions answered and would now be indulging in the spa treatments and complimentary pedicures that come with the *EE*). Instead we ask: What are the reasons we all keep going back to Python over and over again? Just as most readers have favorite authors they reread not just to reimmerse themselves in a particular prose, but also to find new meanings and insights augmented by subsequent life experience, the same thing can be said about Python. The two authors of this book are much like you, the readers, in that when we return to Python after a break of months, or even years, we always come away with something that wasn't there before. As one of us happily posted on Facebook (Time-Suck!) recently: "... after almost two years of pondering Python semi-professionally, I still think they're fucking runny ... err ... funny." So, what did we get out of Python?*

Here are some lessons from Python that Dr. Brian thought were important:

Most comedy isn't funny, meaning we don't really *learn* anything from it. It's junk food that provides momentary satisfaction but leaves an empty taste at the end of the day. Most of the things you believe in are wrong. Not necessarily things such as religion, philosophy, or theory, but the idea that reality is coherent and logical and that most man-made structures are not arbitrary. What is true is that the universe is an absurd and arbitrary place and that the sooner we realize that and laugh at it the better off we are.

Most of the things that you see in other people that look ridiculous or sound silly really reflect how ridiculous and how silly you are. The preva-

---

*Other than everything we have written in the previous chapters, of course?

lent humor that tears down not to build up but simply to ironically smirk at how silly things are is just as great a problem in the world today as any rigid ideological stance. Comedy only works with the extremes of empathy (where the real target is the capriciousness of authority and the people who choose to be involved without questioning why they are obeying orders) or where comedy tears down everything in order to rebuild it.

Most of what we accept about the media is unreal and silly. Media critic Neil Postman was right: the forms of media we use to express ourselves are biased towards certain forms of expression. And some, such as television, are biased towards the trivial and the absurd. Python merely pointed this incredibly obvious but much-ignored fact out to those who chose to engage with them.

Most of what we learned in school is inherently silly and arbitrary. The problem is that we were taught from our earliest years to absorb facts instead of to question authority. We should unlearn as much as we were taught as soon as possible, if not sooner. We also learned that asking a teacher "why" was usually discouraged. Unlearning not facts (gravity does exist; if you don't believe in gravity you are either severely deluded or a wicked anti-gravite), but certain interpretation of facts is definitely possible and desirable.

And an unofficial bonus lesson: when you meet someone who can recite "The Argument Clinic" sketch or sing "The Lumberjack song," this probably means you have met a new friend or loved one. Keep anyone close who thinks the world is as silly as you do. There, are of course, many more of these lessons, but they are in the *Executive Edition*.

AFTERWORD II: ELECTRIC BOOGALOO
"And you try telling that to the kids these days, and they won't believe you."

In the interest of fair play, here are a few lessons learned by Dr. Jeff:

> Never get involved in a land war in Asia.
> Always get the name of the gentleman before . . .

No, no, that can't be right. Let me check my notes. Ah, here we are:

> Words matter. Names too.
> The most serious people in the room are not always the most
>   smartest.
> And, of course, never forget the most important lesson of all:
>   There is *not*, in fact, always room for an after-dinner
>   mint.

But in addition to these core koans, Python taught me a plenitude of factoids both great and small.* Among them:

> I learned how not to be seen and how not to be heard.
> I learned how to recognize different parts of the body.
> I learned how to recognize different types of trees from quite a
>   long way away.
> I learned I should read the fine print before signing on for organ
>   donation.
> I learned how to feed a goldfish.
> I learned how to say "Romans go home" . . . in Latin!
> I learned how to defend myself if anyone attacks me with a piece
>   of fresh fruit.
> I learned that that the Earth is revolving at 900 mph and is
>   orbiting at 90 mps.
> I learned that a nod's as good as a wink to a blind bat.
> I learned how to spot the loony and how to recognize a mason.
> I learned that the llama is a quadruped that lives in big rivers like
>   the Amazon; it has two ears, a heart, a forehead, and a beak
>   for eating honey. It is also provided with fins for swimming.
>   Llamas are bigger than frogs.
> I learned how to climb the north face of the Uxbridge Road.
> I learned Gumby flower arranging.

---

* And dull and ugly, of course.

I learned how to make a small plate of goulash go round twenty-six people, how to get the best out of my canapés, and how to unblock my loo.

I learned how to deal with any left-wing uprising by the end of a party.

I learned that the randiest of the gastropods is the limpet.

I also learned how to become a gynaecologist, play the flute, split an atom, construct a box girder bridge, irrigate the Sahara and make vast new area of land cultivatable, and rid the world of all known diseases.

Sadly, I never did learn how to fling an otter. Ah well: there's always next week.

THE END? OR IS IT?

And now for something completely different: a brief quiz. We warned you!

1. Which of the following are *(DRUNKEN) PHILOSOPHERS*?
Plato
Socrates
Wittgenstein
Semprini

2. Which of the following are *(DEAD) COMPOSERS*?
Debussy
Semprini
Gluck
Beckenbauer

3. Which of the following are POLITICAL FIGURES ...
Mao
Marx
Stalin
Semprini

4. Name three *medieval* Knights of the Round Table, not including Arthur.

5. What radio show most heavily influenced the Pythons?

6. Describe the film stylings of director Sam Peckinpah.

7. What sport do the New Zealand All Blacks play?

8. Who infamously led the Spanish Inquisition?

9. What is the official flower of Australia?

10. If a delicious blancmange could play sports, which would it play?

11. According to legend, how did Arthur become King, eh?

12. Who wrote the longest novel ever (while staring at his madeleine)?

13. Who or what are vox pop?

14. Name two ways to get the vaginal juices flowing (and do *not* stampede straight towards the clitoris!).

15. How does the "Cheese Shop" sketch relate to the conversational maxims?

16. Three-part question:
    What is the capital of Assyria?

    What is the airspeed velocity of an unladen African swallow?

    What is your favorite color?

17. What is the first lesson in "not being seen"?

18. Name five synonyms for "dead."

19. What is the etymology of "SPAM"?

20. Spell "Throatwobbler Mangrove": now pronounce it.

21. Catherine and Heathcliff are the protagonists in which of Emily Brönte's novels?

22. Name as many types of cheese as you can.

23. Which of the following is *not* really one of Shakespeare's plays?
    Titus Andronicus
    Gay Boys in Bondage
    Coriolanus
    Two Gentlemen of Verona

24. Name the following:
    American Python:
    Dead Python:
    Medieval Python:
    Spamalot Python:
    Traveling Python:
    Fawlty Python:
    Glamour Stooge:

25. And finally for 90% of your final grade:
    What is the Meaning of Life?

REFERENCES

Aicinea, Stephen. 2010. "Sport as War or a Means to Peace?: Thomas Hobbes' Laws of Nature." *International Journal of Business and Social Science* 1.1 (October): 15–25.

Almost the Truth—The Lawyer's Cut. 2009. Eagle Rock Entertainment. DVD.

Anderson, Sam. 2005. "And Now for Something Completely Deficient: Why *Spamalot* Should Never Have Won a Tony for Best Musical." *Slate,* June 21. http://www.slate.com/articles/arts/culturebox/2005/06/and_now_for _something_completely_deficient.html.

Appleby, Joyce, Lynn Hunt, and Margaret Jacob. 1994. *Telling the Truth About History.* New York: Norton.

Baggini, Julian. 2010. "Who's the Thinker in White?" *Guardian,* April 27. http://www.theguardian.com/theguardian/2010/apr/28/monty-python -philosophers-football-match.

Baker, Keith, John Boyer, and Julius Kirshner, eds. 1987. *University of Chicago Readings in Western Civilization,* volume 7: *The Old Regime and the French Revolution.* Chicago: University of Chicago Press.

Barzun, Jacques. 2000. *From Dawn to Decadence: 1500 to the Present, 500 Years of Western Cultural Life.* New York: HarperCollins.

Bourdieu, Pierre. 2000. "How Can One Be a Sports Fan?" In *The Cultural Studies Reader,* 2nd ed, edited by Simon Durrey, 339–355. London: Routledge.

Brown, Les. 1992. *Les Brown's Encyclopedia of Television,* 3rd ed. New York: Zoetrope.

Bull Durham, 1988. Directed by Ron Shelton. Orion Pictures.

Calkins, Mark. 2009. "Summarize Proust." À la recherche du Temps Perdu.com. http://tempsperdu.com.

Carcopino, Jérôme. 1968. *Daily Life in Ancient Rome.* New Haven, CT, and London: Yale University Press.

Carlin, George. 1997. *Brain Droppings.* New York: Hyperion.

Carlin, George. 1972. "Seven Words You Can Never Say on Television." *Class Clown.* Little David / Atlantic Records. LP.

Chapman, Graham, David Sherlock, Alex Martin, David Yallop, and Douglas Adams. 1980. *A Liar's Autobiography,* vol. 7. Great Britain: Eyre Methuen.

Chapman, Graham, and Jim Yoakum. 1997. *Graham Crackers: Fuzzy Memories, Sillybits and Outright Lies.* NJ: Career Press.

Chaucer, Geoffrey. 1987. *The Riverside Chaucer.* Edited by Larry Benson. Boston, MA: Houghton Mifflin.

Chrétien de Troyes. 1991. *Arthurian Romances.* Edited by William Kibler and Carleton Carroll. New York: Penguin Books.

Cohen, Jeffrey Jerome. 1996. "Monster Culture: Seven Theses." In *Monster Theory: Reading Culture*, edited by Jeffrey Jerome Cohen, 3–25. Minneapolis: University of Minnesota Press.

Copland, Aaron. 1988. *What to Listen for in Music*. New York: McGraw Hill.

Crystal, David. 1995. "Phonaesthetically Speaking." *English Today* 42.2 (April): 8–12.

Debord, Guy. 1983. *The Society of the Spectacle*. Detroit: Black & Red Books.

Di Justo, Patrick. 2012. "What Spam with Bacon Is Really Made Of." *Wired* 20.05 (May): 40.

"Downfall / Hitler Reacts." 2011. *Know Your Meme*. Accessed May 1, http://knowyourmeme.com/memes/downfall-hitler-reacts.

Eliade, Mircea. 1975. *Myth and Reality*. New York: Harper.

Everett, William, and Paul Laird. 2002. *The Cambridge Companion to the Musical*. Cambridge: Cambridge University Press.

Freud, Sigmund. 2002. *Civilization and Its Discontents*. New York: W. W. Norton.

Gilliam, Terry, and Lucinda Cowell. 1978. *Animations of Mortality*. Methuen: New York.

Goffman, Erving. 1959. *The Presentation of Self in Everyday Life*. New York: Doubleday.

Gopnick, Adam. 2012. "Inquiring Minds: The Spanish Inquisition Revisited." *New Yorker*, January 16, 70–75.

Grant, Michael. 1997. *The Roman Emperors: A Biographical Guide to the Rulers of Imperial Rome 31 B.C.–A.D. 476.* New York: Barnes and Noble.

Green, Toby. 2007. *Inquisition: The Reign of Fear.* New York: St. Martin's Press.

Grice, Paul. 1975. "Logic and Conversation." Reprinted in *Studies in the Way of Words,* ed. Paul Grice, 22–40. Cambridge, MA: Harvard University Press, 1989. Originally published in P. Cole and J. Morgan, eds., *Syntax and Semantics,* Vol. 3. New York: Academic Press.

Grimm, Jacob and Wilhelm. 2002. "Rumpelstiltskin." In *The Grimm Brothers' Children's and Household Tales (Grimm's Fairy Tales),* compiled, translated, and edited by D. L. Ashliman. http://www.pitt.edu/~dash/grimm055.html.

Hamilton, Alan. 2003. *We Are Amused: Over 500 Years of Bon Mots by and About the Royal Family.* London: Robert Hale.

Hardcastle, Gary, and Goerge Reisch, eds. 2006. *Monty Python and Philosophy: Nudge Nudge, Think Think!* Peru, Illinois: Open Court Publishing.

Hibbert, Christopher. 2000. *Queen Victoria: A Personal History.* London: HarperCollins.

Hitchens, Christopher. 2008. "England Made Them." *Vanity Fair,* January. http://www.vanityfair.com/culture/features/2008/01/eccentrics200801.

Horne, Alistair. 2004. *La Belle France: A Short History.* New York: Vintage Books.

Ide, Wendy. 2009. "Terry Gilliam on Heath Ledger's Death and *The Imaginarium of Doctor Parnassus.*" *The Times,* May 14. http://www.thetimes.co.uk/tto/arts/film/article2431428.15ce.

Idle, Eric, ed. 2009. *Monty Python Live!* New York: Hyperion Books.

Jewers, Caroline. 2000. "Heroes and Heroin: From *True Romance* to *Pulp Fiction*." *Journal of Popular Culture* 33.4 (Spring): 39–61.

Johnson, Kim "Howard." 1999. *The First 20 Years of Monty Python*. New York: Thomas Dunne Books.

Jones, Terry. 1985. *Chaucer's Knight: The Portrait of a Medieval Mercenary*. London: Methuen.

Kendall, Paul Murray. 1971. *Louis XI: The Universal Spider*. New York: W. W. Norton.

Landy, Marci. 2006. *Monty Python's Flying Circus*. Detroit: Wayne State University Press.

Langer, Susanne K. 1979. *Philosophy in a New Key: A Study in the Symbolism of Reason. Rite, and Art*. Cambridge, MA: Harvard University Press.

Larsen, Darl. 2008. *Monty Python's Flying Circus: An Utterly Complete, Thoroughly Unillustrated, Absolutely Unauthorized Guide to Possibly All the References from Arthur "Two Sheds" Jackson to Zambesi*. Lanham, MD: Scarecrow Press.

Lawner, Lynne, ed. 1989. *I Modi: The Sixteen Pleasures: An Erotic Album of the Italian Renaissance*. Evanston, IL: Northwestern University Press.

Levine, Lawrence. 1993. *The Unpredictable Past: Explorations in American Cultural History*. Oxford: Oxford University Press.

Lines, Gill. "The Sports Star in the Media: The Gendered Construction and Youthful Consumption of Sports Personalities." In *Power Games: A Critical Sociology of Sport*, edited by John Sugden and Alan Tomlinson, 196–215. London: Routledge, 2002.

MacGregor, Jeff. 1998. "The Naughty, Surreal Pleasures of the 'Python' 6." *New York Times*, June 21. http://www.nytimes.com/1998/06/21/arts/televi-

sion-the-naughty-surreal-pleasures-of-the-python-6.html?page
wanted=all&src=pm.

Malamud, Randy. 2011. "Monty Python's Academic Circus." *Chronicle of Higher Education,* January 30. http://chronicle.com/article/Monty-Pythons-Academic-Circus/126062/.

Malory, Thomas. *Le Morte d'Arthur.* Electronic Text Center, University of Virginia Library. http://etext.virginia.edu/toc/modeng/public/Mal1Mor.html.

Marlowe, Christopher. 2005. *Doctor Faustus.* ed. David Scott Kastan. New York: W. W. Norton.

Marsh, Steve. 2012. "The Vulture Transcript: Terry Gilliam Gets Real About the Making of *Monty Python and the Holy Grail.*" *Vulture,* April 4. http://www.vulture.com/2012/04/terry-gilliam-monty-python-and-the-holy-grail-interview.html.

Marx, Karl, and Friedrich Engels. 1985. *The Communist Manifesto.* London: Penguin Books.

McGinn, Colin. 2012. "Philosophy by Any Other Name." *New York Times,* March 4 http://opinionator.blogs.nytimes.com/2012/04/philosophy-by-another-name/?_r=1.

McLuhan, Marshall. 1964. *Understanding Media: The Extensions of Man.* New York: Signet.

Milton, John. 2005. *Paradise Lost: A Norton Critical Edition.* Edited by Gordon Teskey. New York: W. W. Norton.

Moncrieff, C. K., trans. 2008. *The Song of Roland.* Produced by Douglas B. Killings and R. J. Malley. Project Gutenberg EBook. http://www.gutenberg.org/files/391/391.txt.

Monty Python Conquers America. In *Monty Python: The Other British Invasion*. 2009. A & E Home Video. DVD.

"Monty Python: The Original Kings of Gore." 2009. *Newsweek*, October 26.

Morgan, David. 2005. *Monty Python Speaks!: The Complete Oral History of Monty Python, as Told by the Founding Members and a Few of Their Many Friends and Collaborators*. New York: Harper.

Neale, Steve. 2008. "Sketch Comedy." In *The Television Genre Book*, edited by Glenn Creeber, 76–77. London: British Film Institute.

New York Public Library Desk Reference, 4th ed. 2002. New York: Hyperion Books.

Novak, Michael. 1985. "American Sports, American Values." In *American Sports, Culture: The Humanistic Dimensions*, edited by Wiley Lee Umphlette, 34–39. Lewisburg, PA: Bucknell University Press.

Office of the High Commissioner for Human Rights, United Nations. 2012. "Geneva Convention Relative to the Treatment of Prisoners of War." Accessed August 12. http://www.ohchr.org/EN/ProfessionalInterest /Pages/TreatmentOfPrisonersOfWar.aspx.

Orwell, George. 1945. "The Sporting Spirit." *Tribune* (London), December.

Palin, Michael. 2006. *Diaries 1969–1979: The Python Years*. New York: St. Martin's Press.

Palin, Michael. 2009. *Halfway to Hollywood: Diaries 1980–1988*. New York: Thomas Dunne Books.

Perez, Joseph. 2005. *The Spanish Inquisition: A History*. New Haven, CT, and London: Yale University Press.

Postman, Neil. 1985. *Amusing Ourselves to Death: Public Discourse in the Age of Show Business*. New York: Penguin Books.

Postman, Neil, and Steve Powers. 1992. *How to Watch TV News*. New York: Penguin Books.

Pratchett, Terry. 1987. *Mort*. London: Victor Gollancz.

Python, Monty. 1989a. *The Complete Monty Python's Flying Circus: All the Words*, Vol. 1. New York: Pantheon Books.

———. 1989b. *The Complete Monty Python's Flying Circus: All the Words*, vol. 2. New York: Pantheon Books.

Pythons, The. 2003. *Autobiography*. Edited by Bob McCabe. New York: St. Martin's Press.

Rousseau, Jean-Jacques. 1975. *The Social Contract*. Edited by Charles Frankel. New York: Hafner.

Saglimbene, Lauren. 2011. "What Is a Typical Norwegian Diet?" *Livestrong.com*, April 13. http://www.livestrong.com/article/420236-what-is-a-typical-daily-norwegian-diet/.

Savage, Dan. 2003. "G.O.P. Hypocrisy." *New York Times*, April 25. www.thestranger.com/seattle/Sayage Love 14566.

Schlain, Leonard. 1991. *Art & Physics: Parallel Visions in Space, Time, and Light*. New York: Perennial.

Schmidt, William. 1994. "Still Zany, Python and Cult Turn 25." *New York Times*, September 28. http://www.nytimes.com/1994/09/28/arts/still-zany-python-and-cult-turn-25.html.

"Sicarri." 2012. JewishEncyclopedia.com. Accessed July 1. http://www
.jewishencyclopedia.com/articles/13630-sicarii.

Smith, Justin E. H. "Philosophy's Western Bias." *New York Times,* June 3.
http://opinionator.blogs.nytimes.com/2012/06/03/philosophys-western
-bias/.

Sontag, Susan. 2001. *Against Interpretation and Other Essays.* New York:
Picador.

"Spam That Isn't via Email, The." 2003. *New York Times,* April 7. http://
www.nytimes.com/2003/04/07/us/the-spam-that-isn-t-via-e-mail
.html.

Stewart, Alan. 2000. *Philip Sidney: A Double Life.* New York: Thomas Dunne
Books.

Stott, Andrew. 2004. *Comedy.* New York: Routledge.

Stubbs, Phil. 2004. "Terry Gilliam Talks Tideland." *Dreams: The Terry Gilliam Fanzine.* http://www.smart.co.uk/dreams/tidegill.htm.

Terkla, Dan, and Thomas Reed Jr. "I'm Gonna Get Medieval on Your Ass":
Pulp Fiction for the 90s—the 1190s." *Studies in Popular Culture* 20.1 (1997):
39–52.

"Terry Gilliam's Guilty Pleasures." 1991. *Film Comment* 27.5 (September/
October): 70.

Tolkien, J. R. R. 1966. *The Hobbit.* New York: Ballantine.

Topping, Richard. 1999. *Monty Python: A Celebration.* London: Virgin
Books.

Tracy, Larrissa, and Jeff Massey, eds. 2012. *Heads Will Roll: Decapitation in the Medieval and Early Modern Imagination.* Leiden & Boston: Brill.

Vaske, Hermann, dir. 2009. *The Art of Football from A to Z.* Starring John Cleese. Hermann Vaske Emotional Network. DVD.

Williams, Kevin. 2003. *Understanding Media Theory.* New York: Oxford University Press.

Woodham-Smith, Cecil. 1972. *Queen Victoria: From Her Birth to the Death of the Prince Consort.* New York: Dell.

Yeager, Robert, and Toshiyuki Takayima, eds. 2012. *The Medieval Python: The Purposive and Provocative Work of Terry Jones.* New York: Palgrave Macmillan.

Zimmer, Ben. 2010. "We." *New York Times,* October 1. http://www.nytimes.com/2010/10/03/magazine/03FOB-onlanguage-t.html.

Zweig, Stefan. 1935. *Mary Queen of Scotland and the Isles.* New York: Viking Press.

INDEX